AF342133

Employee Drug Abuse

A Manager's Guide for Action

Employee Drug Abuse

A Manager's Guide for Action

Carl D. Chambers, Ph.D.
and
Richard D. Heckman

CAHNERS BOOKS, *Division of Cahners Publishing Company, Inc.*
89 Franklin Street, Boston, Massachusetts, U.S.A. 02110

International Standard Book Number: 0–8436–0718–1
Library of Congress Catalog Card Number: 73–183372

Contents

Introduction

Contrary to popular belief, the drug problem in business and industry is relatively widespread, and it is not confined to minority groups employed in blue collar areas. Drugs are used, legally and illegally, by a number of different employees for a number of different reasons in a number of different work situations. Some employees are drug dependent, others using drugs are not; drug use affects the performance of some employees and has not as yet affected the performance of others; some drug-dependent employees cause trouble in an entire department while others do not and go undetected for years.

While an employee may indeed be using drugs, he is not considered by most managers to be an abuser until it becomes apparent that he is affecting either his department or himself in a negative way. In most segments of business and industry today, a drug abuser is someone who reveals himself. Detection usually has nothing to do with a supervisor's knowledge of drugs and narcotics; rather, judgments are made on factors that do *not* exist, based on traditional guidelines. If an employee is *not* absent a great deal, is *not* subject to chronic tardiness, does *not* steal, and performs satisfactorily, chances are a supervisor does not think that person is using drugs; yet the employee may, indeed, be using drugs, or abusing them. In fact, the employee may be using drugs in order to measure up to traditional guidelines — to maintain a high level of performance or to combat boredom or stress on the job.

We believe that, at present, business and industry may only be looking at the tip of the iceberg as far as the problem of employee drug abuse is concerned. Many employees have not as yet revealed themselves, and recent studies indicate the number of drug abusers now employed is much larger than we had suspected. It is obvious that we are experiencing only the beginning of employee drug abuse and the problem will continue to grow. Management must begin to earnestly address the issues such increases will dictate.

The fact that employees are revealing themselves as users of drugs in ever-increasing numbers is without question. The causes for this supposedly sudden development have been scantily researched and so they are not the primary concern of this book. However, business and industry must contribute to the overall understanding of these problems.

Many managers believe employee drug abuse is primarily the result of character weakness: the inability of individuals to manage a wide variety of personal problems. This is only partly true. Some drug use occurs not so much for pleasure, but to reduce displeasure. If the problem of employee drug abuse has indeed reached the major proportions akin to those documented in the state of New York, business and industry must look within itself to determine what roles they play in producing the problem. The problem of employee drug abuse may relate more directly than we think to the very fabric of our working environments, rather than totally to external elements. We believe that some drug use is a by-product of today's highly impersonal working environments which promote both boredom and stress on all levels of work, and virtually eliminate feelings of personal achievement and importance — the truly satisfying rewards for the individual. We also believe, however, that some drug use is purely social or recreational and has nothing to do with gross personal pathology or with work problems.

The causes of employee drug abuse will be the subject of seminars for months and years to come, and management will be called upon to contribute to and focus these discussions. But discussion of the topic today is restricted by the scanty research. In this limbo, hypotheses must necessarily precede experience. We offer an exploratory mixture of both.

This book has two objectives: to document as well as possible the fact that employee drug abuse is indeed a reality and that it could grow into a problem of significant proportions, and to provide management with information that will help in formulating policy and programs to minimize the problem.

Perhaps "guide" is not the most suitable word to use in the title of this book. A guide presumes that there is a specific itinerary to pursue in order to reach your destination or goal. The subject of employee drug abuse offers no clear-cut explanations or solutions; rather it often leads one off on tangents and into blind alleys.

This book is a guide in the only way it can be at this stage of the game: it shows the surprising scope of the problem and tells how some businesses are trying to cope with it. The most workable aspects of a good many companies' policies and programs have been analyzed and evaluated, as have the pitfalls of implementation. Equally, if not more important, the views of those employees and potential employees for whom these policies and programs are designed were obtained and measured against program goals.

Because the subject of employee drug abuse is relatively new to business and industry and not enough time has elapsed to prove or disprove anything, no policy or program expressed in this book is put forth as a panacea for any company. What the book offers are the actual experiences of companies and employees — firing-line knowledge that can provide a base on which to create your own policy and programs.

All companies that provided us with information go unnamed. The reason is two-fold. Many of the firms interviewed wished to remain anonymous, primarily because their policies are quite liberal and they prefer not to imply that their plants and offices are or could be havens for junkies. Also, we felt that it could be misleading if specific policy positions were linked to specific companies. While some industries require more stringent stances because of the need to minimize public safety risks (airlines, food processors, etc.), the judgment about your company policy should be yours to make on the evidence that primarily exists in *your* plant or office, in *your* community, and in *your* industry. We did not want to encourage "me-tooism"; the need for imagination and experimentation is too pressing. On the other hand, no company is too small to adopt policies now being implemented by many large firms; a large medical or counselling staff, for example, often is not a primary requirement for effectively minimizing drug abuse. Again, we do not want to discourage innovation or encourage defeatism.

Our thanks go to scores of people in business, industry, and the public sector who not only made the tip of the iceberg more visible and gave us a glimpse of the hulking mass beneath the surface, but who also made it possible for us to offer some information that may help managers chart a course.

Carl D. Chambers, Ph.D.   Richard D. Heckman
Miami, Florida   Boston, Mass.

Employee Drug Abuse

A Manager's Guide for Action

Policy in the Making

Two to three years ago, few companies had either unwritten or written policies concerning employee drug abuse. The primary reason was that the problem was slight. But procedures for handling the situation were also scarce because management really did not know how to respond to it, although individual cases of drug abuse had been occurring for 20 years. Basically, most if not all companies operated on an unwritten procedure that went something like this: the company will allow an employee who may be misusing drugs to remain on the job if he maintains a satisfactory level of performance. If the employee fails to conceal his drug abuse and his performance slips, he will either be warned or terminated, depending on his importance to the company. (If terminated, it was usually for reasons stemming from drug abuse, and this remains true in the majority of cases today.)

This seemed like a reasonable approach; besides, what right did a company have to meddle in an employee's private affairs? If he was "weekending" with drugs, or experimenting on his lunch hour, or even if he was popping pills on the job, wasn't this his own problem, just as long as he showed up for work on time and performed properly?

At the time, one would have thought that industry's experience with the alcoholic would have prompted many managers to wonder about this position. And as the drug problem became more than slight, many did begin to question this *live-and-let-live as long as they perform* position. Slowly, business and industry began to understand that the employee who is misusing drugs can, in many instances, conceal his habit and perform properly for some time. But it also became evident that the drug abuser is a hidden problem, affecting the company in costly ways.

Companies saw their theft rate soar — double and sometimes triple. Could this have something to do with employee drug abusers? And could employees misusing drugs be making money to support their habits in other ways — such as selling dope in-house and spreading the illicit use of drugs to other employees? It was not only possible, it was happening, not in any alarming way yet, but the handwriting seemed to be on the wall. Industry learned a few other things too that made management wonder about the soundness of keying policy only to performance.

Employees abusing many kinds of drugs can often appear as though they are performing properly, when in fact they are not. There is a vast difference between appearing to perform and performing, and it is a costly difference. It is estimated that a practicing drug abuser is only 50 percent efficient. Nobody really knows, for example, the cost to business in spoilage due to the bad judgments of employees misusing drugs.

"I think what industry failed to foresee with its unwritten policy tied solely to performance were the invisible costs," said a supervisor for a telephone company. "Let's take an example, which I can assure you is *not* hypothetical. If one of my installers putting a cable in a key system guesses wrong about the length of cable needed — say by two feet — he'll throw out the original and guess again. That single error in judgment has just cost the company hundreds of dollars. And the chances are that if he is swelling his head on pot, he'll make mistakes again the same day."

Drug abusers also lose three times as much time away from the job as normal employees. On the average they are out twenty-seven days a year; most employees average eight days. This does not account for incidental absenteeism. The drug abuser may be performing on the job, but how often is he there? Probably just enough to get by.

So management thought that perhaps performance was not the only consideration and that a drug policy should reflect something more. But what?

"No one really knew," said a director of industrial relations. "Back then most people were talking about stronger law and order programs — 'We can't handle the problem so dump it on the cops.' We thought at one time that the drug problem was a police problem too." But the police had their own problems and they made it perfectly clear to businessmen that while they would help in apprehending in-plant pushers, they could not take over a company's personnel problems.

To reduce the chances of these personnel problems getting worse, management decided that the best thing to do was to state a policy that the company would not hire anyone with a history of drug use, any use at all. Everything possible would be done to screen applicants, especially the younger ones. Again, this seemed logical; you won't have a drug problem if you don't hire youngsters using drugs. Everyone knew that people under 30 years of age made up the largest segment of the population using drugs, and that 47 percent of all known addicts were between the ages of 20 and 30.

But then it was discovered that while incidence of drug abuse had soared with young people, it also had been steadily climbing in all age levels of the population. Would a policy not to hire anyone with a drug history be practical? Even further, would this policy set up just for youngsters be practical? As we have seen in the prologue of this book, many companies need and hire thousands of young people every year. In the case cited, youngsters comprised more than 50 percent of the company's new hires annually.

What Are Your Manpower Needs?

A recruiting man reported:

After thinking about the no-hire policy, we then had to take a long, hard look at our immediate and long-term manpower needs. We seriously questioned whether we could afford a policy quite so strict. We require a good many new young employees every year. Now obviously applicants probably wouldn't admit to a history of drug use; we would have to make additional effort to find out. If we didn't want to make that effort, it would be silly to have the policy. But we had to ask ourselves this question in light of the fact that very shortly 50 percent of the population will be under

25 years of age. And 100 percent of that 50 percent have been raised in the drug culture. Could we afford to write off *immediately* such a large portion of our potential labor supply?

Not really knowing how many young applicants they would have to reject because of past drug use, management decided to hold this question in abeyance, see how things went for a while, and concentrate their thinking on the in-house drug users who were concealing themselves (performing adequately), but who apparently were costing much in terms of theft, safety problems, attendance, spoilage and mistakes, and perhaps spreading drugs. The talk turned to preventative, in-company drug education and perhaps programs of rehabilitation similar to those for company alcoholics. But little happened beyond the discussion stage. One thing was clear: as time passed the drug problem was not getting any better. What was very unclear was the kind of policy positions management could devise that would cope with a good many uncertainties appearing on the horizon.

Then the recession hit. Many members of management simply threw up their hands in disgust; business was bad, profits were down, and the last thing they needed was another problem, especially one so complex, if not as yet overwhelming. Besides, many businesses were laying off. It was management's employment market, not the applicant's. The hell with them! Adopt a hardline policy, make it short and sweet, and that is that. Fire everyone caught using drugs, do not hire anyone who has used them, and let us not worry about preventative employee drug education or rehabilitation; there are no people to handle it, and certainly no money. A typical, terse, hardline policy statement went something like this: "An employee will be subject to discharge without prior warning for consuming or using narcotics or drugs, or being under the influence of, or bringing same onto company premises. The company will not hire anyone who has used narcotics or drugs illegally."

The hardline policy became very popular, and still is in certain circles. Whether they agreed with the hardline or not, some companies necessarily had to make this position known to the public as the drug problem received more and more national panic publicity. Generally, these firms were airlines, food processors, and organizations that could affect public safety. These companies proceeded to do all they could to screen out applicants by utilizing every known technique, including urinalysis for everyone. But behind closed doors they continued to grapple with a host of related problems, i.e., despite so-called foolproof screening techniques, how can they be sure that a "clean" applicant won't start to use drugs once on the job? They cannot, and without saying so, the companies knew that essentially they were in the same boat as everyone else, hardline or no.

Most companies acknowledged the need for flexibility and began to draft policy that offered them options — room to maneuver, a chance to roll with the punches, opportunity to change. Only the most short-sighted committed themselves to an inflexible position before really understanding the drug problem or its potential impact on their operations. Many are now busily revamping and rewriting policy.

Usually, the personnel department, working with its medical people, got stuck with the first draft of a company drug policy. They were told to look into the subject, to write something based on their best estimate of the future, but to fully expect that within a year or so experience might show that what they had created would not stand up.

"Looking into it" usually meant checking with other companies to see what they were doing. But this was like the blind leading the blind. In the few instances that other companies had thought about the problem, it was usually only the hardliners who had rushed out with a terse statement that evil is evil and that they would have no part of it. They were not much help.

A few conscientious personnel men improvised crash courses in drugs for themselves — reading whatever literature was available and talking with ex-addicts, rehabilitation people, and doctors with experience in the field. But initially, this type of research, while interesting, tended to warp opinion; personnel men returned to their companies heavily indoctrinated in elaborate rehabilitation programs for junkies but with little understanding about how it all applied to the company's day-to-day operational problems.

"Most of the outside experts I talked with thought that our company should be our brother's keeper," said one personnel man. "The ex-addicts working in the residential care houses wanted us to hire all their graduates right away and, in turn, they wanted us to send them all of our addicts, at our expense. They really wanted us to go into the rehab business. I didn't even know how many addicts we had on the payroll, if any. Perhaps our policy would include some position on rehab, but to what degree and under what circumstances, I just didn't know yet."

Neither did a lot of other people. But rehabilitation was one aspect that was beginning to get increased attention. Was drug abuse a sickness like so many people were saying? Was it really treatable? If so, would rehabilitation help salvage trained men and reduce turnover? Many men who were drafting policy started taking their statements on alcoholism out of their files and using them as a base on which to draft positions on drugs. They assumed, with some justification, that alcoholism and drug misuse were parallel problems, and with fingers crossed they moved ahead, knowing that only time would tell whether they were right.

To assure that time was on the company's side, they wrote policy that gave management many options: to hire anyone with or without a drug history, or not to hire them; to terminate immediately anyone caught using drugs in-house, or not; to help rehabilitate employees who were hooked, or not. In short, most policies offered management the chance to move in a number of opposite directions, a stratagem that seemed to be then and still remains the only sensible stance to take, whether policy is written or unwritten.

The following is a New York company's drug policy. It is an excellent example of the option-oriented approach. The complete policy is reprinted here; the boldface on the option-offering phrases are the authors':

THE POLICY ON DRUG USE

A. Basic Company Policy

The Company prohibits the sale or medically unauthorized possession or use of narcotics and other dangerous drugs by employees on Company premises, not only because such activities are unlawful, but also because they may adversely affect employees' safety, health and longevity, and seriously impair their value as employees. In addition, such drug use constitutes a potential danger to the security and welfare of other employees, and exposes the Company to the risk of property loss or damage. For these reasons, the Company feels it is important at this time to clarify further its policy with regard to drug use.

1. In the context of this policy statement, the term drug use is defined as the sale, or medically unauthorized use or possession of any dangerous drug, which means any narcotic drug (including marijuana), hallucinogenic drug, or depressant or stimulant drug as defined under State Law.
2. The Company will not hire anyone who is known to be a drug user. **However, in cooperation with public or private agencies engaged in the rehabilitation of drug users, the Company may at its discretion hire a small number of former drug users who have been rehabilitated.**
3. Any employee who is known to be or suspected of engaging in drug use should be reported immediately to the Medical Director and the Personnel Services Unit for evaluation and **consideration of appropriate Personnel action.**
4. An employee who has been discontinued because of drug use or a related problem **may be reinstated** only with the approval of the Medical Director and the Personnel Officer.
5. An employee who is found to be selling or distributing any dangerous drug on the Company premises shall be terminated immediately. **The Company will be the sole judge of the sufficiency of evidence in such cases.** Where the evidence so warrants, the Company will also bring the matter to the attention of appropriate law enforcement authorities.

B. Administrative Procedures

The existence of a drug problem may often manifest itself in an employee's work performance, behavior or appearance in the following ways:

1. Excessive absence and/or lateness and unsatisfactory work performance.
2. Frequent and prolonged absences from the work area.
3. Frequent non-work visits from other employees or strangers.

4. Frequent trips to the washroom or water fountain.
5. Deterioration in personal grooming and hygiene.
6. Drowsiness, slurred speech, lack of coordination, inability to concentrate, nausea, cramps, etc.
7. Agitation, rapid speech, dizziness, dilated pupils.
8. Bloodshot eyes, runny nose.
9. Drastic weight loss.
10. Marked change in mood, attitude or behavior.

The presence of any or all of these signs may not necessarily be the result of a drug problem. They may be merely symptomatic of some other underlying problem that requires immediate attention. However, where these signs are evident, or there is a suspicion of drug use, the employee should be interviewed confidentially. It should be made clear that the discussion arises from unsatisfactory performance, excessive absence and/or lateness, attitude or behavior. The subject can be approached discreetly by asking if the employee has a health problem or is taking any kind of medication or drug. However, under no circumstances should the employee be accused of using drugs.

If the employee acknowledges a drug problem or the need for medical counseling, an appointment should be made with the Medical Director through the Departmental Personnel Representative. A memorandum detailing the facts of the case should be sent to the Departmental Personnel Representative for transmittal to both the Medical Director and the Personnel Services Unit.

However, where the employee denies the existence of a drug problem or refuses medical counseling, it should be made clear that unless there is an immediate and sustained improvement in over-all performance, the Company will have no alternative but to consider appropriate disciplinary action. The facts should then be documented and sent to the Departmental Personnel Representative for referral to both the Medical Director and the Personnel Services Unit for possible future action.

Following diagnosis of drug use by the Medical Department, **continued employment may be permitted during rehabilitation** only if the employee cooperates fully in the therapeutic program prescribed by the Medical Department and, at the same time, maintains an entirely satisfactory work performance and attendance record. Failure to comply with any of these conditions will result in termination.

However, should the employee's problem require long-term therapy or institutional care, **the Company will usually have no alternative but to terminate** employment. In this situation, referral to an outside source of help will be made, if the employee is interested.

C. Implementation of the Policy
  1. Supervisors and Managers
      (a) Be alert to the signs of drug use among employees, particularly changes in normal behavioral patterns.
      (b) Interview suspected drug users to get the problem out in the open. Document the facts.
      (c) Promptly refer cases (known or suspected) to the Departmental Personnel Representative. Prompt referral may help prevent hopeless addiction or even loss of life. It may also help prevent the involvement of other employees in drug use.
      (d) Cooperate with the Personnel and Medical Departments in following-up on employees under rehabilitation.

  2. Personnel Department
      (a) Assist Managers and Supervisors by explaining the Company policy and procedures with regard to drug use.
      (b) Cooperate with the Medical Department in educating employees to the hazards of drug use and in the rehabilitative aspects of the drug use program.
      (c) Screen out applicants **who may be users** of dangerous drugs.
      (d) Cooperate with the Security Force in the investigation and detection of drug and related activities.
      (e) Take appropriate disciplinary action based on all available facts.

  (f) Develop and maintain contacts with outside public and private drug agencies.

 3. Medical Department
  (a) Screen out applicants who are involved with dangerous drugs.
  (b) Educate employees to the dangers of drug use with the cooperation of the Personnel Department.
  (c) Identify Company employees with drug problems.
  (d) Prescribe therapeutic programs for employees with drug problems. Follow-up on their progress during rehabilitation with the assistance of the Personnel Department.
  (e) Consult with Supervisors and Managers who need advice about possible drug users in their work areas.
  (f) Counsel employees who may have drug problems in their families.

 4. The Security Force
  (a) Investigate incidents involving the sale and distribution of dangerous drugs in the Home Office in cooperation with the Personnel Department.
  (b) Maintain contacts with the law enforcement agencies and cooperate with them in investigating criminal drug activity in and around the Home Office.
  (c) Advise Personnel Department regarding the suspected or known use, sale, distribution, or other activities involving dangerous drugs.
  (d) Recommend changes and innovations in security procedures.

Here is another example, offering a little less flexibility:

COMPANY POLICY CONCERNING THE
MISUSE OF DRUGS OTHER THAN ALCOHOL

The illegal sale, purchase, transfer, use or possession of drugs by employees on Company premises or while on Company business is prohibited.

This prohibition applies to all forms of narcotics, depressants, stimulants or hallucinogens whose sale, purchase, transfer, use or possession is prohibited by law. The only exception is the use of prescribed drugs under the direction of a physician.

Any employee who engages in the illegal sale of these drugs on Company premises or while on Company business is subject to disciplinary action up to and including dismissal.

Any employee who is found illegally purchasing, transferring, using or possessing illegal drugs on Company premises or while on Company business **is subject to disciplinary action up to and including dismissal.** However, it is the Company policy to attempt rehabilitation **whenever appropriate.**

The disciplinary action to be taken **will be determined by consideration of all circumstances.** Efforts toward rehabilitation should be made where there **is a likelihood of success.** Consultation with Personnel, Labor Relations, Benefit, Medical, and Legal people is often warranted before final determination of rehabilitative or disciplinary action.

Where the circumstances do not warrant immediate disciplinary action, the employee will be informed that if he participates in similar behavior in the future, he will be subject to disciplinary action up to and including dismissal.

An employee committing any of the above acts off premises while not on Company business, and whose behavior does not adversely affect his job performance or is not detrimental to the business should be guided by supervision toward rehabilitation. However, if such behavior does adversely affect his job performance or is considered so serious as to be detrimental to the business, he will be subject to disciplinary action up to and including dismissal.

Identifying the Problem

A supervisor should be as knowledgeable as possible about the signs and symptoms of drug misuse, and should inform his own supervisor, the Personnel Representative of his Department and the Medical Office as soon as he suspects that an employee has a drug problem. He should never be without the advice and assistance of experts, since diagnosis is complex and a false accusation should be avoided. Nor should he undertake independently the counseling or rehabilitation of an employee who misuses drugs. Delay in reporting a suspected problem can be dangerous for the employee, his associates and the Company.

Common signs of drug misuse are:

1. Changes in attendance and discipline.
2. Change from normal capabilities (work habits, efficiency, etc.).
3. Poor physical appearance, including inattention to dress and personal hygiene.
4. Wearing sunglasses at inappropriate times (indoors or at night, for instance) to hide dilated or constricted pupils.
5. Long-sleeve shirts worn constantly to hide needle marks.
6. Association with known drug users.
7. Stealing small items.

Supervisory Procedures

A supervisor who suspects an employee of drug misuse should take immediate action as follows:

1. Inform his own supervisor and the Personnel Representative of the Department; then, with their agreement, proceed to Step 2.
2. Consult the Medical Department, describing the employee's behavior and symptoms.
3. Discuss with the employee his deficiencies in job performance, personal appearance, absences, lateness, etc., but with no suggestion of suspected drug misuse.
4. Refer the employee to the Medical Department for evaluation and counsel, informing him that his record is being made available to the physician. If the employee refuses to visit the Medical Department, explain that this may be grounds for dismissal.
5. After the medical interview, decide on further action through consultation with his own supervisor, the Personnel Representative and the medical consultant. Rehabilitation should be attempted if there is a likelihood of success. The physician will suggest appropriate sources of treatment in the community.

6. Explain to the employee exactly what improvement in performance and behavior is expected, ascertaining that the employee understands that improvement is necessary if he is to continue in the job. The supervisor should not engage in counseling or in therapeutic discussion; because of the complex nature of drug involvement, rehabilitation should be directed only by experts.
7. In conjunction with the Medical Department maintain a close follow-up of the employee's progress. Follow-up should be undertaken whether the employee continues work or is institutionalized.
8. If rehabilitation is ineffectual or if the employee is uncooperative, resort to further disciplinary action — suspension or dismissal.

A supervisor who observes an employee selling, purchasing, transferring, using or possessing drugs while on the job should take prompt action which may include suspension pending investigation. If he suspends the employee pending investigation, he should tell the employee that disciplinary action including separation from the Company may be forthcoming. The supervisor should then confer with his own supervisor and the Personnel Representative of the Department about the nature of the offense and the action to be taken. The discipline may be:

1. Warning that repetition will result in further discipline, possibly dismissal.
2. Suspension.
3. Dismissal.

All circumstances of the case should be considered and the Medical Department should be consulted before a final decision is made. If appropriate, advice should be sought from the Legal Department and others.

Documentation of Case

Observations about an employee's behavior, as well as each contact and discussion with him, should be documented in detail for use by higher levels of supervision if necessary.

Drug Misuse Off the Job

An employee who illegally sells, purchases, transfers, uses or possesses drugs off the job and whose behavior does not adversely affect his job performance or is not detrimental to the business should be guided by supervision toward rehabilitation. However, if such behavior does adversely affect his job performance or is considered so serious as to be detrimental to the business, he will be subject to disciplinary action up to and including dismissal.

Who's Doing What?

The preceding policy statements are about as complete and option-oriented as any your authors reviewed. But, you may ask, are they typical? You may think, "If it is working for a lot of people, it should work for us." While this may or may not be important, it is indeed reasonable to wonder what other companies are doing.

A study conducted by *Industrial Relations News* asked 108 companies about their drug problems. A formal drug policy, either written or unwritten, had been thought through and was being used by 34 percent of the 108 companies. These companies represented both large and small organizations, ranging from 275 employees to over 80,000. The 108 companies were also geographically dispersed, some located in large metropolitan areas, others in rural communities.

Of those 34 percent with a formal drug policy, 95 percent made no distinction in their policy between physically addictive drugs, like heroin, and softer drugs which are not classified as physically addictive. There was no distinction between sellers and users in company policy of 60 percent of those companies that had policy. Penalties such as dismissal were applicable to both. Immediate dismissal was the policy for both seller and user in 51 percent of those companies having a policy. Within this 51 percent, a minuscule number of companies had procedures for referring dismissed employees to rehabilitation agencies.

A warning to first-offense drug users — not sellers — is the policy for 49 percent of the companies reporting. Accompanied with this warning is a policy that the employee must begin outside rehabilitation if he wishes to remain in the employ of the company, and that the employee would not be dismissed unless rehabilitation failed. In some cases, companies gave employees two or three warnings, depending on the value of the employee.

Of the 108 companies surveyed, three-fifths make an effort to find out whether a job applicant has a record of drug use; of the 51 percent who have a written or unwritten drug policy, 81 percent of these make an effort through various means to find out whether a job applicant has taken drugs in the past. Of the 49 percent of companies who do not have a drug policy, only 58 percent attempt to secure information about a job applicant's drug record.

The survey went on to reveal that "the two most common ways of getting information are the interview and the physical." Other ways used with considerably less frequency are reference checks, background investigations, and police checks. Many organizations use more than one means since medical checks are not an infallible guide. If a candidate shows an armful of needle tracks, the alert examiner will not ignore them. Moreover, urine tests give a positive reading only when certain drugs have been used recently.

Only 3 percent of the companies are giving supervisors specific information about recognizing signals of drug use or abuse, and one other company says it will start such training this year. In no case is the supervisor expected to be a diagnostician. In most instances, supervisors reaching the end of their counselling resources are expected to refer problem employees to someone else.

The survey went on to point out that drug misuse is not getting much discussion in general employee publications. Only 11 percent of the organizations go beyond employee handbook prohibitions and take up the matter in the newspaper, magazines, or widely distributed booklets.

So it seems that there is no band-wagon approach to adopting drug policy; many companies are doing many different things, generally with their fingers crossed. Some are doing very little. Industry simply has not had enough experience to know who is right and who is wrong.

Rehabilitation is the one aspect of policy, however, that is continuing to raise questions in nearly every company which is thinking seriously about a drug policy. Is it worthwhile? Is it effective? Is it business's bag?

What are the best procedures? If an effort is made to help employees, should a company also consider hiring rehabilitated addicts?

"We have no intention of becoming a haven for people who are actively using drugs, either our own people or outsiders," said a personnel director. "We have a rehabilitation program of sorts for employees, but a guy has really got to want it, cooperate with the company in every way, including sustained and satisfactory performance."

By and large, this sums up what most companies are doing in rehabilitation (and these are relatively few). The commitment is far from total and the burden of success is placed on the employee rather than the program. This is understandable since most companies have not thought through their role vis-à-vis rehabilitation, and it is a tacky question. Rehabilitation presents a question of corporate conscience, in a way. A business must decide — on the basis of a drug problem, in the company and the community, now and in the future — whether it has an obligation, if not practical then moral, to help people who are misusing drugs. The company must decide this on the basis of virtually no record for rehabilitation in business and industry. Time consuming, costly, and often frustrating, business-connected rehabilitation programs generally have not been too successful. But then there have been few to assess. Almost all companies with rehabilitation written into their policy say that should the employee fail to rehabilitate, he is dismissed. If the employee stays off drugs, he is kept on the payroll.

It seems the reason the rehabilitation programs have not been generally successful is that management has not been motivated to spend any money. Effective company-community rehabilitation programs require both the time of company professionals and funding. Either the drug problem has not reached the upper executive suites with sufficient impact to justify necessary expense, or the extent of business's drug problem is not bad enough yet.

Yet some companies, seeing storm clouds on the horizon, are looking to the future and are thinking seriously about establishing workable drug rehabilitation programs now. These are usually the larger, urban firms with a growing rate of drug incidence and a sizcable in-house medical staff.

Also, a special counselor is required who must be able to give the extra time and help that workers with drug problems need. Most businessmen agree that management should not assign this kind of problem to the personnel officer, who has neither the expertise nor time.

Since industry is only now beginning to understand the extent of its drug problem, let alone the cost of rehabilitation, some companies are coordinating efforts and going to outside experts for help and advice. A group of companies in New England, for example, have helped fund a rehabilitation center for young addicts in the community (see the chapter, "Organizing a Community Drug Council") and, possibly later, for their own employees. In the future, this guarantees these firms a place to refer drug abusers for rehabilitation.

When do you take a chance with someone as far as rehabilitation is concerned? According to one medical director,

It is easier to determine whom you wouldn't take a chance on. If we have an employee whose performance has been marginal for some time, although he is not on drugs, and perhaps we are on the verge of firing him, if he starts misusing drugs, then it is unlikely that he would be recommended for rehabilitation. But suppose an employee had a period of good performance, followed by a decrease in performance due to drugs; then I think that we would try to give that person a chance, if he wanted help.

We also believe that it is the company's responsibility to the community to hire a few rehabilitated addicts, to give them a chance to make good. So far we have taken people who have graduated from recognized rehabilitation programs in the area, although we have two men right now who are still connected with a rehabilitation facility and are approaching graduation. They had been under residential treatment for a year and it was the judgment of the head of the facility that they were ready to reenter the world of work before graduation and that employment would be a necessary part of their rehabilitation.

But if somebody came to our company looking for work, said they had had a drug problem, but had licked it on their own, we'd have serious questions about him. Now and then we hear also from ex-addicts who want employment, but who haven't worked in over a year, although they maintain they have been *clean* all this time. They say that no one would hire them because of their drug history. This may be true, but we feel this is a very risky individual. We'd like to know more about him, and more about his so-called cure.

ELIMINATE THE GUESSWORK

This leads to something a company across town is doing that we are very interested in. They want to hire certain numbers of people from depressed neighborhoods, and they know they are going to get some unknown drug misusers that will be uncovered after they begin work. Instead of dealing with the unknown, they think it might be a good idea to go out into the neighborhoods and select some people who have had drug problems and who have been under appropriate rehabilitation; these people actually are a better risk, and they can also be helpful in influencing their peers in the neighborhoods. They have had the problems and they have been rehabilitated, and they are working.

Anyway, perhaps one of the reasons our company has been willing to take a chance on people is that we do not have the fear of the unknown that many companies have because of our experience. I guess in the last six months or so we have had between 35 and 40 kids in treatment, ex-addicts or addicts. Perhaps we've just had more experience than other companies, and once you come face-to-face with someone who is undergoing rehabilitation, the stereotypes in your mind about the addict disappear. You find out you're really dealing with people, you're not dealing with monsters.

Did the medical director have a difficult time selling top management on employee rehabilitation or the hiring of ex-addicts?

That's not in our policy. But there is no policy against it either. We are hiring them, that's the way it is. And generally, it has worked out. In fact, I would say that many ex-addicts are probably better employees than some of the young drug-free kids we have. They are disciplined, highly motivated, and they know what it is all about.

Hiring people from depressed neighborhoods who have had or still have known drug problems and then working with them, rather than hiring unknowns and then coping with problems as they arise, can provide management with invaluable experience for formulating a finished rehabilitation policy.

Already this approach has revealed a problem that one company is trying to solve in a very imaginative way. The company has said that it wants more than a *seek and destroy* posture with drug abuse. A company spokesman describes their program thus:

It is our objective to give the employee with a drug problem a chance to rehabilitate himself while remaining in the company's employ.

Unfortunately, the rehabilitation facilities currently available are not geared for treating the drug abuser who is employed in a company full time. Most of the therapeutic communities — quite properly — are concerned with handling the hard core addict who is part of the street culture. Their programs involve long term, full time, residential treatment, or daytime programs from 9 to 5.

For the drug abuser who is employed and needs his job both for economic survival and self-respect, existing facilities cannot solve his problem. Additionally, it may well be that the manner of treatment — the ways of reaching the drug abuser with a job and a different pattern of drug use — may differ from the approaches used on the hard core street addict.

So we are proposing that several companies in our community join together to fund a pilot project, establishing an experimental downtown community drug rehabilitation clinc. The clinic would be open from 4 to 8 P.M. three or four weekday evenings. It would be exclusively devoted to drug rehabilitation (and would not be a community center or coffee house). To qualify for treatment, patients would have to be currently employed by companies in this area.

Ideally, the clinic will be an unmarked storefront facility with space for two meeting rooms and a small office/reception area. It would not be housed in the headquarters of any participating company.

To handle an estimated 20 patients, three staff people will be required. They would have had solid experience as staff members in other drug treatment facilities. Two psychoanalysts, who have also had long experience in drug rehabilitation programs, would serve as consultants. The participating companies would not be involved in program administration.

Privacy is a basic requirement if this program is to succeed. When a potential patient is a "walk in" rather than a referral, his employer would not be apprised of the employee's drug problem. In the case of a referral, a joint decision would be made by patient and employer as to the advisability of continuing progress reports.

Treatment methods, based on the group therapy techniques used successfully by therapeutic communities, would necessitate withdrawal from all drugs. This would preclude admission of patients on a continuing methadone maintenance program.

The clinic cannot be conceived of as a corporate public relations gesture. Rather, it is a serious — if experimental — attempt at drug rehabilitation. As such, no mass media publicity would be permitted. Only internal announcements within participating companies would be made to let employees know the facility exists. Local and state government drug agencies, as well as local police precinct and hospital personnel, would be informed of the clinic's existence but would not be otherwise involved.

If the proposal works, the company says the experiment would be of approximately three months' duration, after which time the participating companies and the clinic staff would evaluate the program and determine collectively whether a broader-based facility should be established. Assuming a rent-free facility can be found, with furnishings and supplies contributed by the participating companies, costs (primarily salaries and upkeep) should be in the order of $13,000 for the three month trial period. It is recommended that not more than four companies be involved in funding this pilot project.

Finally, what is changing the minds of many managements about a positive position on rehabilitation is that they are beginning to understand that, in many cases, an addict or drug misuser is someone who can be worked with; he is not a raving lunatic. More and more, it is believed that addiction is a sickness. Users are passive when under the influence; they commit crimes only because the illegality of their habit makes it tremendously expensive. More and more, businessmen are beginning to think of narcotics addiction as a health problem instead of a crime problem. With this understanding is coming a desire to help lick or at least reduce the problem through rehabilitation and employment.

In the final analysis, a company's drug policy will be as individual as its products and services. It will reflect a variety of things common only to itself — top management's opinion about the morality of drug misuse, the sensitivity of the company's operations and its ability to assume the risk of rehabilitated employees, the availability of local services for treatment, and the time and money available to organize and implement a drug program that includes detection, screening, supervisory training, employee education, or rehabilitation.

In the end, drug policy must be tailored to the depth of a company's immediate problem and perhaps to the prospect of future troubles, as well as the company's and community's ability and desire to cope with them. A truly key policy decision, of course, is whether or not your company, with community participation, should work toward a program of treatment and rehabilitation of drug-dependent employees. In order to make this decision, management must understand more about this complex issue. The following chapter has been designed to shed some light on the subject.

Treatment and Rehabilitation of Drug Abusers

Can drug abusers be treated? Who should treat the drug abusers? Is the treatment of drug-abusing employees like any other kind of medical problem? Is drug abuse a medical problem *only?* How successful is the treatment of drug abusers? These and many other questions have been addressed verbally and in print. Unfortunately, as with any complex issue, the answers have been ambiguous, contradictory and incomplete. Because of this state of the art, we would recommend that management conduct a review and assessment of *all* the statements which seem relevant to their specific company situation. We believe, however, that there are a number of universal truths which define a frame of reference wherein this review should occur.

1. Drugs do something *for* the abusers as well as *to* him. What they do or have done *to* the abuser is indeed a medical problem which must be addressed by very skillful, specifically-trained medical personnel. What they do *for* him is normally something far more complex, requiring interventions from a number of specialties.

2. No one starts out to be a drug abuser. Why a person began to use a drug may have little relation to why he chose to continue that use. For example, to be curious about the reaction of a specific drug may be a valid reason for "tasting" the drug, but it cannot explain its continued use or the relapse to its use after treatment. Successful rehabilitation demands an understanding of all the "whys."

3. The treatment of a drug abuser is *not* synonymous with the detoxification of his body. Placing an abuser's life into an appropriate perspective, understanding his personal needs, resolving his interactional processes, and so forth, require long-term involvements with him. Without these ancillary services, however, treatment will not succeed. The alleviation of the physical dependency is always much easier than the elimination of the psychological dependency and resolution of the social problems associated with addictions.

4. When conceptualizing the physiological and psychological dimensions of the drug abuse problem, for example, chronicity, relapse, dependency, and so forth, if you look at drug abuse as a disease, the "contagion" aspect of the "disease" is more appropriate for some forms of drug abuse than others. Marihuana use does have a significant social dimension and is, therefore, highly "contagious." There is no contagion from the executive who abuses tranquilizers or other sedative-hypnotics.

5. Most persons identifiable as drug abusers have progressed through a number of stages — experimentation, social and recreational use, involved use where one spends the significant portion of his time in drug-related activities, and finally total involvement where this one behavior results in his becoming personally and socially dysfunctional.

6. Not all forms of drug abuse will require medical intervention. For example, there is no medical treatment needed for marihuana abuse.

The Treatment of Narcotic Addiction

When one first encounters the pessimism with which most people discuss the treatment and rehabilitation of those addicted to narcotics, it is very easy to accept narcotic addiction as a permanent illness. This pessimism stems from the accumulation of frustrations associated with learning to intervene in a process characterized by chronicity and relapse. This frustration is only partly warranted. For example, although relapse to drug use among treated heroin "street addicts" is extremely high, relapse among physicians who became addicted to morphine or some other legal narcotic is extremely low. Persons with medical onsets to drug use relapse less often than those who pursue euphoric reactions. As with any other complex "disease," the successful treatment and rehabilitation of any narcotic addict will depend upon the selection of the appropriate treatment regimen, the quality of the care provided, the physical and psychological strengths of the patient at the time treatment begins, and the diligence with which the aftercare recovery phase is planned and carried out.

Our experience has been that the addict who possesses the greatest psychological and physiological strengths when he begins treatment, and who receives support from his family and peers during and after treatment, will have the greatest chances of being cured. The less these are in evidence, the less the chances of successful rehabilitation.

The successful rehabilitation of the narcotic addict will include three phases of treatment: initial detoxification, initial abstinence and extended abstinence.

The *initial detoxification,* or withdrawal, takes only a few days — 6 to 14 — and can be accomplished in a hospital or on an ambulatory basis. No significant discomfort will occur under appropriate medical management of the process with therapeutic reductions of a substitute drug, for example, methadone. Until quite recently, clinicians mistakenly believed the person was completely detoxified with all physiological effects of the addiction reversed at the completion of this initial phase. Recent studies show a secondary detoxification, an imbalance of the body, lasts for many months. While the cramps, vomiting, and so forth, indeed do pass rather quickly, the former user will experience vague, diffuse discomfort for at least four to six months.

The *initial abstinence* phase of treatment must address the vague physical discomfort indicated above as well as the psychological dependency which always accompanies the abuse of drugs. Most relapse occurs during this initial abstinence phase. We believe it is because most clinicians are insensitive to complexities and potencies of the secondary-detoxification difficulties and psychological dependencies. They treat the things the drugs do *to* you without appropriate concern for what they do *for* you. High-frequency, extended counselling is an absolute necessity during this phase.

The final phase of treatment is the *extended abstinence* phase, which can last indefinitely. It consists of providing supportive counselling at any time the former user finds himself in a crisis situation where relapse becomes an alternative.

The advantage to the above program is that the employee may never need to leave the job to secure treatment. At most, the employee might have to be off the job for the one or two weeks required for the initial detoxification. If the above abstinence regimen is not successful, one might want to consider the appropriateness of one of the drug substitution regimens, for example, narcotic maintenance or narcotic antagonism.

In narcotic maintenance, usually with methadone, you substitute for the individual's drug use with medically prescribed and managed drug use. The user becomes stabilized and theoretically is capable of functioning normally. Unfortunately, while the advantages of such narcotic maintenance are extensive and the procedure has reclaimed thousands of dysfunctioning addicts, we do not have sufficient hard data on the working potential of these maintained persons. While we do know of many methadone-maintained workers who are performing in a wide variety of work situations, we do not have information sufficient to establish predictable risk levels. For example, we do not know what effect this regimen has on motivation, concentration, attention span, muscle coordination, reaction time, and so forth. It may have no significant effect. Our point is, however, that the studies have not been done.

In narcotic antagonism procedures (for example, cyclazocine, naloxone, and so forth), one neutralizes or in some other way antagonizes the effects of narcotics. In theory, if the user cannot receive any of the anticipated desired effects of the narcotics he uses, or if they make him violently ill when he uses them, he will cease using them. One then keeps the antagonist in his system to prevent relapse. While these regimens hold much hope for the future, at the present time they are plagued by extremely high costs, gross inconvenience and undesirable side effects.

The Treatment of Barbiturate Addiction

It has been our experience that barbiturate abusers can be grouped into three fairly distinct types:

1. There are persons who, in order to deal with states of emotional distress, will abuse the barbiturate solely for their sedative-hypnotic effects, and in so doing remain constantly in a highly sedated state.
2. There are persons who, during the course of therapeutic usage, have discovered the paradoxical reaction which occurs when sufficient tolerance has been developed with the barbiturates. At these dose levels, barbiturates stimulate rather than depress, and the person begins now to take the drug for exhilaration effects.
3. There are persons who, during the course of abusing another class of drugs, ingest large amounts of barbiturates to alter the effects of the other drugs, for example, to counteract the abuse effects of amphetamines, to enhance the effects of intravenous use of opiates, to substitute for an opiate during the times when opiates are unobtainable, and so forth. This frequently sets up a consecutive cycle of abuse.

As with the narcotic addict, the abuser of the barbiturates does not ordinarily seek treatment until such time as his abuse has precipitated some crisis, for example, the threat of losing his job, marital difficulties, a police contact, the loss of a drug supply, and so forth. Once the abuser does seek treatment or it is imposed, the detoxification phase of treatment, since it can be life-threatening, should occur in a hospital under close medical supervision.

Once primary withdrawal has been completed — in two to three weeks — the rehabilitative and psychotherapeutic treatment of the barbiturate abuser is identical with that of the narcotic addict. While there is, of course, some pragmatic expediency in this approach, there is precedence for some variation. For example, post-detoxification treatment should be guided by the type of barbiturate abuser the patient has been. For example, it would probably be appropriate to treat the concurrent barbiturate-opiate abusers as you would an opiate addict. It would, however, be clinically inappropriate to treat the individual who has kept himself in a constant hypnotic stupor the same way as the individual whose sole abuse was for the exhilaration effects of the drugs. While both types of individuals perceive themselves to be inadequate, how they used the drug to counteract this inadequacy, that is, what the drug was doing *for* them, provides the cues for the focus of the therapeutic process. In the one case, the individual abuses the barbiturates not only to avoid interacting and competing, but also to block out anxiety or worry about this noninteraction and noncompetitiveness. In the other case, the stimulation derived from the drugs and the increased activity which follows are interpreted as increasing one's efficiency and effectiveness in interactions and competition.

High-frequency, individually supportive counselling is a valuable procedure during the initial abstinence phase of treatment. The main therapeutic emphasis should be on the acquisition or sharpening of coping skills. While these abusers are more likely to have more competitive skills, that is, education, jobs, status, intact families, etc., than the narcotic abusers, they seem to be deficient in their ability to adapt and adjust to new or stressful situations. While it is possible to impart and acquire these coping skills in group settings, individual sessions are probably more appropriate for initiating the process. Once some minimal insight and success are accomplished, the group setting where testing can occur and be analyzed is usually indicated.

The same tendency to relapse, which is characteristic of addiction to opiates and alcohol, is present in addiction to barbiturates, so that the prognosis must be guarded. (Isbell, and Fraser, 1950)

Contact with the ex-abuser should be maintained for an extended period of time. As with the former narcotic abuser, it may be necessary to have someone available to provide supportive counselling at any time the former user finds himself in a crisis situation where relapse becomes an alternative. The management of patients during this extended aftercare phase can be effectively accomplished in regular, but infrequent, group sessions. Groups with enduring histories appear most appropriate for the rapid discovery of anxieties or depression, which too frequently signal relapse in these patients. Both multiple-diagnoses groups, as well as groups comprised only of barbiturate abusers, have produced favorable results. Neither, however, has been rigorously studied for measurement of results.

Special Considerations for the
Treatment of Barbiturate Abuse

1. The incidence of suicide during the initial detoxification and abstinence phases of treatment is apparently much greater than that found among narcotics addicts. There is sufficient evidence to warrant the implementation of special suicide prevention procedures during these phases of treatment.

2. If chemotherapy appears indicated after detoxification, there is evidence that these former drug abusers will be less inclined to abuse the phenothiazines, reserpine, or the tricylic antidepressants than the minor tranquilizers.

3. Except for the persons who abuse barbiturates concurrently with other drugs, for example, opiates or stimulants, most barbiturate abusers should not be treated in close proximity with the narcotics addicts. These barbiturate abusers normally will not have had any involvement in either the criminal or illicit drug subcultures, and the possibility of seduction and contamination should be minimized. Those who have been concurrent abusers or who have multiple addictions have usually been involved in both the criminal and illicit drug subcultures. One can, therefore, treat these abusers with the narcotic addicts without the concerns of seduction and contamination.

4. Individuals addicted to nonnarcotic drugs may be beginning to seek public and private mental health facilities for treatment. Not only will the addicted individual need extensive treatment, but other family members may also need concurrent treatment. It was noted in one study that the incidence of a family member concurrently abusing drugs was high (30.0%), with most of the abusers being spouses.

The Treatment of Sedative-Hypnotic and
Minor Tranquilizer Abuse and Addiction

Several of the newer nonbarbiturate sedative-hypnotics and minor tranquilizers have been shown to produce intoxication, physical and psychological dependence, coma and/or death, resembling those symptoms associated with barbiturate abuse.

Symptoms of Sedative-Hypnotics and Minor Tranquilizers

| Drugs | | | Physical | |
Generic	Brand	Intoxication	Dependence	Coma/Death
Meprobamate	Miltown, Equanil, etc.	Yes	Yes	Yes
Glutethimide	Doriden	Yes	Yes	Yes
Ethinamate	Valmid	Yes	Yes	Yes
Ethchlorvynol	Placidyl	Yes	Yes	Yes
Methpyrylon	Noludar	Yes	Yes	Yes
Chlordiazepoxide	Librium	Yes	Yes	—
Diazepam	Valium	Yes	Yes	—
Oxazepam	Serax	Yes	—	—

While these drugs are indeed addicting when misused, the available evidence would suggest this addiction will occur only at dose levels considerably in excess of those therapeutically prescribed.

Experience with treating these abusers is limited. It is anticipated that the treatment process should parallel the three phases which have been effective with other abusers — initial detoxification, initial abstinence and extended abstinence. One of the major contributors in the assessment of abuse potential and addiction liability for these drugs has provided the clinician, who is confronted with the necessity for detoxifying this type of abuser, with an appropriate regimen for doing so.

Treatment must be carried out in the hospital and requires barbiturate substitution, followed by its gradual withdrawal at a rate not to exceed 0.1 gm. daily. (Essig, 1966)

. . . Phenothiazine derivatives should not be used to combat withdrawal convulsions, and their use may aggravate the hypotensive aspects of the abstinence syndrome. (Essig, 1966)

Postdetoxification treatment, at least with glutethimide (Doriden) abusers, has been effective when conducted in the same manner as indicated earlier for the barbiturate abusers — high frequency, individually supportive counselling sessions during the initial abstinence phase and less frequent group therapy sessions during the extended aftercare phase.

Specific research needs to be accomplished to validate which therapeutic techniques are most appropriate for which type of abuser. It is best to remember that in pioneering fields such as drug-abuse treatment, therapeutic success, regardless of the technique, is intimately related to the skills of the therapist.

The Treatment of Amphetamine Abuse

Amphetamine abusers appear to fall into two somewhat distinct, contrasting types. While the authors are, of course, aware that a dichotomous characterization of amphetamine abusers would not be totally distinct and that there will be many gradations and exceptions, it does provide an appropriate frame within which to provide treatment services. We have chosen to label these two types of abusers as *adaptive* and *escapist*.

The *adaptive abusers* can be generally characterized as using the amphetamines to bolster their functioning within conventional interpersonal and social activities. This type of user tends to deny that he abuses upon initial confrontation. When the denial is no longer possible, he will contend that drugs prevent or eliminate problems rather than cause them. This type of abuser usually has enjoyed some success in his interactions and social competitiveness, but mistakenly believes that the drug permits him to recapture or increase this success.

In contrast, the *escapist abusers* can be generally characterized as using the drugs so that they will not have to function within conventional interpersonal and social activities. This type of user does not tend to deny the abuse when confronted, but he has ready multiple rationalizations as to why it occurs. He readily admits that drugs are a problem to him. He has not normally enjoyed any success in his interactions and social competitiveness; and he escapes these activities, at least at the conventional level, through his abuse of drugs.

As with all other types of drug abusers, we suggest the treatment of

The Two Kinds of Amphetamine Abusers (Selected Characteristics)

Adaptive Abusers	*Escapist Abusers*
Onset was accidental medicine abuse and the medicine rationale continues	Onset was deliberate experimentation for a predefined euphoric effect and the euphoric rationale continues
Onset occurs after adulthood and after the acquisition of most major individual and social roles	Onset occurs prior to adulthood and before the acquisition of most major individual and social roles
Extensive experimentation with other drugs	Extensive experimentation with other drugs
Nonaggressive reaction to amphetamines	Aggressive reaction to amphetamines
Amphetamine of choice is not methamphetamine	Amphetamine of choice is methamphetamine
Oral use of drugs from a legal source	Intravenous use of drugs from an illicit source
Solitary abuse (hidden)	Group abuse (highly visible)
Regular, noncyclical abuse with any mood elevation a byproduct	Spree – cyclical abuse specifically for euphoric-stimulating effect

amphetamine abusers must include three phases — initial detoxification, initial abstinence and extended abstinence.

The initial detoxification phase of treatment is a medical process and should be accomplished on an in-patient basis. While there is apparently no harm in the abrupt withdrawal of amphetamines, the psychiatric reactions to amphetamine abuse, which reportedly range from acute anxiety to full-blown psychosis, may require medication, for example, sedatives or phenothiazines. Concurrent medical problems primarily associated with the intravenous, high-dose abusers may also require attention during this phase of treatment. There are a whole host of secondary medical problems associated with amphetamine abuse, such as hepatitis, malnutrition, skin problems, some acute respiratory distress, and occasionally gastric distress.

Excluding those cases which require extensive attention for concurrent medical problems, the initial detoxification phase should be completed within one week. This initial phase will usually be characterized by sleepiness. Social withdrawal, severe depression with suicidal ideas and neurasthenia have also been reported. These characterizations appear to be appropriate for both the adaptive abusers as well as the escapist abusers and, at least during this phase of treatment, the treatment procedures are basically the same for both types of abusers.

Even though there is evidence that portions of the primary withdrawal distress may continue for several weeks, it is recommended that the second phase of treatment — initial abstinence — be conducted on an ambulatory basis. The recently detoxified amphetamine abusers of both types can be expected to display chronic fatigue, flattened emotions and depression. The chronic fatigue, which continues for several weeks, has been interpreted variously as a lack of initiative, apathy and lethargy. An exaggerated sense of guilt occurs in most patients during the initial abstinence phase.

Individual, high-frequency, supportive counselling has been successful during this phase of treatment. The main therapeutic emphasis during the frequent contacts, for example, three one-hour sessions per week, has been on counselling only on present and future behavior. While both types of abusers profit from intensive supportive counselling in the areas of drug usage, general attitudes, domestic relations, peer relations and employment difficulties, the primary focus is somewhat different for the two types.

Supportive counselling for the adaptive abusers should be focused upon the alleviation of neuroticlike reactions to normal interpersonal relations and social activities. This type of abuser frequently is unable or unwilling to recognize his drug use as being the cause of any of his problems. His rationale, of course, is that the drug eliminates his interaction difficulties, and so forth. Coping with the awakening feelings of frustration which were dormant throughout the period of heavy drug use becomes a primary therapeutic task.

In contrast, the escapist abusers have more frequently presented psychoticlike reactions to their interactions and activities. Unlike the "uncovering" (i.e., bringing-out-into-the-open) counselling techniques utilized with adaptive abusers, the opposite (i.e., covering) approach has proven effective with escapist abusers. Other contrasts are: (1) the escapist abuser tends to blame all of his problems on the drug with an assertion that if the therapist can assist in the maintaining of abstinence, he will have no problems, and (2) being younger, as a rule, the escapist abuser has not acquired educational or occupational skills nor the values our system attaches to them. This disability usually continues beyond detoxification, resulting, in part, from disabilities in functioning which predate drug use. Competitive skills, both at the individual and social levels, must be acquired. Habilitation rather than rehabilitation too frequently is the need.

During this initial abstinence phase of treatment, the patient should receive frequent supportive sessions as he explores his intrapersonal and interpersonal capacities without the use of drugs. The ambulatory situation with frequent therapeutic contact seems best suited for this exploration. These explorations will probably occupy several months. Once the individual patient has demonstrated some degree of continuity in conventional functioning, therapy should continue, but within a different context and within a different frame of reference.

The long-term aftercare phase of treatment appears to be managed most appropriately in regular but somewhat less frequent group sessions. Indices of anxiety or depression, inappropriate changes in mood, inabilities to cope with stresses, and so forth, any of which may signal a relapse episode, seem to be more readily detected in group sessions. In addition to early detection, concentrated support and guidance are more available in group therapy settings. Reality therapy techniques seem appropriate during this continuous care phase until such time as a crisis is presented or detected. At that time, the more buffering techniques of supportive therapy will probably produce favorable responses.

In summary, after the initial detoxification is completed, very frequent, individual, supportive counselling provides the therapeutic method for reintegration into society. When the patient demonstrates adequate functioning, the mode can be switched to less frequent, but reenforcing, group therapy sessions.

The amphetamine abusers of the adaptive type should *not* be treated in proximity with the escapist type of amphetamine abusers or most narcotic addicts. It would appear appropriate to treat them in proximity with other medicine abusers, that is, abusers of tranquilizers, antidepressants and some analgesic addicts who had medical or accidental onsets.

There seems to be little reason to segregate the escapist type of amphetamine abusers from narcotic addicts. Both have shared common drug experimentation patterns — illicit subcultural involvements, and so forth — and seduction from one group to another is unlikely. While both have their preference drugs, heroin users will also shoot amphetamines to enhance the effects of the opiate, and amphetamine abusers will shoot heroin to "taper a run and prevent crashing."

Special Considerations in the
Treatment of Amphetamine Abusers

1. Amphetamine abusers of the escapist type characteristically abuse their drugs in a cycle. The cycle has two basic phases — an *up* or active phase and a *down* or reactive phase. The two phases are approximately equal in duration. Typically, an experienced abuser would inject the drug, usually methamphetamine, at two- to four-hour intervals for four or five days (the action phase), during which time he will remain awake continuously and then collapse from exhaustion and remain in a semi-comatose state, sleeping intermittently for the next four or five days (the reaction phase).

At the onset of a "run," doses are relatively small, for example, 50 to 100 mgs., but as the run progresses, the doses increase. The highest maximum dose known to us was a dose in excess of 1 g. taken every two hours, probably close to 15,000 mgs. in one day. At the peak of a run, no quantity of drug produces the desired effects. Throughout the run the abuser will continue to desire to function in all of the conventional roles, but his ability to do so will deteriorate in direct proportion to the time he has been in the action phase of the cycle.

One clinician has provided us with a detailed description of what one may expect to encounter while the abuser is in the action phase of the cycle:

During the first 24–48 hours of drug use, underlying conflicts, although never far from the surface, seldom escape the usual ego controls of the drug user. During and after the second day, however, this control may be lost and distinct psychotic behavior and personality changes develop. Most striking are changes in affect [mood] which become at first inappropriate, then quite blunted, and assume a sham quality. . . . Accompanying [this] is a distinct loss of reality testing. Thought processes take on a distinct paranoid quality which eventually replaces more rational thinking. . . .

Such delusional systems are poorly organized — grandiose verbalizations are quite common and are concerned with such items as immunity from arrest, strength, money and women. (Griffith, 1966)

The adaptive abusers do *not* abuse their drugs in such a cycle. This type of abuser ingests drugs in a very steady, regular and at a fairly stabilized dose level for extended periods of time. As indicated earlier, in contrast to the escapist abuser, his subjective desires to function in conventional activities and his objective ability to do so also remain fairly stable. This, of course, is not meant to suggest that this type of abuser does not think he is functioning better than he is.

2. There is considerable disagreement concerning the incidence and degree of permanent organic damage to the brain with amphetamine abuse. Representing one extreme, researchers report that clinical, pathological and experimental studies have demonstrated permanent organic brain damage; and, for this reason, the associated psychiatric condition would be even more difficult to treat than spontaneous disorders. Others, while not testing specifically for brain damage, did discover that about a third of their respondents indicated memory and concentration impairment after their experience with high doses of amphetamines. Most recently, the issue was summarized in the following manner:

The present position would seem to be that there is no conclusive evidence of permanent brain damage, but there may well be a basis for such an eventuality in terms of the clinical, animal, physiological, neurochemical, and neurophysiological findings. (Connell, 1970)

If indeed permanent brain damage does occur, the employers should consider this when establishing expectations and goals with this type of abuser. In the few cases where standardized psychological tests were available, the authors have not encountered any organic brain damage which could be attributed to drug use.

3. Numerous writers have addressed themselves to the aggressiveness of those we have labelled the escapist type of amphetamine abusers. This behavior, variously labelled as aggressive, assaultive, violent, compulsive, suspicious, paranoid and impulsive, may in some patients present a major management problem. While the physical danger to other patients or treatment personnel is probably no greater than that

encountered in the treatment of psychotic patients whose problems were not drug-induced, it does warrant the clinicians' awareness. Many clinicians suggest that high-dose mainliners of amphetamines are the most — and probably the only — dangerous drug abusers to treat. Our own experience would support this contention. Unfortunately, it has not been possible to predict when a violent eruption will occur with this type of abuser. While paranoid reactions and impulsive violence most frequently occur during the initial detoxification phase of treatment, episodes have been encountered throughout the treatment process. Violence during the initial detoxification phase seems best countered with a general, nonthreatening calmness. The episodic eruptions which occur after detoxification are best countered with more direct methods, namely, by the direct use of authority and the labelling of the behavior as inappropriate and not to be tolerated. This authoritative setting of limits does not appear to feed the paranoid delusions or suspiciousness, and this is undoubtedly related to the insights gained during treatment.

4. The question of the incidence of amphetamine psychosis and whether it is dose related deserves close clinical and research attention. At the present time, the literature reflects opposing positions. Some work would indicate that this psychosis is dose related; that is, the greater the dose the greater the probability of producing the psychosis. Others suggest this relationship is not so predictable.

If indeed a paranoid psychosis occurs with any regularity at low doses, a special problem is presented to the social system. For example, at these low doses the person taking the drugs will still be capable of conventional functioning throughout his drug-taking career until the paranoid psychosis erupts. If this eruption should include the all-too-common components of aggressiveness and violence, a significantly dangerous situation could ensue involving those around the abuser, namely, his fellow workers, fellow commuters, family and so on.

The Treatment of Hallucinogenic/Psychedelic Abusers

The hallucinogenic/psychedelic drugs include LSD, a semisynthetic derivative of ergonovine; mescaline, a phenethylamine present in the buttons of a small cactus (mescal, peyote); psilocybin, an indole found in a mushroom (teonanacatl); DMT (dimethyltriptamine), a synthetic indole derived from the seeds of a South American plant; DOM or dimethoxyamphetamine, otherwise known in Haight-Ashbury as STP, an abbreviation for "serenity, tranquility, and peace"; and the seeds of some morning glory varieties (Oloiuqui), the active principle of which is closely related to LSD. Marihuana, which has hitherto been mistakenly classified as a narcotic and with hard drugs, is increasingly being viewed as a mild hallucinogen. Most of our knowledge concerning these drugs has been accumulated with that of LSD. This section is therefore concerned primarily with the LSD abusers.

LSD was first described as a "psychotomimetic" drug, producing a "model psychosis" because it was assumed to have many similarities to psychosis; that is, it mimicked psychosis. A similarly, inaccurately used description has been "hallucinogenic," although it is agreed LSD does not produce true hallucinations since the subject may be aware of what is happening. That is, there is a "spectator ego" witnessing all the excitement — a sort of split of self, with one part observing, the other participating. The most recent term of "psychedelic," meaning "mind-manifesting," is deemed more acceptable today, though it, too, raises a question as to whether LSD is indeed generally consciousness-expanding in the sense implied by some advocates.

LSD is *not* physically addicting in the sense of barbiturates and narcotics. The dependence is psychological, not physical. Tolerance develops rapidly after a few days of repeated use, but is usually lost in two or three days. Some users have built up their LSD doses to 1000 and 2000 μg. over a period of days. The first, or threshold, dose is about 25 μg., and an average dose is 200 to 400 μg. Cross-tolerance exists among LSD, psilocybin and mescaline, though tolerance to mescaline develops more slowly than to the other two. Paradoxically, some users report a state of increased sensitivity to LSD once they have lost their tolerance. Unexpected return of the drugged state without ingestion of LSD for months or even a year has been reported. Some people in the drugged state may pay attention to auditory frequencies they normally ignore and thereafter continue to be sensitive to these frequencies.

To date, neither the mode nor site of action of LSD is known, but it has various effects within the central nervous system. Physiologically, the effects of psychedelic drugs resemble those of sympathomimetic drugs, such as increased pulse rate and blood pressure, dilated pupils, tremor and cold, sweaty palms, and, at times, flushing, shivering, chills, pallor, salivation, disrhythmic breathing, nausea, anorexia and urgency.

Drug-induced activity lasts 8 to 12 hours, with the most intense changes in sensation, mood and perception occurring during the first half of the experience; the latter part is marked by introspection and hypersuggestibility. A change in mood is the first obvious behavioral change observed. Along with this comes a tremendous increase in sensory observation, a kind of flooding, with perceptual distortions and hallucinations. "Synesthesia" often occurs, that is, a crossover of the different senses: subjects can "hear" colors, visualize music as colors, or "taste" sounds. There is also tunnel vision, the focusing on minute detail not observed before.

The literature reports three different kinds of experiences under LSD: (1) *the good trip* — a predominantly pleasant experience; (2) *the bad trip* — a dysphoric experience characterized by anxiety, panic, feelings of persecution, fears of loss of ego boundaries, loss of control and time perception and impaired performance; and (3) *an ambivalent state* where the subject may simultaneously experience contrasting feelings as of happiness and despair, relaxedness and tenseness.

The bad trip has been well-documented in the literature. Most describe these experiences as psychological and attributable to panic upon experiencing a host of overwhelming sensations. The negative experiences which one may encounter during the management of these persons have been summarized as follows.

Acute Reactions

The acute reactions — the bad trips — are of two types:

1) *Psychotoxic reactions* which are characterized by confusion and/ or acute paranoia, feelings of omnipotence and invulnerability, which may cause the user to expose himself to dangers resulting, at times, in injury or death.
2) *Panic reactions* which occur as a secondary response to the drug-induced symptoms.

One may anticipate fairly rapid recovery from these two acute states. Remission usually occurs within two or three days with the recommended treatment of sedation and verbal support.

Recurrent Reactions

These reactions are the spontaneous return of perceptual disorders or feelings of depersonalization, occurring up to a year after the last use of the drug. Some believe these recurrent symptoms are associated with stress or anxiety in the person.

Prolonged Reactions

These reactions are the chronic anxiety states and chronic psychoses resulting from LSD administration, persisting beyond the period of acute intoxication.

Significant variables determining the result of any LSD trip are: the personality and expectations of the subject, the presence of a dependable guide, the nature of the setting in which the drug is taken, and the age of the subject. Younger subjects were noted to have experienced acute reactions more frequently.

Treatment

For the acutely intoxicated state, it is usually recommended that the LSD abuser have an immediate trial with phenothiazine medication, preferably administered intramuscularly, since the phenothiazines block the action of LSD. Barbiturates can be used in lieu of, or in addition to, the phenothiazines. Because the hallucinogens do not cause physical dependence, there are no physical complications of withdrawal. Care should be exercised, however, to learn whether other addicting drugs were taken concurrently with the LSD, which may require a separate detoxification regimen. Once the acute reaction or panic has subsided, sedatives or tranquilizers have been recommended.

You have to be particularly careful what you do with a patient like this because his altered perceptions will color everything you do. . . . A gruff manner may send a patient on LSD into a screaming panic, or a sympathetic manner may be treatment enough. Even with the most severe case of LSD intoxication, we've been able to turn a bad trip back to a good trip with nothing but the talk-down. (Smith, 1969)

Some clinicians place more emphasis upon pleasant surroundings and psychological supports during the initial treatment phase than upon medication.

We get a patient into as pleasant an environment as possible and try to make him comfortable. If he's got sympathetic friends with him, keep them around and then just talk. Try to find out what is actually causing the panic. . . . Keep emphasizing that all these things are effects of the drug and that they'll pass. . . . Very often you may want to use a tranquilizer, too — you can give 50 mg. of Thorazine orally to begin with and then repeat it every three or four hours depending on the patient's anxiety — but the psychological support is more important. (Smith, 1969)

The duration of the initial treatment of the acutely intoxicated abuser is relatively short — 12 to 72 hours. Once this period of intoxication is over, and if symptoms of mental illness are apparent, any medication prescribed should be on the same basis as for a similar type of mentally ill person who has not been involved with hallucinogens.

Postdetoxification treatment during initial abstinence is probably best managed if it is focused upon coming to grips with any psychological dependency produced by the abuse. As with any drug which produces a psychological dependency, the dependency produced by LSD abuse continues long after the physiological effects have dissipated. Sympathetic supportive counselling seems to be most effective during postdetoxification treatment. As one clinician puts it, "The compulsive user, and often the initiate as well, usually has severe underlying psychiatric problems, and it's almost impossible to break a pattern of abuse without treating these problems." (Smith, 1969)

Extended therapeutic contact with the ex-abuser of LSD is imperative for two reasons. First, after psychedelic intoxication there is always the possibility of spontaneous recurrence; and second, this contact is the only way in which the clinician can ascertain if the acute reactions are indicative of a chronic abuse pattern.

In our discussions of treatment and rehabilitation, we have purposefully provided more information about nonnarcotic drugs and the abusers of them. We have chosen to do so because the abusers of these soft drugs far outnumber the abusers of narcotics, because they are more frequently in the labor force, and because less is known about them. We have also purposefully avoided any success predictions in discussing treatment and rehabilitation. We have chosen not to do so because no one knows how many succeed. We have attempted to show that success is a matter of how much the abuser wants to succeed, how much you and others significant to him want him to succeed and what help he gets in the endeavor. The medical officer has the pivotal position in this entire process. It is he who must have the largest repertory of knowledge and the largest number of skills whereby he can advise both management and the employee who is abusing drugs. If the medical officer and his related health services staff do not keep abreast of the explosion of information in these areas, there is little hope of intelligent company policy concerning the drug-abusing employee and even less hope of rehabilitating these employees. As one medical officer has stated, too often the medical officer's primary allegiance and obligation to his company have made him unappreciative of the fact that what is good for the employee is almost always good for the company.

For a summarization, we are unable to improve upon the statements of a chief medical officer for a major insurance company concerning this new role of the medical officer.

He must immerse and educate himself in the drug epidemic and the drug scene so that he can lend his expertise to his company in formulation, implementation and expansion of a company philosophy, policy and program on drug abuse.

. . . He must develop an awareness and a know-how so that, as much as it is possible to do so, he can protect the company from hiring the unknown user, to establish a medical environment which offers concentrated help to those employees turning to drug abuse, to aid in every capacity in rehabilitation and a return to life, and to help fulfill the company's community obligation to hire or rehire the handicapped but rehabilitated ex-user.

. . . Lastly, to critically involve himself and his company not just in the corporate scene, but in the community drug scene as well within practical limitations.

Employing the Former Abuser

If society is to have any hope for successfully rehabilitating the hundreds of thousands of persons who have become dysfunctional as the result of abusing drugs, business and industry must provide the former users with meaningful occupational roles. This must be done in spite of the fact that we know of *no one* or *no agency* who can certify that a former abuser will not return to drugs. At the present time, it is relatively easy to predict who will return to drug use but extremely difficult to predict who will not. The only meaningful certification which is possible is a probability statement based upon ill-defined clinical judgments and past experiences. While no one can guarantee abstinence, high levels of work performance, punctuality, absence of theft, and so forth, there are a few rules-of-thumb which one can consider while one decides whether to hire a former abuser. These rules are themselves only probability statements.

1. *No one* knows the actual success potential for any treatment program. All programs have more failures than successes, and it is not possible at this time to predict with any certainty which will be the case for any one individual. Do not be confused or misled by those who present high comparative success figures, for example, self-help abstinence programs versus methadone maintenance.
2. The longer a former abuser has been in a formal treatment program or the longer he has been drug-free, the greater are the chances he will remain drug-free.
3. Those former abusers who began their drug use during a legitimate medical regimen have greater success rates.
4. Those former abusers who primarily used only one drug or one class of drugs have a greater success rate than the poly-drug abusers.
5. Former abusers who had marketable employment skills prior to using drugs have greater success rates. Even with those former abusers with no prior marketable skills, the maintaining of a legitimate work role significantly increases the probability of a successful rehabilitation.
6. Former abusers who work in supervised situations, where their duties are clearly defined and structured, have higher success rates than

those who must function independently or where performance expectations are not clearly defined.

Because of the risks in employing the former abuser, common sense dictates that each applicant be independently considered. If the assets which the former abuser brings to the job outweigh the known risks he presents, he should be given the opportunity of marketing these assets.

It is unfortunate that those social agencies which treat and rehabilitate drug abusers have not adequately evaluated the ability of their clients and former clients to perform and compete in the normal work world. In their need to appear successful, these agencies too frequently publish exaggerated or otherwise misleading claims on work performance, lack of impairment, and so forth. It seems advisable for business and industry to independently consider addressing these issues. For example, various segments of business and industry could collaborate with several specially designed and controlled experimental work programs for former abusers. Such a pooling of resources could establish data bases and subsequent guidelines appropriate to the various types of former abusers in various types of work settings.

Some companies have experimented with the employment of former users to function as liaisons between employee drug users and management, as "gatekeepers" between employees who use drugs and appropriate treatment services, as detectors of users who are applying for employment or who are undetected on-board users, and as educators of the nonusers or potential users. While there is some utility in all of these roles, we must caution management about expecting too much from former abusers employed in these capacities. When one considers hiring former abusers in these capacities, one should also consider the following:

1. Even if a former abuser understands his own abuse of drugs, this is no guarantee he will understand someone else's abuse of them.
2. Former abusers who were rehabilitated in a formal treatment program too often hold unrealistic, positive beliefs about the efficacy of that program's approach and corresponding unrealistic, negative beliefs about all other approaches. These identifications with specific treatment programs quite often are maintained with such religious

fervor that the graduate is unable to view objectively that or any other program.

3. Former abusers as a group have not been shown to be more qualified than aware, observant medical and personnel officers in the assessment of the motivation of former abusers seeking employment, or in the detection of hidden abusers among those already employed.

In summary, we believe there to be some utility in having former abusers functioning as liaisons, gatekeepers, and so forth, if one's expectations of them in these roles are rationally and realistically based. Being a former abuser is not a skill, but insightful, feeling and skilled people can be former abusers.

About Employee Education, and Yours

The greatest long-range problem, many managers feel, is not the present drug abuser in industry, but employees who do not use drugs. The challenge is in keeping them able to withstand the pressures that push them in the direction of experimenting with drugs. Employees, especially younger ones, are beginning to accept drugs as a socially acceptable, "in" thing. Important as it may be to find ways of reaching present drug users, to rehabilitate them, to identify them among job applicants, these activities alone cannot stem the tide of misuse. The problem must be stopped before it starts, or at least minimized.

Only through education can the in-house spread of drugs be reduced. Business and industry must create a new awareness and a better understanding among all employees of the many and varied aspects of drug use and its impact on family, job, and health. Needed are programs that give employees the latest medical evidence, that correct misconceptions about drug use, that cut through myth and adult hypocrisy, and that allow for response.

It has been said that industry is about three years behind the public schools in developing educational programs to combat drug abuse. Perhaps this is good, because by-and-large the schools have done a poor job. In the intervening years, industry has learned from the schools' mistakes. It has learned, for example, that to be effective, employee drug education must:

1. Communicate within the context of a drug-using society.
2. Develop programs based on participatory education.

Industry may have learned from the schools' mistakes, but it has yet to act on that knowledge in a meaningful way. For the most part, educational efforts have not taken the two important points mentioned above into consideration. Instead, business, if it is doing anything, has followed its traditional pattern of employee communications: tell them what management thinks they should know. Communication has been a one-way street with information about drugs (much of it inaccurate) emanating from management, and none returning. The subject of drugs is too complex, managements are too naive, and today's young people are too cynical for this old approach to work any longer.

Payroll inserts, booklets, posters, house organ articles, and films explaining the dangers of drugs do not hurt, but do they help meet your educational objectives? We do not think so — not by themselves. They are useful only as adjuncts to a broader employee education program that communicates within the context of a drug-using society and allows for active employee involvement.

There are no short-cuts to effective employee drug education. It requires much more time and effort than one-way communication. One-way worked when you were explaining an addition to the benefit plan. But the subject of drugs demands more sophisticated education, and there is simply no alternative.

When considering an employee education program to combat drug misuse in your company, you must acknowledge that young people at almost every age level are the first to point out that ours is a drug-dependent society. Almost everyone uses drugs for one reason or another — to cure a headache, to relieve depression, to gain energy, to go to sleep, to diet, for endless physiological and psychological reasons.

Television and other advertising media tell us daily that pills, tablets and capsules are the panacea for almost everything, from the prevention of birth to a mild headache. Tranquilizers and antidepressants are hawked as the answer to many if not most of life's trials and tribulations. We are told that it is difficult if not impossible to get through life without the aid and comfort of these drugs.

Remember, your younger employees were weaned on a welter of advertisements that urged them from infancy to use drugs to feel better. What is wrong with drugs, the kids ask; everyone uses them. Popping pills is as normal as brushing your teeth.

A publication titled, *Drugs and Drug Abuse Education Newsletter* — a fine source published by Scope Publications, Inc., Washington, D.C. — recently cited an advertisement for a tranquilizer that ran in a magazine for doctors. The ad pictured a coed at the beginning of her college career. The headline said: "A Whole New World of Anxiety!" In copy surrounding the attractive, worried young lady, the advertiser noted that the exposure to new friends and other influences may force her to reevaluate herself and her goals. "Her newly stimulated intellectual curiosity may make her more sensitive to and apprehensive about unstable national and world conditions." The ad suggests that the tranquilizer, along with counselling, could counteract this.

In all likelihood, your younger employees see no difference between a middle-aged housewife using tranquilizers to reduce anxiety, a man using alcohol to relax, and themselves using marihuana for their own reasons. The difference, they are told, is only in the type of drugs being used; some are legal and some are not. It is as simple as that. But is it? Not as far as the kids are concerned, who quickly point to adult discrimination and hypocrisy.

Your employee education program should reflect this duality in standards; otherwise your efforts will be met with skepticism and doubt. The important point is that if you want to communicate about the drug scene and be convincing, you have got to tell it the way it is. Your information must be complete and it must be accurate. You will have to be honest enough to deal with the complexities of the subject — adults' hangups as well as the youngsters'.

Nor can you sensationalize drug use, using fear as a base on which to build your educational program. Overkill destroys your credibility. You cannot hope to convince a pot smoker that marihuana can lead to the use of hard drugs if his experience and the experiences of his peers fly in the face of such statements. And the facts are, you may be wrong. You can, however, point out that facts seem to indicate that the use of marihuana *may* lead to the use of hard drugs, leaving the conclusion to employees.

Your younger employees who have been brought up in the drug culture may be smarter than you are about what is happening "on the scene." Any false statements, any moralizing based on insufficient evidence, will destroy the effectiveness of your message. Your words will be measured carefully; they will be measured against a drug user's own experience, against what he knows about the experiences of others, and they will be measured by employees not now using drugs on the basis of what they have seen and heard.

Employees, especially those using drugs or those on the brink of experimenting, will delight in underscoring untruths and inconsistencies in your educational program. This could be more detrimental in the long run than not having any educational program at all. Needless to say, there are inconsistencies on the drug scene — in terms of legislation, penalties, and medical evidence about the results of use of drugs. These inconsistencies are beyond your control. Do not try to defend them. You will be building your credibility if you describe them, giving equal time to various points of view and giving employees an opportunity to question your facts. The old one-way approach to communication — "tack this memo on all bulletin boards" — does not allow for this.

Mutual Trust the Key

What is the best method to reach your people? There are literally hundreds of companies that will tell you they can take your problems of employee drug education off your hands. With each passing day, scores of new instructional tools and materials are coming onto the market — films, reading-rack booklets, drug kits, packaged articles for house organs, and so forth.

Some are worthwhile, but all too many of these devices are ineffective simply because the authors have failed to design their materials around even a superficial understanding of today's youth. They have created their educational tools on myth and wishful thinking, using a profile of youngsters that is what we would like them to be rather than what they are. Unless discussion of the decision to use or not to use drugs is placed into the context of the way kids feel about drugs, and the way they view society, your drug education program will be a waste of time and money.

The most important thing in a successful drug education program is mutual trust between you and your employees. If you are alienated from each other (the generation gap exists in business as well as in the home), education will not work. Even face-to-face discussion between generations will only serve to widen the gap if there is not mutual trust. And trust is only born of understanding.

How well do you understand your employees' feelings about drugs? If you do not know (not *think* you know) what your people believe about drugs, you are in a poor position to evaluate materials or tools that will be beneficial to your education program. Begin with these three steps:

1. Familiarize yourself with the drug scene as it is known in the "straight" world — doctors, social workers, your top management, government literature.
2. Familiarize yourself with how the younger generation thinks about the drug scene. There is a difference. You will have to listen a lot, not just talk.
3. Develop imaginative ways of communicating with youth about drug abuse, preferably based on participatory education. The old ways do not work.

One company helped accomplish steps one and two with a single procedure. Groups of employees were invited to hear the company medical director discuss the dangers of drug abuse and the head of the personnel department explain the company's concern about the problem. After the lectures, the personnel man asked for six young employees to discuss the program with the two speakers. The personnel man was scrupulously honest in describing to the employees the reason for the rap session and the objective he hoped it would accomplish. The employees were told that this was the beginning of a plan for what hopefully would be an effective, all-company employee education program. Before designing a program the company wanted to find out how their younger employees felt about the problem. Three girls and three boys accepted the invitation; four white and two black. They ranged in age from 18 to 23, and nothing was known of their records — whether they were using drugs or ever had. The employees represented a broad cross section of occupations — clerical, manufacturing, and inspectors. The personnel man reported:

We learned a good deal about our younger people from the rap session, there's no question about it. We learned, for example, that they cannot be spoon-fed information; they disagree with some of our beliefs; that if we hope to reach them, our education program would have to be far more creative than a few scare articles in our company magazine. The kids learned something too, I think. They learned that we are capable of listening and that we are interested in their views and ideas; they learned that we can begin to admit that we don't know all the answers. Out of the meeting came a certain degree of mutual trust and understanding, and this was a good beginning.

It was a beginning, but that is all it was. For it is almost startling how little adults know (or perhaps care to know) about how youngsters feel about drugs. The following transcript is a portion of the rap session. It serves to underscore that all-too-familiar gap in understanding between generations. While managers may not agree with what some of the kids have to say, they can better understand the need for creativity when it comes to trying to communicate with them:

DOCTOR: You have just heard me discuss drugs and drug abuse and I would like to know whether you agree with me, whether you disagree with anything, or whether you have any questions.

EMPLOYEE: I'd like to know whether you have ever tried any of these drugs you knock. Like, do you speak from experience?

DOCTOR: I have taken some. But let me say that I have also delivered many babies — about 100 in my first 12 months of practice — but I never had a baby. I just want you to understand that you can know a subject in detail without ever having experienced what is involved in it. I also was administered morphine during World War II, so I know the kind of feeling you get from some of these drugs.

EMPLOYEE: Have you ever smoked marihuana?

DOCTOR: Yes, I tried it once. It was a very pleasant experience.

EMPLOYEE: But you said it can have bad effects. What can you really know having only tried it once?

DOCTOR: Does one have to try every drug many times to really know? As a doctor I know what a depressant does, I know what alcohol does, I know what barbiturates and amphetamines do. I know what the long-term effects of most drugs are.

EMPLOYEE: I don't think adults know anything about it, especially parents. They don't even know the difference between pot and heroin. They say all drugs are bad, and that's it.

DOCTOR: Parents need good information about drugs, as we all do. If they have that then at least there is some base for common discussion. In the absence of accurate information, there is a real barrier to communication. It is pretty tough for parents today with the widespread increase in heroin addiction. It is a very frightening thing for them and it is easy to understand why they may look at you in a different way because of it. They see every day that young people like yourselves have been busted and they wonder if their child is involved. And this creates fear. I sympathize with them. Don't you?

EMPLOYEE: Sort of. But usually a kid has to open a discussion with his parents about drugs. They won't. I know they are under a lot of pressure now, with the whole world blowing its mind, and they are afraid their kids are going to blow their minds too. They hear from their neighbors that grass is bad, and that it is all over the place, and they tighten up. But everything is publicized so much these days, it is tough to open a discussion with them. They are running scared, even looking for such things as loss of weight and then accusing you of using drugs. They see some kids in the neighborhood who have freaked out — kids from so-called good families — and it really tightens them up. It is a new thing for them, and they almost don't want to understand it. They want to ignore it, and maybe it will go away.

EMPLOYEE: They won't talk about it, but they do it themselves. What do you do when the parents turn on — with booze or grass or tranquilizers? They discourage their children, but they turn on.

DOCTOR: You mean alcohol?

EMPLOYEE: And pot and pills.

DOCTOR: Well, that is hypocritical, isn't it? I don't think they have a chance of communicating with their children about right and wrong.

EMPLOYEE: Now wait a minute, Doc. What's right and what's wrong?

DOCTOR: Well, I think my discussion this morning made some points about this. Let's take a simple statement we can kick around: do we all agree that heroin addiction is bad, it's wrong? And do we all agree that helping a heroin addict is right? As I mentioned, many companies are trying to work with employees who are hooked. Rehabilitation, and we are thinking about this. What do you think?

EMPLOYEE: You can't change the world, man. You can change a person maybe, but you can't change the world. You can't make someone fit in a world that he never fitted into in the first place. If a man fits in the world, maybe he wouldn't be on drugs in the first place. If he were born white, let's just say. I know a lot of guys that say shooting dope isn't bad for them. It's your white establishment that it's bad for. Sometimes a black man is using dope just to buy himself some escape, but then he goes too far and crashes. Then he is a problem, a white man's problem. But junk isn't the problem to begin with.

EMPLOYEE: Yeh, maybe he is a hype to keep from going nuts in this world. We all have our escape valves. The other day a buddy of mine was brought into personnel because they thought he was smoking pot. I know the guy he saw and I bet just before my pal came in, the guy popped his fourth tranquilizer.

EMPLOYEE: So rehab is o.k., man. Clean 'em up, but make a place for them in this world after. Make them a part of it. See, they can be a part of something in the world of junk. Everyone's the same; they are dependent on each other. You have people you rely on, and people who rely on you. You are part of a scene. It is a bummer, but at least you are part of it.

DOCTOR: So you think an important part of rehabilitation should be the hope of a good future for someone?

EMPLOYEE: The hell with rehabilitation! Give them a chance before they get hooked. Once they're hooked, it really changes them. You straighten them out, but they are scared. They don't want to go out into the world again, because they know they may not be cured. Stopped, yeh. But they've got to get through every day, every hour, without anybody's help. That's why a lot of so-called ex-hypes stay on as employees of the residential rehab houses. They feel part of something and they need the constant reassurance. Anyway, the straight world looks at the ex-addict like he was some kind of monster. An ex-alcoholic gets a medal; an ex-addict gets strange looks.

DOCTOR: How would you suggest we get to people before they get hooked?

EMPLOYEE: When they are kids, I guess. Like, it's that group thing again. If no one takes an interest in them when they are kids, they'll stick with the bunch and go for dope if it is around.

DOCTOR: That gets us back to the parents again.

PERSONNEL MAN: You know one of the problems I think we have here is that for a long time we have been dealing with alcohol out in the open. Even though you know that you are going to have a hangover, for example, you know what the end result is going to be. So maybe some of the parents and older people are really scared because they don't know about marihuana or heroin or other drugs. It is fear of the unknown. They know about alcohol. They may know it is not good, but at least they know it. So I suspect that you can communicate with your parents about alcohol a lot better because they know something about it. So maybe the answer is getting more information to the adults about drugs.

EMPLOYEE: I don't think so. There has been a ton of information for them, if they wanted it. But all they say is that it is bad and don't go near it. If you ask them questions they just say it's illegal, don't use it. They say, "I don't want to talk about it anymore." They won't discuss it.

DOCTOR: Are you suggesting that there is something good about using drugs?

EMPLOYEE: Maybe not, but I think there is a lot to be talked about. Like how do adults get away with making a distinction between alcohol and marihuana? Booze is a drug too, but it's legal. Marihuana is a drug but it is illegal. I've tried both, and it seems to me that alcohol is worse. I get sick with booze and feel rotten the next day. I feel good with marihuana and I don't have a hangover. I don't lose time on the job with marihuana, but I did when I used booze. I just don't like the idea that the only difference between booze and grass is that one is legal and the other isn't. And that's it, with no more discussion about it.

DOCTOR: Marihuana is often presented as you have just presented it — as being a mild hallucinogen, and you can use it and the effects are most pleasant; it doesn't cause a hangover, you don't get sick, it makes you enjoy things and people more. So you say, well, what is really wrong with it? Suppose I say to you that by using it you are running the risk of damaging your brain structure. Does that have any impact on you?

EMPLOYEE: Well, you run the risk of ruining your liver with alcohol. I also think that a booze high is a bummer — you blow your mind, get overconfident and do things you'd never do sober. You don't with grass. But the next question, I think, is how many people can use marihuana steadily without going on to stronger drugs?

DOCTOR: Well, we don't have good statistics about drug abuse. It is illegal and we are handicapped in our studies, so we have to go on limited surveys and then extrapolate. We don't know, but we suspect that 20 million people have used marihuana and there are about 200,000 heroin addicts in the United States. This would suggest that the vast majority of people who use marihuana don't go on to use heroin. We don't know. But the real risk is that you might start fooling with other kinds of drugs that are worse. I have heard that you can't be around any kind of stuff without running into all the other stuff.

EMPLOYEE: I think it depends on the individual. I've known friends who just smoke pot and they hang with a group of people who are on ups and downs and some of them are into junk. But the pill poppers and the junkies don't try to force the marihuana smokers to turn on with their stuff; they know that if you don't want to turn on with other drugs, it's no good; it will make things worse and turn you against barbs or junk.

EMPLOYEE: Sure, it's up to the individual. But I think if you want to hang with a group you like, you are influenced by what they do. If they smoke pot, chances are you will too, if you want to be part of the group. It isn't the group itself that forces you, it is the individual who feels he has to do something to belong. You either do it, or walk away.

DOCTOR: Do you know anyone who graduated from grass to junk? Do you think they knew what they were getting into?

EMPLOYEE: Yeh, I know people who have gone all the way. One guy had real family problems and he wanted to be accepted by the group. He was looking for a place to be; but I don't think he knew what he was letting himself in for when he started shooting. He first really knew weeks later when he woke up with one hell of a Jones — upset stomach, achy, cramps. He was hooked.

DOCTOR: Peer pressure is a very strong force. But drugs are illegal and I'm wondering if you think the law is a stronger force. Do you think so?

EMPLOYEE: The law is hypocritical too. I know the fuzz keeps half of the stuff they catch you carrying. And they sell it again. I know this. So I don't have much respect for the narcos.

DOCTOR: Unfortunately, you may be right. A few years ago, federal narcotics agents in New York — as I recall thirty-one of them — were accused of selling drugs. Some resigned, some went to court. Let's face it, it is a dirty, messy business. Sometimes the agents are involved; we shouldn't evade that. But the laws themselves — do you think they are just?

EMPLOYEE: No. I think the laws should be as strict as the drugs involved. Like if you have LSD or mescaline, the law should be strict. But not for pot. The more powerful the drug, the more powerful the punishment.

EMPLOYEE: Right. A felony for carrying a little grass is all out of whack. A felony is not something you want on your record. A lot of places won't give you a job with it on your record, and that makes everything worse because more and more guys are on the street just because of a little pot.

DOCTOR: Do you think enforcement of just laws, better laws, will work?

EMPLOYEE: No. It didn't work during prohibition. Sure some people got busted. But it didn't work.

DOCTOR: Well, if we can agree that excessive use of drugs is bad, how then do we get at the problem?

EMPLOYEE: Make it legal.

DOCTOR: Why would that help?

EMPLOYEE: There seems to be a certain attraction about something that is illegal. O.K., so there will be a mad rush in the beginning, just like for booze after prohibition. But after that it will taper off.

DOCTOR: But booze and cigarettes in excess are bad too, and legalizing them has not cut down on the number of people using them. How, for example, would legalizing pot help?

EMPLOYEE: First of all, I don't think pot is bad for me. That's your story. If I want to swell my head with pot now and then, I will, but I won't go to skin pops. How much can pot hurt me? Anyway, it should be my choice.

DOCTOR: Suppose I told you it causes permanent damage with respect to recent memory, so that the more you use it, the less able you are to remember things that happened in the recent past.

EMPLOYEE: That would make a dent with me.

DOCTOR: But it would have to be factual information?

EMPLOYEE: Yeh, you would have to prove it, and I don't think anyone has yet.

DOCTOR: How can we make people believe that there is a risk using drugs? That is a tough one.

EMPLOYEE: It doesn't work with cigarettes, even with proof. There is a health risk, and it is even spelled out on the package. But it doesn't work. It is up to the individual. It is excessive use of anything that is bad. Excessive use of cigarettes, booze or marihuana. You can abuse all of them if you want to. The only thing is, booze and cigarettes are legal; but even in moderation, pot is illegal.

EMPLOYEE: Right, it is all up to the individual. It depends on how you feel. You can smoke a carload of grass and not get high if you don't want to. Or, you can just sniff it sometimes, and you get high. Anyway, people are going to use pot whether it is legal or not. Kids are finding marihuana an easier way than booze of getting a high. You don't get a hangover or sick, and it is tougher for the parents or your superviser to find out.

PERSONNEL: Why is that? Marihuana has a strong aroma — something like burnt palms.

EMPLOYEE: Parents or supervisors just don't know. Last week a friend of mine had a bunch of guys up his house smoking pot and his parents came home early. They had finished smoking but the odor was there; the parents thought the television had burnt out.

DOCTOR: Well, you know, adults do not understand much about the drug scene, but they are worried about young people using more and more. And they ask themselves, "Why?" Why do young people abuse these substances?

EMPLOYEE: For the same reason you drink. To get away from reality for a few hours. Whether reality is trouble or monotony, you need an escape. You know you are not doing anything beneficial. It's just an escape for a little while. Your generation does it with booze; ours with drugs. We don't like your way. You've got to do your own thing.

Will these employees and thousands like them respond to one-way communication? Certainly not. But they are receptive to discussion, to rapping, to the sharing of ideas. To be effective, then, your education program must allow for employees to participate in the process, or if not that, then create instructional vehicles that utilize their peers; kids believe other kids.

Kids Believe Each Other

Just how well kids believe other kids is exemplified by a seven-minute film produced by a New York company and used as part of its employee orientation program. The cast of the film is two young company employees — a girl 19 and a boy 21. The setting is a mailroom where they work, and the film describes the company's drug policy in the language of the young. A company spokesman explained:

Our drug policy was written in corporate and legal gobbledegook, and we felt that many of our new people didn't understand it or didn't even read it. So what we did was to ask two youngsters here to give us their ideas about presenting the policy to newcomers. They reviewed the policy and started talking about it together, and then the idea came to someone to make a film based pretty much on their discussion and improvisation. The two kids had definite ideas about how to get the policy across. Out of their thoughts we created a boiled-down version of our policy, which is given to every new employee after they see the film. In essence, the two kids created everything; we simply produced it.

Is the film working? It is too early to tell. But one thing is clear: the company now has kids talking to kids about its drug policy, and the feeling is that this *has* to be more effective than simply passing out a policy statement.

"The film has one purpose," said the company spokesman: "to let the kids know what the rules are here. Nothing more. We don't get into the dangers of drugs in this film. One thing at a time, and I believe this peer-to-peer approach is working for us."

The film is short and interesting. The kids began only with a script outline and improvised most of their dialogue. They are believable and, in turn, convincing, primarily because they are employees, they are kids, they know the drug scene, and they know company rules. Everything is authentic:

MAILROOM

Hi. My name is George. What's yours?

Joan.

Are you new? I haven't seen you around before.

I just started a few days ago.

Nice to have you here.

Thanks. You know, you're the first person that really noticed me. People notice, I guess, but they don't say much, so I'm really glad we are talking like this.

Me too.

How long have you been working here?

I've been here almost a year now.

You must know a lot about what happens around here.

Yeh, I do. I know a lot of people, mostly because I'm a messenger and I get around a lot. Do you have a lot of friends in the company?

No. I know one girl upstairs, but not very well.

Well, if you don't mind, how about having lunch with me and some of my friends today?

Hey, I'd really like that. Great! What time do you go to lunch?

Twelve o'clock.

Hey this is great. What do you do on your lunch hour?

Oh, not much. A bunch of us will go to the park and hang around. We rap a little and generally have a good time.

Oh, I've been to the park before. In fact, I turned on down there.

Oh yeh?

Yeh. Do you turn on around here at all?

Wait a minute, what do you mean by turning on?

You know, turning on, drugs. Because when we go to lunch today I have this friend that works right around this area who can take care of us and . . . .

Hold it, hold it. That may be your thing but around here it isn't ours. Being new around here I guess you don't know very much about the company's drug policy. You know, this is a place of business. We all come here to work. That's what you came here for, right? That's why you were hired. Like you come from 9 to 5 and you have your responsibilities like everyone else. You can't come in here just to blow your mind and get high. You can't do it. This company is against it, other companies are against it. And I'm sure you know it is against the law too. So if you think you can come here and blow your mind, baby, and let everybody watch you, you got another think coming.

Company policy, huh. O.K., what if I don't use stuff here myself? I can get real good stuff, you know, the best, and we might be able to sell some of it around here.

Now wait a minute. That's the main thing; they're really looking for pushers. That's big trouble. It's bad enough that you come here and want to use it, but it is even worse if you are going to try and push it to other people in the company. You'll be right out the door.

O.K., so forget about dealing. Suppose they caught me using something here in the building, would they fire me just for that?

No, you would probably be warned. It wouldn't be an easy warning; you'd get a harsh warning, baby. You'd have to knock it right off. Some things will be held against you, but you'll get a chance. Like you may not get a raise you are up for, or a promotion, and you might get suspended from the company for a while. But the main thing is that if you are going to come here and try to deal and push around the premises, baby, you'll be fired.

O.K., so what would happen if I were really strung out and I wanted help? Would the company help me?

That's where our company is different from other companies. If you are really hooked on drugs, the company will try to help you, but only if you want help.

But how can they help me?

Well, we have a medical center downstairs on the third floor and you could go down there and they'll discuss your problems with you. They'll let you know where you can go for help, and all this will be kept confidential. Nothing will be held against you. They'll help you after hours if you'd like, and you can still stay with the company, if you can work.

Really? I've never heard of a job like that.

I told you, you don't find too many companies like this. But everybody's got their own thing; this is our company's thing.

Hey, that's great. I've got to split now, but I'll be talking to you.

But what about lunch, like we said?

Out of sight, man. Do you really mean it?

I wouldn't have asked you if I didn't mean it. You can meet a lot of people today, o.k.?

Beautiful. See you at noon.

Getting policy across is one thing, but convincing employees about the dangers of drug misuse is quite another. It takes even more imagination. "But," says a personnel gal for the same New York firm, "it becomes easier when you listen to the kids and find out that they really want to know more about the effects of drugs, more than the usual facts and statistics fed them. And you can reach them if you *show* them what it is like, not just tell them. You find out, too, that they really relate to novel educational approaches utilizing other youngsters."

One novel approach used by the company was a play about drug addiction performed by young people who had experienced it. The play, titled "The Concept," was presented to employees in a company cafeteria. The program was for nonmanagement people only and nobody over 25 was permitted to attend. The play was part of an afternoon-long program which included person-to-person conversations and informal discussion groups.

"The Concept" was created in 1966 when eight residents of Daytop Village, a New York self-help center for drug addicts, were chosen to write a scenario of their personal histories, based on ideas, and recollections. Originated as a method of group therapy and not intended for theatre, the play has no formal script. It is built around the basic plot devised three years ago.

> "I'm Mark, and I need LOVE!"
> "I'm Diane, and I'm ANGRY!"
> "I'm Leon, and I HATE YOU!"

So begins the hard-hitting performance. From the moment they walk on stage, the Daytop actors engage in a wild and wooly dramatization of the experiences of a teenage junkie.

Daytop Villagers, whose average age is 21, have together experienced a total of 40 years of heroin addiction. With such a history, they are well qualified to give a down-to-earth dramatization of the horrors of drug abuse, complete with screams for help, name-calling, and physical contact with the audience.

The play is a loosely sequential account of a young man's first heroin experience, his inevitable breakdown and arrest, his night in prison, his trial, his sentence of either a jail term or Daytop Village, his first days at Daytop, and finally his rehabilitation and renewal. Along with the scenes from the young man's actual experience with heroin, there are routines, tableaux, processions, and even little allegories depicting the various crises of the hooked generation.

Some of the scenes are little horror shows with the pusher as villain. Others are statements of philosophy. Still others are short climaxes of emotion, as when the junkie fancies himself drowning in his own weakness and screams for help. Some of the highpoints are pure farce — belly-laugh scenes of a kiss in the park interrupted by a low-flying pigeon, or a sequence in which the big bruiser turns out to be something less.

The theme of "The Concept" — the search for the true self and a means of expressing it — confronts the audience in the final moments when the players ask, "Will you love me?" and they walk out into the audience to embrace the people who are willing. What begins as a play about drugs ends as a play about people — not just the people who were once addicted to drugs, but everybody who was ever afraid and wanted to be loved.

Judging from the employees' reaction to the final scene, as well as their comments in the discussion groups following the play, "The Concept" had a much stronger impact than the usual antidrug program. It would be hard for anyone — no matter how much they know about drugs — to turn a deaf ear to the climactic speech of the play. It sums up the Daytop philosophy, as well as the play's importance to employees:

"Until a person confronts himself in the eyes and hearts of others, he is running. Until he suffers them to share his secret, he has no safety from it. Afraid to be known, he can know neither himself nor any other; he will be alone."

"I just never knew it would turn out so well," said the personnel gal. I've seen the play three times, and every time, I learn a little more. A lot of our people say they wish they could see it more than once."

But there is one warning that goes with this type of education. While participation of former drug addicts can be useful in teaching sessions, watch out not to sensationalize the drug education process by glorifying the role of the former addict and presenting him as a model for young employees. Glorification of the addict, particularly those who can display the stigmata of needle tracks to awestruck youngsters, is dangerous. Do not ignore the fact that to become a successful ex-addict, one first must be an addict. According to Dr. Melvin Weinswig of the University of Wisconsin, "One of the basic problems with drugs today is that there is a narrow line between that which will convince users of the hazards of misuse of drugs and that which will encourage drug abuse by creating a morbid curiosity in turning one's self on."

Essentially, however, that fine line can be walked, and the positive results of the excellent instruction provided by "The Concept," for example, is a good trade-off against the risk of glorifying addiction. Remember, the objective in all of this is prevention, to help reduce the spread of drugs in your company. The means is participatory education, or at least peer-to-peer instruction.

The best program for your company is one you design yourself, geared to your needs and aims. But there are guidelines that may be helpful in creating your approach:

1. Ideally, base your education on a dialogue with your employees. Make the process a two-way street, involving them in the action.
2. Do not indoctrinate; rather, convey information that is as accurate as you know how to make it, and then answer questions. The subject requires a give-and-take exchange of views. For example, films or lectures should be followed by rap sessions; panel discussions with question and answer time. One-way communication, such as booklets and house organs, does not allow for this. If a house organ is to be utilized as part of the overall program, articles should be written by young employees with experiences to impart. The best printed instruction consists of booklets containing edited transcripts of employee–management rap sessions.

3. All members of management participating in the education process (or the search for answers) should either know the drug scene well or admit that they do not. Do not try to "con" the employees with an "understanding" you do not have. They will see right through you and turn off.

4. An educational dialogue, to be effective, must be a continuing exercise. The format of the dialogue may change — from workshop atmosphere to personal counseling. For example, supervisors should be available for followup sessions.

5. If possible, broaden rap sessions and group discussions to include a family night; parents usually need more information about drug abuse than the kids.

Incidentally, parents can be an important asset to your overall preventative drug education program. One company has produced a booklet specifically for parents which is mailed to the homes of employees under 25. The booklet not only explains drugs to the parents, but it details what the company is doing in its in-house education program. While the company has received some criticism from parents who do not want their children "to learn about drugs," the majority of parental opinion is enthusiastic.

There is no shortcut to understanding how your own employees feel about drugs. You have to ask them. There is no shortcut to learning about the drug scene yourself. You simply have to do your homework, including the active aspect of talking with ex-addicts, doctors, social workers, rehabilitation people, and so forth. Only then can you design a message and a format that is right for your company and its employees.

Once you feel you are ready to begin thinking about an approach, look at all the tools and materials on the market today and evaluate them. Consult with your communications people, your medical staff, and your personnel department. There are several outside sources that will provide this team with advice, ideas, and information. Some are better than others. Most manufacturers of pharmaceuticals, for example, have people who can help. Smith, Kline and French Laboratories in Philadelphia is one of the more helpful companies. Also contact:

The National Institute of Mental Health
5454 Wisconsin Avenue
Chevy Chase, Maryland   20015

The Pharmaceutical Manufacturers Assn.
1155 15th St., N.W.
Washington, D. C.   20005

The American Pharmaceutical Assn.
2215 Constitution Ave., N.W.
Washington, D. C.   20037

The National Association of Retail Druggists
One East Wacker Drive
Chicago, Illinois   60601

Specific literature about drugs can be obtained by writing the organizations listed under References in the rear of this book.

Communicating
with Supervisors

There is no question that the supervisor's role was always a difficult one. The drug problem only makes it tougher. In fact, there is probably no employee relations problem a supervisor now has that demands or will demand more time, intelligence, and patience. Short of alcoholism, few personal problems can affect his people and in turn his department's productivity more than the misuse of drugs. Unlike alcoholism, drug abuse can spread rapidly through his area, requiring an acute understanding of *all* of his people, their performance, and their problems.

Traditionally, the supervisor's key role has been that of a manipulator and coordinator of people. He manages manpower. And he has been successful, operating much of the time on the principle that if you cannot solve someone's problem, you salve it. But the enigma of drug abuse casts a new light on the supervisor's contribution as a good "people person." Drugs and the unique problems they present are alien to most supervisors' experience.

In the past, supervisors have been effective counselors because they understood both their employees and their problems. But few supervisors fully understand the younger generation or the drug scene. Their continuing effectiveness as managers, however, requires they do.

It is important to the maintenance of the supervisor's traditional effectiveness that employees continue to come to him for help with both work-related and personal problems. This enhances a supervisor's stature and, in turn, his efficiency with all of his people. But seldom will a drug abuser seek help from a supervisor, because he knows that in all likelihood the supervisor cannot relate to the problem. This can reduce the supervisor's effectiveness, in his own mind and those of his people — *all* of his people. Thus the problem of employee drug abuse can have a psychological impact on a department far more insidious than the obvious one-to-one troubles of communication between a supervisor and a single drug user.

It is for this reason, as well as for the reason of coping with employee drug abuse per se, that it is critical that supervisors be encouraged by management to learn about drugs and drug abuse. Coupled with encouragement must be an instructional program that does not overwhelm the supervisor with medical details he cannot assimilate, yet provides him with all the facts about what the company expects him to do. A vague company policy about the supervisor's role will only create more misunderstanding and trouble on the operating level.

While formats for communication with supervisors vary according to the size and scope of a company, the following two-step program is working for firms both large and small. But it must be underscored that this is only a beginning; education, policy and procedures about employee drug abuse, at this stage of the game, are in a constant state of flux, and instructional programs should be made a regular part of a company's ongoing supervisory training program.

The first step is to instruct supervisors as quickly and effectively as possible about what the company is going to do vis-à-vis the drug problem, and what management expects supervisors to do. The information included in the following examples of a two-step instructional program may describe elements of policy that your company has considered and rejected. The purpose here, however, is to include everything so that managers can get ideas about implementing their own individualized programs. This two-step program provides for necessary discussion after supervisors have familiarized themselves with written communications:

1. *Written Communications*
   A. A covering memo should set the tone of the company's position
      and indicate how supervisors will be expected to react to the

problem of employee drug abuse. The memo should include sufficient detail to show the supervisor that he will be expected to
act on the problem. The best way to set the appropriate tone and
to introduce policy is in a memo. The subject of drug abuse is
an emotional one and requires study and thought before open
discussion.

   B. A guide should accompany the memo detailing company policy
(repeated, if already published). It should also include drug education and suggestions for detection, counseling, rehabilitation,
and benefits. All of this information should be designed to provide the supervisor with enough facts to be able to ask intelligent questions during a follow-up group meeting. Do not overwhelm the supervisor with "textbook" instruction about drugs.
Technical material at this early stage is likely to produce a negative response.

2. *Rap Sessions*
   A. Follow-up meetings between supervisors, the company medical
director or outside authorities, and the head of the personnel department should be held to answer questions about written policy, counseling techniques, and drugs in general. Most companies make these meetings part of their regular supervisory
training programs.

COVERING MEMO EXAMPLE

Re: The Drug Problem
To: Supervisory Personnel

The attached guide has been prepared to help you to deal with
possible drug problems that may occur. We are sure you will find
this informative and useful in meeting your supervisory responsibilities in this area. Please familiarize yourself with it, because in
the weeks ahead we will be discussing the subject in special training sessions.

At the outset, it should be reemphasized that there is no evidence of any significant drug problem in our company. However,
medical authorities and social agencies are more and more con-

cerned about the increasing prevalence of drug usage among young people. They are considered particularly vulnerable to drug experimentation and, contrary to popular opinion, they are usually introduced to drugs by friends and not "pushers." Since a majority of our new employees each year are young people, we should be alert to the possibility of this problem developing.

Drug addicts — habitual users of hard drugs, such as heroin, morphine, and other opiates — may not be found in industry, because they are largely unemployable. Among working personnel there may be individuals who use the so-called soft drugs (marihuana, amphetamines, barbiturates) which erode self-control, lead to psychological dependency, and perhaps ultimately lead to the use of hard drugs which cause both psychological and physical dependency and addiction.

There are certain signs which may indicate the existence of possible drug abuse. Some of these are: erratic behavior, stupor, confusion, frequent agitation, lack of coordination, excessive absence and unsatisfactory work performance. The presence of any or all of these signs may not necessarily be the result of a drug problem. They may merely be symptomatic of some other underlying problem that requires immediate attention.

However, where these signs are evident, or there is a suspicion of drug abuse, the employee should be interviewed. It should be made clear that the discussion arises from poor performance, excessive absence, attitude or behavior. The subject can be approached discreetly by asking if the employee has a health problem or is on any kind of medication (or drug).

If the employee acknowledges a problem or the need for medical counseling, arrangements for an appointment with the Medical Director should be made. A memorandum detailing the facts of the case should be sent to the Personnel Department for transmittal to the Medical Director. They will determine what steps, if any, will then need to be taken.

Where the employee denies the existence of a problem or refuses medical counseling, make it clear that an immediate improvement is expected or there will be no alternative but to consider disciplinary action.

We must depend upon your good judgment in obtaining and evaluating the facts so that the few individuals who may be drug abusers can be referred promptly to sources of help. Your alertness and prompt action may spare an employee from irreparable harm.

A schedule of meetings for all supervisors is now being developed so that any questions you have about policy or procedure may be answered.

Supervisor's Guide

The following example of a supervisors' guide does not include a description of the different types of drugs; this information was covered in the chapter, "The Extent of Drug Abuse in Business and Industry." It does not include a description of company policy; examples of policy are included in the chapter, "Policy in the Making."

SUPERVISORS' GUIDE EXAMPLE

Introduction

By technical definition, drugs are chemicals that act upon the body's own chemistry. Most adults take, or have taken, drugs for medical reasons. Drugs such as aspirin, taken for various aches and pains, and antacids, used for heartburn, are in common usage. When taken on the advice of a physician or according to directions on the label, drugs can contribute to restoring and maintaining good health. When misused, they can be harmful to health and after varying periods of constant use, they produce a condition of drug dependence.

In the most simplistic terms, one can view drugs as falling into two main classes. One class has as its purpose the relief of physical symptoms or conditions. The other class serves to alter one's mood or mental state, and these are known as the "mind-affecting drugs" or "mind drugs." It is this latter group with which this guide is concerned. [Here include a description of drugs in your guide.]

It has been determined that a small percentage of our employees may have a drug problem. Only a few of this number are known to supervision or to the medical department. Since we feel that much can be done to rehabilitate many people with a drug problem if it is discovered at an early stage, this guide has been developed to help you deal with the situation when it arises.

It must be remembered, however, that the company's desire to facilitate the identification and possible rehabilitation of drug-dependent employees is necessarily subordinate to the overriding interest in protecting all employees. Accordingly, any case of employee misconduct resulting from the imprudent or intemperate use of drugs may require the company to terminate employment. [Here include specific company policy in your guide.]

Drug abuse can best be defined as any nonmedical use of drugs purely for their euphoric effect, which use results in physical, psychological or social dysfunctioning. It creates continuing difficulties in many areas of the individual's life. It is characterized by drug-seeking behavior at times to the exclusion of all other behavior. When this happens, the drug abuser allows drugs to outweigh all other considerations, including his family, his friends, and his job.

While prevalent among the young, drug abuse is found at all social levels and in all businesses and professions. It has no respect for sex, social rank, or employment status.

There is no single cause for drug abuse. Many drug-dependent employees may have some emotional rationale for their behavior. This may stem from a variety of unfortunate experiences, or may be a means of escaping from problems and tensions. The drug abuser may continue to use drugs to escape from the problems caused by his habit. Drug abuse is **not** caused by lack of will power or lack of sense of responsibility. Your company feels that the drug abuser is not morally bad; in most cases he is a sick person who needs help.

Change in Approach

For years the only method of handling the drug abuser was dismissal. This led to ignoring or covering up an individual's problem until the situation became so bad that punitive action was taken. Sometimes not only the misuser but his family were affected, and the employer often lost the services of a skilled employee.

The current trend in dealing with drug abusers is toward treatment rather than punishment. By adopting definite policies to be carried out conscientiously and uniformly, industry can help solve many of these problems. Not all drug abusers, however, are motivated to cooperate in their rehabilitation, so termination of service will be the only solution in some cases.

To contribute to your understanding of the position this company has adopted in the management of drug abuse, management's present thinking is stated below:

1. Drug dependence is recognized as an illness requiring treatment.
2. Early recognition of the problem is a proper function of supervision. Once recognized, every reasonable effort should be made to encourage and assist the employee in his rehabilitation.
3. If rehabilitation is unsuccessful, the services of the employee will be terminated by resignation or dismissal.

The Supervisor's Role

As a supervisor, you are in a better position than perhaps anyone to identify and guide an employee with a drug problem. Because of your close association with the employee under your supervision, you know his attendance record, his condition and appearance on the job, his habits and, very likely, his family and community relationships.

It is important not to let close friendship and sympathy lead you into the mistake of covering up for him or her with the idea that you are helping. In almost all cases the drug-dependent employee needs the help of others to overcome his problem. The sooner this help is provided, the better are his chances of arresting the progress of this condition.

Often you are the only person who can motivate him to seek treatment. He probably has failed to listen to friends and family who have urged him to do something, but he may be stimulated to action when confronted with the realization that his job may be in jeopardy.

The company considers a drug problem to exist when:

1. Efficiency and dependability of the employee are reduced because of drug dependency.
2. Such drug abuse is not an isolated experience, but more or less repeats itself.
3. Such drug abuse results in recognizable interference with the employee's health, and his or her personal relations with fellow employees or customers.

One, or several, or all of the following signs frequently are seen; and when they are present in combination, they may indicate a high probability that the employee is regularly using drugs.

1. Attendance pattern: frequent Monday, postholiday, and post-payday absence. The drug-dependent employee usually will have from six to eight times as much incidental absence per year as the normal employee. (The usual excuses are headache, upset stomach, colds, or just "feel rotten.")
2. Frequent tardiness
3. Job performance: decreased reliability; erratic performance; tendency to put things off; neglect of details; blaming other workers; desire for job changes; unexplained absence from an assignment.
4. Frequent on- and off-the-job accidents: these may be mostly minor, such as cuts, scrapes, bruises or bumps.
5. Personality changes: moodiness, irritability, chronic complaints and gripes, giddiness, disinterest in work, reports of family or financial difficulty, and memory gaps.

Once the problem is suspected or identified, a specific series of steps should be followed, designed to acquaint the employee with the seriousness of his or her problem, to refer the employee for medical evaluation, and to maintain close supervision during the rehabilitation process.

It should be emphasized again, however, that initial observation should be circumspect. Confronting the drug user requires tact. Requiring a medical examination raises civil liberties questions, or accusation without proof could invite suits of various kinds. Because of these problems, many supervisors are reluctant to report an employee who may be suspected of drug misuse. Although supervisors are aware that illicit use of drugs is a criminal offense, they are also aware of the heavy penalties specified by the law. Knowledge of these stiff penalties often inhibits supervisors from seeking out suspected employee users and trying to help them. Too often, they simply find some "other" excuse to dismiss a suspected user.

At this writing, the facts are that a company has no legal obligation to report an employee user to the police. No crime is committed by failing to notify law enforcement officials. We do feel, however, a moral obligation to report rehabilitated addicts who have had relapses to the appropriate social agency. Drug sellers, the pushers, are to be reported to the police. Any employee suspected of selling drugs on company premises should be reported immediately to the personnel department.

The First Interview

When it is recognized that the employee's attendance, job performance or conduct is becoming unsatisfactory due to suspected drug abuse, you, the supervisor, should have a frank and firm talk with the employee. This often is a difficult task because of personal friendship and the above-mentioned considerations. The interview must be well planned in advance. It is advisable to have a general plan prepared for conducting the interview. The interview should be held at a time when the employee is alert, and should be done in a calm manner and with an attitude of constructive help.

It often helps to jot down the points you wish to cover. These might include:

1. Aspects of the work performance that are not meeting expectations.
2. His personal record of tardiness and sickness absence compared with the other employees in his group or area.

3. His safety record on and off the job.
4. His personal relations with other employees.
5. Changes in his personal and physical appearance.
6. Any other points you may feel are pertinent.

After discussing the above points with him or her, ask the employee if the use of drugs could be a contributing factor to this record. Again, do not accuse him of being a drug abuser or addict. **Suggest** that drugs may be a reason for his record. Remind the employee that there is a company policy on drug abuse. In doing this it is wise to stay close to the wording of the policy.

You will need to remain patient and firm throughout the interview, as at some point the employee can be expected to react to your statements. His reaction usually will be in the form of strong denial and disagreement. Professional people who deal with drug-dependent employees soon learn that many of them can almost convince you that black is white. Others will have vague, general excuses, such as, "I've had a lot of troubles lately." Many drug-using employees do not believe this drug use constitutes a problem for them. The biggest hurdle is to show the employee that a problem does indeed exist. Offer the employee the assistance of the medical department in eliminating the problem.

Be sure that before the interview ends the employee understands that if the situation is not corrected within a reasonable time, there will be a further interview and consultation with higher management. The employee should clearly understand that although the company will assist, it is **his** responsibility to achieve complete control over his problem; that the company expects evidence of favorable progress toward complete rehabilitation; and that continuing unsatisfactory job performance and attendance will not be tolerated.

If Improvement Does Not Occur

If the employee does not improve, you should consult with higher management and arrange for an examination by a physician at the company medical department.

For this purpose, a form should be used, summarizing the employee's absence record, commenting on his job performance, and giving your appraisal of the situation. It is helpful to discuss this in advance with one of the physicians in the medical department before the examination is scheduled. The employee should understand that the physician who examines him or her will have this information.

A physician is the only person qualified to make a diagnosis of drug dependency and to determine the seriousness of the problem. Upon completion of the medical examination, if the employee is cooperative, the physician will counsel him relative to the steps necessary to achieve rehabilitation. The physician will recommend and assist in the initial contact with an appropriate treatment and rehabilitation source in the community. The employee will be informed that any treatment costs will be his own responsibility, and that rehabilitation must take place during off-job hours. The physician also will advise supervision of the steps recommended and/or taken and will arrange appropriate follow-up. This does not mean that supervision abdicates its responsibility in overall management of the case. The physician's role remains advisory.

If the drug user is represented by a union, it is advisable at this time to acquaint the local union officials with the situation. Experience has demonstrated that the union can be of great help in encouraging and providing additional stimulus to the employee to make a sincere attempt to rehabilitate himself.

One must remember that the rehabilitation of a person with such complex problems may be marked by occasional relapses. If the overall progress continues to be satisfactory and the employee remains sincerely interested in his own improvement, one should be supportive during any such occasional setback.

Many drug-dependent employees can be treated and remain at work. Occasionally, in special circumstances, a period of hospitalization may be advised to get the employee detoxified and properly started on treatment.

Under certain circumstances, an employee absent from work because of drug abuse may be eligible for sickness benefits under provisions of the benefit plan — hepatitis, liver problems, etc. This usually requires that he or she be under active medical treatment in a recognized hospital. The medical department will advise the benefit committee on the facts in each case.

When Rehabilitation Is Unsuccessful

When it becomes evident to supervision that no appreciable progress is being made toward rehabilitation, disciplinary action should be considered. If it has not earlier been consulted, higher management should be acquainted with the situation at this time.

No rigid pattern of procedure should be established. The type and severity of any action to be taken should be determined only after consideration of such factors as age, length of service, prior job record, potential future value to the company, family conditions, and community relations.

For an employee with more than a few years of service, the following general guidelines may be used, varying the steps at the discretion of the department to fit each individual case:

1. After the first relapse, suspension for a relatively short period.
2. After the second relapse, suspension for a longer period of time with a warning that termination of services may follow the next offense.
3. After the third relapse, termination should be considered. In exceptional circumstances, after consultation with the medical department, a longer leave-of-absence might be recommended. (Remember that any leave-of-absence in excess of one month requires benefit committee approval.) If such a longer leave-of-absence is to be recommended, it should be with the understanding that it is preliminary to termination unless during such period the employee demonstrates to the satisfaction of management that he or she is making a sincere and sustained effort to achieve rehabilitation.

The importance of continuing management and medical supervision during all periods of suspension cannot be overemphasized.

Pensions

If an employee whose service is terminated because of illness attributed to drug abuse is eligible for a service pension by reason of age and length of service, application for pension should be made to the benefit committee. In no case should supervision tell the employee that he or she is going to be pensioned. The procedure is termination, followed by benefit committee consideration of a pension application. Drug abuse in itself does not qualify one for a disability pension.

In Conclusion

As a supervisor you can be a key person in identifying the employee drug user and initiating the rehabilitation of that employee. If you are successful, you will have rendered a fine service to the employee, to the company, to his family, and to the community. Remember these important points:

1. The earlier the problem is recognized and rehabilitation started the greater the chances for success.
2. Before rehabilitation can be successful, the drug-dependent employee must admit to himself that he has a problem, and he must accept the idea that he is responsible for making the effort to overcome his problem.

Rap Sessions: Step Two

It is important to follow-up written communications to supervisors with discussion groups; drug abuse is not only a complex subject which is sure to generate many questions, it is also an emotional subject. Many middle-aged supervisors will be reluctant even to discuss the subject, let alone help minimize the problem.

At these follow-up meetings, it must be stressed that successful employee relations depend largely on the supervisor's attitude toward his people. All supervisors should demonstrate by their actions and their attitudes that they are interested in their people, not only as employees

STEPS FOR HANDLING THE DRUG–DEPENDENT EMPLOYEE

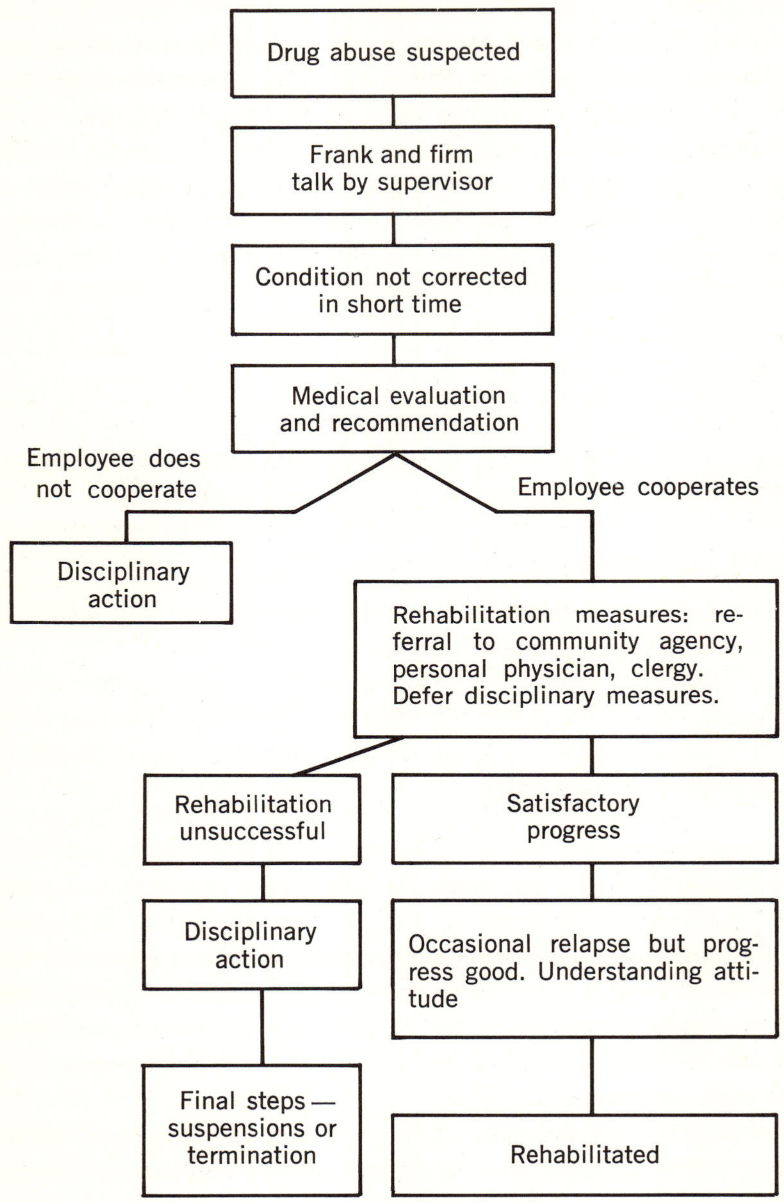

but also as individuals. Supervisors should be reminded that they should give all problems fair and impartial consideration.

In an effort to enhance fair and impartial consideration of the drug problem, one company published a counseling guide for supervisors and reviewed salient points during the rap session. In introducing the subject of counseling suspected drug users, a company official told the supervisors that they should try to view the problem of drug abuse as objectively as possible so that counseling will be useful. He continued,

Too often a discussion about drugs between generations becomes a heated debate laced with emotion and misinformation, and little but further alienation is accomplished. To be perfectly frank, we do not want alienation; we want good communication between supervision and employees with the ultimate goal being a forthright but enlightened approach to the drug situation.

There are facts that help make your end of the discussion more meaningful. And when facts and persuasion don't work, we have rules that we must fall back on. These facts and these rules are what we must base our attitudes and actions on, nothing else; not long hair, not someone's way of dressing, not our own biases. So please familiarize yourselves with the counseling techniques you have been given.

COUNSELING TECHNIQUES EXAMPLE

The Supervisor Can Help

It is most important that all employees know where they can get advice about possible or potential drug problems and understand that the company has a sincere and genuine interest in the welfare of each employee. Early identification of problems and prompt action in trying to resolve them are the keystones to maintaining good employee relations. Experience has shown that such actions can pay high dividends in the form of improved employee morale and better performance.

Often an employee with a drug problem will feel better about discussing the situation with someone outside his immediate work area. This is not a reflection on the attitude or the ability of his supervisor. It is simply that at one time or another all of us find it easier to talk with someone with whom we are not closely associated.

With this in mind, supervisors should take the initiative in reminding their people that they are free to contact their medical department or the personnel department. This should be offered without the employee fearing reprisal.

Regardless of whom they contact, it is important to assure employees that their problem will be handled objectively and confidentially. All cases should be treated objectively and with understanding. Where corrective action is indicated, such action should be consistent with company policy and sound personnel practices.

Counseling Techniques

Interviewing or counseling is a personal experience for the supervisor as well as the employee. We all react differently to various situations, and one person may stress certain factors more than others. Below are a few points on effective counseling which you may find helpful in determining the proper action to take in each case:

1. Conduct all interviews in a friendly atmosphere. It is important to try to conduct employee interviews in private and where there will be no interruptions. Try to put the other person at ease. Show him that you are sincerely interested in him, and that he can feel confident that you will consider the matter in a fair and impartial manner.
2. Listen carefully. Be a good listener; let the troubled person explain the whole situation. Don't interrupt with questions unless absolutely necessary.
3. Avoid arguments. Demonstrate that you are impartial. Avoid arguing and never criticize his point of view during an interview. This is inconsistent with the purpose of the counseling interview, which is to get the facts. However, any obvious errors or misunderstandings about company policy that come to light during the discussion should be corrected.
4. Don't jump to conclusions. The action you take will depend primarily on the accuracy of your information. Examine the

facts carefully and check them out wherever possible. Look at the problem from all angles. Evaluate it completely so that you can form a sound basis for action. Obtain the advice of others in the medical department, if necessary.

5. Take prompt action, once you have reached a decision. Tell the employee your decision and discuss the reasons with him. If any new developments have occurred, determine whether they should affect your decision. If the problem requires additional consultation with higher management, don't delay in obtaining it.

6. Continue to show your interest. Maintain an interest in the employee until the situation is resolved one way or another. Successful employee relations depend largely on your own attitude toward your people. All of us should demonstrate by our actions and our attitudes that we are sincerely interested in our people not only as employees but also as individuals. They should know we are anxious to give the problem fair and impartial consideration.

In the final analysis, supervisory training about employee drug abuse will have to be tailored to your own company's personality and its needs. Communications with supervisors is a subtle thing that cannot be packaged for you. All companies react differently to various situations, and one company may stress certain factors more than others. For example, one company felt that their employee drug problem was so severe that it was well worth the time and expense for a full-day, follow-up seminar. The seminar, designed to further increase the supervisors' awareness of employee drug abuse, consisted of one day of presentations by experts, followed by a question and answer period. It was conducted on three separate occasions, with each seminar attended by about 100 of the company's 300 first-line supervisors. The program included talks by a psychiatrist in the mental health field, a consultant for the Narcotic Addiction Service Center in the community, the physician-in-charge at the regional clinic of the State Department of Mental Health's Drug Dependence Division, and a former employee and ex-addict working with a local drug rehabilitation program.

The two-step procedure outlined in this chapter for beginning to instruct supervisors may be too inflexible for your company, as it was for the above. With this in mind, the following topic outline for any supervisory training format may be helpful in creating your own program.

OUTLINE FOR SUPERVISORY INSTRUCTION

1. Growth of drug abuse nationally and in business and industry
   A. Explain high number of students and other young people using drugs. Comment on company's possible experience on basis of appointments of young people
   B. Describe widespread increase of drug use by adults (see chapter 1)
   C. Explain extent of the drug problem as it relates to company now, and estimate future problem
   D. Relationship between legal use and illicit abuse of drugs
2. Explain present company policy and rationale in terms of hiring, preemployment screening, dismissal, rehabilitation, and benefits
3. Explain what the company wants supervisors to do to help implement policy and minimize drug abuse
   A. Why supervisors must become knowledgeable about drugs
      1. Keep drug abuse from spreading
         a. Detection. (See "A Guide to Drug Abuse Detection" at the close of this chapter.) Discussion on types of drugs
            1. Amphetamines. General description of how these drugs work, their legitimate uses, and examples of the brand and generic names
               a) Physiological dangers of misuse
               b) Psychological dangers of misuse
               c) Observable signs of misuse
               d) Potential impact on performance
            2. Barbiturates, heroin, morphine, and so forth. Same explanations as above
               a) Physiological dangers of misuse
               b) Psychological dangers of misuse
               c) Observable signs of misuse

        d) Potential impact on performance
     3. Marihuana. Controversial subject. Research not complete. General description of how this drug works and what it is
        a) Physiological dangers of misuse
        b) Psychological dangers of misuse
        c) Observable signs of misuse
        d) Potential impact on performance
   b. Other company detection methods
     1. Preemployment controls
        a) Employment interviews (supervisor's role in terms of observing appearance, behavior, work records, references, and so forth)
        b) Working with the medical department
           1. Medical examinations are not foolproof. Explain why
     2. Postemployment controls and supervisor's responsibilities
        a) Reports to security people. Observations of pushers, thefts, and so forth
        b) Reports from other employees about signs of possession, sale, or use

4. Explain legal ramifications of accusing an employee of drug abuse
   A. Legal rights of employer and employee
   B. Explain delicacies of counseling techniques
5. Explain what the company will be doing in terms of in-house, employee education programs, as well as any programs in the community
6. Outline programs for further supervisory training
7. Question and answer period

A Guide to Drug Abuse Detection

Because of the large number of employees in some plants and offices, drug abusers may go unnoticed by supervisors for quite some time. Supervisors unaware of some of the symptoms of drug abuse may

A GUIDE TO SOME DRUGS WHICH ARE SUBJECT TO ABUSE

Drugs	What they are	Primary effect
HALLUCINOGENS (LSD, Acid)	LSD–25 is a lysergic acid derivative. Mescaline is a chemical taken from peyote cactus. Psilocybin is synthesized from Mexican mushrooms.	All produce hallucinations, exhilaration, or depression, and can lead to serious mental changes, psychotic manifestations, suicidal or homicidal tendencies.
HEROIN (Snow, Stuff, H, Junk and others)	Heroin is diacetylmorphine, an alkaloid derived from morphine; it does not occur in opium. A white, off-white, or brown crystalline powder, it has long been the drug of choice among opiate addicts. Its possession is illegal.	Like morphine in all respects, faster and shorter acting.
MARIJUANA (Cannabis) (Pot, Grass, Joints, Weed, Mary Jane, Reefers, Sticks)	Marijuana is the dried flowering or fruiting top of the plant Cannabis sativa L., commonly called Indian Hemp. Usually looks like fine, green tobacco. Its possession is illegal. Hashish is a preparation of cannabis, taken orally in many forms.	A feeling of great perceptiveness and pleasure can accompany even small doses. Erratic behavior, loss of memory, distortion of time and spatial perceptions, and hilarity without apparent cause occur. Marked unpredictability of effect.

LEGITIMATE (PERMITTED) DRUGS   (Essential to practice of medicine;

AMPHETAMINE (Bennies, Co-pilots, Footballs, Hearts, Pep Pills)	Amphetamines are stimulants, prescribed by physicians chiefly to reduce appetite and to relieve minor cases of mental depression. Often used to promote wakefulness and/or increase energy.	Normal doses produce wakefulness, increased alertness and a feeling of increased initiative. Intravenous doses produce cocaine-like psychotoxic effects.
BARBITURATES (Red Birds, Yellow Jackets, Blue Heavens, Goof Balls)	Barbiturates are sedatives, prescribed to induce sleep or, in smaller doses, to provide a calming effect. All are legally restricted to prescription use only. Dependence producing, both psychic and physical, with variable tolerance.	Small amounts make the user relaxed, sociable, good-humored. Heavy doses make him sluggish, gloomy, sometimes quarrelsome. His speech is thick and he staggers. Sedation and incoordination progressive with dose, and at least additive with alcohol and/or other sedatives and tranquilizers.

How to spot abuser	Dangers
Abusers may undergo complete personality changes, "see" smells, "hear" colors. They may try to fly or brush imaginary insects from their bodies, etc. Behavior is irrational. Marked depersonalization.	Very small quantities of LSD may cause hallucinations lasting for days or repetitive psychotoxic episodes, which may recur months after injection. Permanence of mental derangement is still a moot question. Damage to chromosomes, and hence potentially to offspring, has been demonstrated.
Morphine-like.	Like morphine; dependence usually develops more rapidly. Dependence liability is high.
Abusers may feel exhilarated or relaxed, stare off into space; be hilarious without apparent cause; have exaggerated sense of ability.	Because of the vivid visions and exhilaration which result from use of marijuana, abusers may lose all restraint and act in a manner dangerous to themselves and/or others. Accident prone because of time and space sense disturbance. Dependence (psychic but not physical) leads to antisocial behavior and could be forerunner of use of other drugs. (The effects of marijuana, as with so many drugs, have never been fully demonstrated. The effects noted here are those suggested by many competent authorities. —Editors)

legitimate manufacture and distribution confined to ethical drug channels.)

An almost abnormal cheerfulness and unusual increase in activity, jumpiness and irritability; hallucinations and paranoid tendencies after intravenous use.	Amphetamines can cause high blood pressure, abnormal heart rhythms and even heart attacks. Teen-agers often take them to increase their "nerve." As a result, they may behave dangerously. Excess prolonged usage can cause hallucinations, loss of weight, wakefulness, jumpiness and dangerous aggressiveness. Tolerance to large doses is acquired by abusers; psychic dependence develops but physical dependence does not; and there is no characteristic withdrawal syndrome.
The appearance of drunkenness with no odor of alcohol characterizes heavy dose. Sedation with variable failure of muscle coordination.	Sedation, coma and death from respiratory failure. Inattentiveness may cause unintentional repetitious administration to a toxic level. Many deaths each year from intentional and unintentional overdose. Potentiation with alcohol particularly hazardous. The drug is addictive, causing physical as well as psychic dependency, and withdrawal phenomena are characteristically different from withdrawal of opiates.

Drugs	What they are	Primary effect
COCAINE (The Leaf, Snow, Speedballs — when mixed with Heroin)	Extracted from the leaves of the coca bush. It is a white, odorless, fluffy powder that looks like crystalline snow.	Oral use is said to relieve hunger and fatigue, and produce some degree of exhilaration. Intravenous use produces marked psychotoxic effects, hallucinations with paranoid tendencies. Repetitive doses lead to maniacal excitation, muscular twitching, convulsive movements.
CODEINE (Schoolboy)	A component of opium and a derivative of morphine, in most respects a tenth or less as effective as morphine in individual doses.	Analgesic and cough suppressant with very little sedation or exhilarant (euphoric) action. Dependence can be produced or partially supported, but large doses are required and risk is minor.
METHAMPHETA-MINE (Speed, Crystal)	Stimulant, closely related to amphetamine and ephedrine.	Effects resemble amphetamine but are more marked and toxicity is greater.
MORPHINE (1 M, Dreamer, many others)	The principal active component of opium. Morphine sulphate: white crystalline powder, light porous cubes or small white tablets.	Generally sedative and analgesic (rarely excitatory). The initial reaction is unpleasant to most people, but calming supersedes and, depending on dose, may progress to coma and death from respiratory failure.

Reprinted with permission of The American Social Health Association.

How to spot abuser	Dangers
Dilated pupils, hyperactive, exhilarated paranoic.	Convulsions and death may occur from overdose. Paranoic activity. Very strong psychic but no physical dependence and no tolerance.
Unless taken intravenously, very little evidence of general effect. Large doses are morphine-like.	Occasionally taken (liquid preparations) for kicks, but large amount required. Contribution of the alcohol content to the effect may be significant. Degree and risk of abuse very minor. Occasionally resorted to by opiate-dependent persons to tide them over with inadequate result.
Extreme restlessness and irritability; violence and paranoid reaction possible.	Excessive psychotoxic effects, sometimes with fatal outcome.
Constricted pupils. Calm, inattentive, "on the nod," with slow pulse and respiration.	Man is very sensitive to the respiratory depressant effect until tolerance develops. Psychic and physical dependence and tolerance develop rapidly, with a characteristic withdrawal syndrome.

never suspect an employee, attributing unusual behavior to eccentricity. While it must be emphasized that only a trained physician can diagnose drug abuse, supervisors should be instructed about the symptoms of drug abuse, although it should be emphasized that observation should be circumspect. Detection is at best difficult. Marihuana, for example, can be used by many people with no discernible signs of trouble, or even of superficial, observable signs. Some users can appear perfectly "straight." Also, a marihuana "high" may affect the same individual differently each time; it depends to a great extent on the user's mood, the purpose for which marihuana is used, and the quality of the drug. The effects of marihuana can duplicate both the depressing and exhilarating effects of alcohol.

The guide on pages 82–85 details what a supervisor's drug problems might be. It indicates how drug abusers may be spotted. All supervisors should have some basic knowledge about certain drugs and symptoms associated with the abuse of these drugs. Unfortunately, our knowledge does not always permit comprehensive guides to be formulated. We believe the guide reflects the current consensus of the field.

An Avocation Ends

For years, employee drug abuse was one of many topics discussed superficially by managers during lunch; it competed with the latest ballgame scores, the weather, and company politics. It was not sufficiently detrimental to warrant more than a passing mention between dessert and coffee. It was a minor aggravation that popped up now and then in the shipping department or the mail room.

Today, however, the problem of employee drug abuse is the topic of seminars, workshops, and planning meetings. Company legal departments are immersed in the subject. Supervisors, labor relations people, and the personnel and medical departments are busy trying to understand how the problem affects them. What was an avocation has quickly become a full-time job for many company specialists.

Actually, employee drug abuse is an all-company problem. Labor relations people will have to deal with the unions' growing involvement in drug abuse; security people must cope with a skyrocketing theft rate, much of which points to drug abuse; company lawyers must understand the pitfalls of the law as it pertains to drugs and company liability; and personnel people are being asked to understand the often confusing ethical and discriminatory aspects of preemployment screening. All of this can directly affect a company's profit and loss statement. As one company president put it, "This is no joke, and damn it, my people better get with it."

So your company specialists have their work cut out for them. In order to put their problems in better perspective for managers who are sure to be involved peripherally in discussions about numerous aspects of employee drug abuse, the following sections offer a summary of labor's aims and goals, preemployment screening techniques, and some advice about the legal considerations of drug abuse.

Labor's Concern

Labor unions, like most companies, have no ready answers to the drug problem. But they are now beginning to search for some. Like a good many organizations, they have in the past been extremely silent about the situation, preferring to let management cope with the few instances of employee drug abuse that came to light. In most cases, unions have gone along with the dismissal of drug abusers for other reasons (the effects of drug abuse — absenteeism, chronic lateness, and so forth) and they have been conspicuously absent when some firms have talked about rehabilitation programs for drug-dependent employees.

In all fairness to labor, it has been honest about its tardiness in developing antidrug and rehabilitation programs, admitting that until recently the problem has had a low priority. But as research has revealed the rapid growth and potential extent of the drug problem, several union officials have spoken out, indicating some of the cooperative steps labor may soon ask management to take.

During the last year, many large unions have been trying to determine the extent of the problem vis-à-vis their members, formulating general position statements, and deciding how best to work with management in minimizing drug abuse. For example, the United Auto Workers was one of the first unions to request major corporations with whom it has contracts to join in cooperative efforts to deal constructively with employee drug abuse.

The UAW's International Executive Board also has called on federal, state, and local governments in the U. S. and Canada to intensify their efforts to develop new knowledge of causes and methods of treatment of drug addiction and to augment support "for the pitifully limited treatment resources available."

After considerable study, the UAW Board said that there are indications in plants of widespread drug abuse which significantly contributes to increased absenteeism and tardiness with resultant disruption of work assignments. At this writing, the UAW plans to propose joint efforts to secure expansion of referral and treatment services, greater research efforts in the development of cures for drug addiction, education programs for nonusers on the dangers of narcotics, and prevention of drug sales on plant property. Agreement on joint efforts to seek solutions to drug problems has already been reached with some companies under UAW contract.

The following statement, issued by the UAW's Board on June 8, 1971, is the base from which the union begins its attack on drug abuse as well as its discussions with management about cooperative approaches:

The UAW is deeply concerned over the serious and growing problems of drug abuse and narcotic addiction in our society. We believe the spread of these "illnesses" is a reflection of the alienation of many, particularly the young, from our society; it is a reaction to the tensions and pressures of the harsh, real world, feelings of inadequacy and social conflicts which come from a value system which gives higher priority to material achievement than to people; it is an unhappy attempt to find "fantasy" solutions to gnawing personal and family problems; it is often a reflection of the dissatisfactions with the school, the home and the work-place.

We see what we believe to be widespread use and abuse of drugs by workers in the plants, with resultant adverse effects on their ability to function. Drug use contributes to increased absenteeism and tardiness. This in turn disrupts work assignments, with consequent dissatisfaction among the majority of workers who are sincerely trying to do conscientious jobs. The combination of factors has a potentially damaging effect on plant efficiency.

The community at large, including our members, is disturbed by the close relationship of the drug "culture" to crime and violence, and bewildered at these spreading sicknesses in our country.

We recognize that there are no easy solutions, no well-accepted cures for these sicknesses which are social, personal and medical in causation. We have no ready answers to these problems, but we have the conviction that answers must be found if the health of the society and of the work place is to be preserved.

Accordingly, we call upon the federal, state, provincial and local governments to intensify their efforts to develop new knowledge of the causes and methods of treatment of drug addiction and to augment support for the pitifully limited treatment resources now available.

These problems, however, cannot be solved by government alone, or by industry alone, or by the trade union movement. The UAW has already made provisions with some employers for union and management jointly to seek solutions to the drug problem in the plants.

Such joint activities at a minimum should develop new efforts to:

a. Discourage the use of drugs among those who are not users.
b. Apprehend the narcotics "pushers" in an intensive effort to prevent the sale of drugs in plants and on plant property.
c. Work with the community to provide meaningful referral and treatment resources to rehabilitate drug users.
d. Develop new knowledge and understanding in depth of the causes and cures of narcotics dependence among workers.

We shall call upon managements in the major corporations where our members work to join with us in developing cooperative efforts to deal constructively with these grave problems.

Many other unions will soon "call upon" management with specific suggestions for the prevention and treatment of drug abuse among their members. While most unions think that their suggestions for a cooperative antidrug campaign will not be a part of collective bargaining, they are not ruling this out; and it may be that some unions will ask that certain aspects of an antidrug program be part of a union contract.

While labor as well as management suffers from a lack of substantial research, which hinders the creation of specific proposals, union officials have talked enough about the subject of late to indicate the types of steps they will probably ask management to consider:

1. Reversing past experience, unions will advise that any company procedures adopted to combat drug abuse be the result of joint union-management efforts. Success of any drug program, labor will contend, depends on a union's active involvement in a worker's problem. This involvement will be achieved through newly created union-management committees on drug abuse.
2. Many unions are thinking seriously about advocating in-plant union manpower for overseeing the drug problem. They will ask that these

people be trained, union counselors who will function on company time much like shop stewards.

3. It may be that additional health insurance benefits will be proposed, including new programs for the coverage of in-patient and out-patient rehabilitation of drug dependent union members. This issue, of course, will confront squarely the question about whether drug abuse is a crime or a sickness. (This point, however, may be academic, since most medical claims are not made for drug use; rather they are reported as hepatitis and other drug-related illnesses that usually are covered.)

4. Unions will take a harder look at management's policy of immediate dismissal of all employee drug abusers. Questions will be raised concerning development of specific policy as it pertains to rehabilitation vis-à-vis tenure, with emphasis on in-patient leaves-of-absence.

5. With this in mind, joint union-management efforts will be encouraged, aimed toward the creation of residential rehabilitation centers for drug-dependent employees. These will include both out-patient and in-patient facilities, the latter of which is opposite to industry's present view that employees may be offered help only on their own time and if they can continue to perform.

Evident in all this is the fact that unions are finally becoming more interested and involved in the drug problem. Little else is clear now, except that management can expect to be hearing from labor about the problem and it should be ready to evaluate the proposals.

Preemployment Screening

As pointed out earlier in this book, the value of preemployment screening by itself is seriously questioned as a long-term solution to a company's problem of employee drug abuse. You simply cannot keep all drug abusers out of your company, nor can you insure that "clean" applicants will not begin using drugs once on the job. Yet preemployment screening is and probably will continue to be part of policy for a majority of companies; it is a worthwhile adjunct to a comprehensive antidrug program.

According to all experience, however, there really is no foolproof method for screening out drug abusers in preemployment testing.[1] The best one can do is to instruct employment interviewers to look for and question certain warning signs, prior to requesting a physical examination. In addition to the usual observance of the stigmata of needle marks on the inner surface of the forearm (although most addicts wear long sleeves), there should be careful scrutiny of the employment application for evidence of unexplained gaps in the work record, frequent job turnover, reasons for quitting previous jobs, and reference checks.

Reference checks, however, seem not to be working very well when it comes to suspected drug abuse. The reason is that seldom is drug abuse listed as a cause for termination on an individual's personnel record; instead, improper performance usually is recorded, which, of course, is only a by-product of the cause. This same sort of evasion has been used in other sensitive dismissals, such as homosexuality.

It has been said that this really is not an issue because personnel people can talk with each other indirectly, and somehow each gets the proper message. But this does not pertain to drug abuse. Although it is the responsibility of businesses to provide factual and truthful referential reports — or reports that are guarded but understood such as in the case of dismissal for theft — companies truly hedge about the subject of drug abuse for reasons of liability. Too many firms have been stung too many times. It is virtually impossible to prove that a person has used drugs in the past, and some companies that have dismissed a suspected drug user and recorded drug use as the reason for termination on the employee's personnel record have lived to regret it; they have been sued by ex-employees when they found out that possible drug use

1. Many people are feverishly working on the problem, hoping to develop a foolproof method. The most recent example is a study of fingerprint patterns by a Massachusetts deputy sheriff who believes that drug addicts might have similar fingerprints. Louis Cataldo of Barnstable, Massachusetts, began noticing the similarity of print patterns among drug offenders arrested in his county. Discussing his theory in an article in the Boston *Globe,* Cataldo said, "My study involving drug addicts shows that their prints are similar, favoring arch, tented arch and radial fingerprint patterns. Considering that arch and tented arch patterns have always been the lowest percentage (six or seven percent) of all fingerprint patterns, the information is of great interest. This is not to say that everyone with this type of fingerprint is a drug or potential drug user; but it is unusual that so many drug addicts have the pattern. Most addicts with this fingerprint pattern range in age from 17 to 21 years." Cataldo says a member of the Pittsburgh police department said he likewise noted similar observations.

was the reason they failed to secure another job. It has been claimed in some circles that a few employees have actually planned such a tactic with the hopeful, specific intent of being able to sue a company for libel or defamation of character later.

Hence, in many companies, when an employee is dismissed for drug use it is not recorded as such on his personnel record. Other more traditional reasons are listed. So reference checks can be unreliable and also misleading. If there is no indication on a personnel record that an ex-employee was dismissed for using drugs, a new man in the personnel department may answer a reference question with, "No, he was not using drugs; he was dismissed for excessive absenteeism." This is the only reason the new man knows about. Also, the new man may have been instructed to be tight-lipped when it comes to answering questions about drugs. So while it is good practice to check with employers about whether an applicant has used drugs, beware of the information you receive.

Incidentally, colleges and universities generally will not divulge information concerning drug use of students. Students have the right to request of colleges and universities that information of this kind be withheld or deleted from their files, and schools usually comply. Generally, this type of information includes arrests in connection with drugs, and, in most cases, colleges and universities go along with student requests not to record or divulge information of this kind. In most instances, colleges would not divulge this type of information even if the student did not request that they not do so. As one personnel man puts it, "No wonder the kids raise hell in school, they know they can apply for a job without a blemish on their record; this is a lot of crap and only serves to encourage kids to experiment with drugs." Whether it does or not is a question that is unclear; what is clear is that college reference checks about drug use are a waste of time.

One new procedure may help to enhance the value of reference checks concerning applicants who are suspected of drug use. In some states, companies are being asked to report all employees terminated for drug use to the appropriate city health department. The reason is both for valuable research and to assist in possible follow-up rehabilitation. But this is an extremely controversial topic. Listen to one New York City businessman:

When we discharge an employee for abusing drugs, I've long had the feeling that the company has a responsibility to report that person to some sort of public health agency, for help. We don't have to report them to any law enforcement agency, but I think we have a moral obligation to try to help them, not just heave them out on the street.

In New York City, there is a strong appeal from the people in the health department that companies be made to report cases of dismissal for drug use for epidemiologic purposes. Right now, it is voluntary, and the health department has assured us that all the information will be confidential. But I know that in the past there have been several attempts on the part of law enforcement agencies to use the health department's records for their own purposes. The police know that the health department's records would contribute toward finding sources of drug sales. I think this is fine, but I also think it would have a negative impact on the rehabilitation efforts of a health department. It is that old bugaboo again about drug use being a crime or a sickness, and I am not about to get into the middle of that argument.

If it ever became mandatory for companies to report employees who have been dismissed for drug abuse to health departments, chances are the health departments would not share the information with other companies anyway. Yet it *is* a possibility — the only one that seems to make sense as far as reference checks of drug abusers are concerned.

Applicants who are suspected of drug use by employment interviewers, yet in all other ways appear to be a suitable potential employee, should be and usually are referred to the medical department for a physical examination. Although there is no known medical test to detect the use of marihuana, recent use of other drugs usually can be detected by chromatography, which finds the presence of drugs in body fluids.

In the New York area, for example, these types of tests are performed for industry by the Laboratory of Chromatography in Bayside. Addressing the American Management Association, Dr. David Sohn, Medical Director of the Laboratory, reported that the biological fluid used in detecting all of the drugs except LSD and marihuana is urine.

Most drugs are excreted via the urine which provides the greatest amount and concentration of material for study. Obviously, no special techniques, technicians, or sterile materials are needed to obtain the specimen and there is no discomfort to the contributor, as might be the case with blood samples. There is also no serious difficulty or discomfort in obtaining multiple, sequential specimens on the same or subsequent days, as might be the case were blood to be used.

LSD can be detected only from blood serum. It is metabolized too rapidly to be retrieved. The normal dose is so small that it cannot be found subsequently. Marihuana, at present, cannot be detected in any body fluid.

Urine tests can pick up recent use of heroin. But some addicts simply refrain from using it for a few days before their physical examination. Others bring in hidden vials of "clean" urine and substitute it for their own. Yet, on the whole, urinalysis is a worthwhile screening technique.

Several questions are now being raised by many companies anticipating extensive use of chromatography and other preemployment medical tests. Are these tests ethical? And unless all applicants are tested, are they discriminatory? The director of industrial relations for a large utility sums up the beliefs of many of his counterparts:

I don't believe these tests are either unethical or discriminatory. Our applicants are made to understand that they must take a preemployment physical exam before they can be hired. The results of this exam are evaluated both by the medical department and the personnel department. The applicant is told this, and he is also told that if he doesn't measure up in all preemployment tests, including the medical exam, he cannot be hired. I think this is being honest and ethical. As far as medical tests being discriminatory, I say this: I don't believe that they are discriminatory or not discriminatory. You have to think in terms of the type of job to be done. If we are testing someone for a job involving some of the secrets on which this country's security is based, I think that applicant would receive a different kind of scrutiny than someone else. There are many types of preemployment tests for many types of jobs in many different companies. A clerk typist may not get the same type of examination as an applicant who will be required to lift 75 to 100 pounds every day. If a person is going to be a cable splicer, for example, he gets more than an ordinary color test. Different tests are designed to determine whether applicants are capable of doing different jobs. And there aren't too many jobs you can do well if you are abusing drugs.

A Word to the Wise, About the Law

With the problem of drug abuse in business and industry comes a paper problem — the understanding of a host of statutes, regulations, and court decisions concerning the legal aspects of drug abuse. This is a continuing challenge for your company's legal department or outside counsel because of the newness and complexity of the subject, and because federal and state laws that affect drug abuse are changing constantly.

Employee drug abuse can present legal problems in just about every segment of your company, including security, medical, personnel, and production. Beginning with the illegal possession and sale of narcotics and dangerous drugs on company premises, drug-related activities requiring expert legal advice can range through theft of company property, product liability, false claims for workmen's compensation, union arbitration, equal employment opportunity charges, occupational safety and health, surveillance of suspected employees, suits by employees for slander, libel, and defamation of character, death benefits as they relate to drug abuse, privileged communication between doctor and employee, and many more.

The point is that drug abuse is indeed a legal threat to every company, and while managers and supervisors should be briefed by the company's legal people during regular training sessions about the possible legal ramifications and risks in their dealings with employees, it should be made absolutely clear at the outset that this is an area in which supervisors should rely totally on legal specialists.

The realities and responsibilities of the legal department vis-à-vis drug abuse and its mélange of possible legal problems are beyond the ken of supervisors, and this should be strongly suggested to them. A little knowledge is extremely dangerous, and supervisors who are given a superficial understanding of the legal considerations of drug abuse might cause irreparable harm by thinking they can cope with incidents or situations that could lead to possible litigation.

What then do you tell your supervisors? You tell them first that they are not lawyers and are not expected to be. You tell them that in every instance where there is a question about the legality of a situation, they should do nothing before checking with higher supervision, who, in turn, will check with the company's legal specialists. Impress them most forcefully with this point. Apprehending a thief is one thing, apprehending a suspected thief is quite another.

Because business and industry's experience is still limited, a suitable training session for supervisors designed and implemented by your legal department may be difficult to create. An excellent source for research, however, is a book titled *Legal Considerations: Drug Abuse in Industry and Business,* by Sidney H. Willig, Professor of Law and Director of Drug Law Unit, Temple University. The book is published by Symposium Enterprises, 1460 N.E. 129th Street, P. O. Box 356, North Miami, Florida 33161.

While most of today's legal questions about drug abuse deal with unsettled areas of the law, and varying interpretations may be possible in various jurisdictions, Mr. Willig's book provides a fine base on which one can begin to build an individual company's supervisor training meeting.

That there are numerous interpretations of the law in various jurisdictions is easily shown when one looks at the penalties now on the federal and state books for illegal manufacture, possession, and sale of narcotics and dangerous drugs. They not only vary widely, but they could soon change. While managers probably will have little direct experience with the implementation of these laws, their diversity serves to show current inconsistencies and underscores why supervisors should refer all legal questions to specialists.

At this writing, for example, state laws for the possession, sale or manufacture of marihuana vary widely. In Nebraska, a conviction of first offense possession of marihuana can mean only seven days in jail and a course in drug education. On the other hand, in Texas you can receive up to life imprisonment for possession and sale. In California, conviction of possession can bring one-to-ten years; in Ohio it brings two-to-twenty-five years and a $10,000 fine.

Aside from this type of diversity, there are also the differences in certain types of drug penalties:

Opiates (*opium, heroin, morphine*)

The illegal manufacture, sale, and possession of opiates is a felony and, upon conviction, sentences range from 2-to-10 years imprisonment for first-offense possession to 10-to-40 years for second offense sale. In all but first-offense possession, suspension of sentence, probation or parole are prohibited. These are federal penalties; state laws vary and in most instances they are more severe than federal law.

Marihuana

At this writing, marihuana is also classified as a narcotic by federal law (this is a very controversial issue). Hence, the penalties that can be applied are the same as for heroin. There is one important exception: unlike a second-offense heroin crime, suspended sentence and probation is permitted for unlawful possession of marihuana, but not for the unlawful sale of marihuana. Penalties for the unlawful sale are the same as for heroin. Some state laws provide alternatives to prison sentences, which could be taken as an admission that the punishment concept is not working. First offenders for all marihuana drug abuses other than its manufacture and sale often have the legal right to receive physical and psychological treatment for drug dependency instead of a prison sentence or a fine, depending on a medical examiner's certification. These state laws often cover both hard-core addicts of heroin and other opiates and users of marihuana. But, again, there are qualifications; for example, if a person convicted of using marihuana can "function effectively," he cannot benefit from the rehabilitation provision and is subject to the same penalties as before.

In short, the "ifs" in the law seem endless and this also pertains to areas of the law that can have a direct effect on your company. Debates will continue to effect changes. Keeping abreast of many changes that are coming and will continue to come, and acting on them, is your legal department's job; yours is to assure that your supervisors understand the delicacy of their actions in all legal matters and to institute immediately a training session to familiarize them with the type of procedures your legal department believes they should follow.

As One Manager Sees It

Frank's second floor office in corporate headquarters overlooks a lush courtyard. Willow trees are swaying in a soft spring breeze.

In this quiet suburban office just outside New York, the immensity of his company is not felt. Its 20,000 employees — most in the urban Northeast — make little impact in this remote setting. Then you spot a 3 x 5 card file marked "Employee Drug Abuse." You wonder how many "strung-out" employees Frank and his staff of personnel counselors had to see in order to fill the file.

Frank is in his late 50s and he has been with the company for thirty years. He looks as though he came up through the ranks, starting in a plant right out of high school. There is still an aura of the blue-collar man about him. He is easy to be with — amiable, but kindly tough.

There is no trace of the cynicism one would expect in a man who for the last 15 years has been coping with the personal problems of his company's employees — alcoholism, venereal disease, compulsive gambling, and, during the last few years, drug abuse. People have come to him with a variety of miseries. He tries to help them and on the whole he has. Perhaps better than he gives himself credit for.

Frank is honest and candid. His comments about his company's drug problem reveal a good many things common to most businesses — the surprising scope of the problem, the difficulties in dealing with it, the search for workable approaches, the mistakes, the frustration of being unable to communicate well with young people.

Frank is a practical man. He has had to walk that fine line between his company's best interests and the well-being of troubled employees. He would like to believe that they are always one and the same, but on occasions they are not, and he knows it.

He is the last to say that what his company is doing about its drug problem is right for everyone. In fact, some of his friends in other companies think Frank is soft on drugs. But he believes that what he is doing is right — for his company, for its employees, and if you press him, for the communities in which his plants and offices are located.

His comments offer background to the problem as a whole, summarizing the array of new problems drug abuse presents to every manager, and showing how one company is trying to minimize them:

Back in 1968 we felt there was something really wrong happening here, but we couldn't put our finger on it. Too many employees were having too many problems. Odd things were happening on the job — weird behavior and poor work performance. Attendance slipped and it seemed related to the pattern of alcoholism — Monday absences, Friday absences, partial days off with the usual alibis.

Yet it couldn't all be booze. We asked ourselves whether it might have something to do with drugs. We had read about it and we heard about it on television. But like most people, we felt it couldn't happen here; we hire only the finest people, you know.

But then we began to realize that it was probably impossible for us to escape the problem. If drug abuse was a reality outside in the schools and ghettos, we certainly must be exposed to it. We hire anywhere from five to eight thouand young people every year — out of high schools, colleges, right off the street. That's when we really started looking into the thing, talking with supervisors, looking more closely at some of our own people with problems. In many instances, drugs came up as the root of the trouble, and we didn't know what to do. We knew nothing, absolutely nothing, about drugs.

So, we arranged to get around and talk with some experts. We talked with doctors, we talked with social workers, people in the enforcement agencies. We got reports from the Narcotic Addiction Control Commission and we visited some of the rehabilitation facilities, such as Phoenix House and Daytop Village. We wanted to get the same feel for the drug scene as we have for alcoholism, and you don't do that from the seat of your pants. You can try, but you are not going to help many people.

Basically, we are sort of a mental first-aid station in this department.

We listen a lot to people's problems and then we talk some. But you've got to know what you are talking about; they know immediately if you don't. I'm an ex-alcoholic — I know.

We have six counselors who do nothing but try to help our employees with their personal and work-related problems. It has its payback — in lower turnover, in keeping trained men on the job, and in indirectly helping the communities in which our plants and offices are located. Alcoholism is still our biggest headache. In handling the alcoholic, not all of my counselors have had the experience with drinking that I have had. But I don't believe that you necessarily have to be a recovered alcoholic to function effectively in this job. But if you are not, you certainly must get around to AA meetings, you must get out to the hospitals to understand rehabilitation and group therapy, you've got to go into the homes and talk with the families. You've got to get the feel of the problem from the inside out if you are going to work with alcoholics. You can't con them.

Empathy Needed

I don't think you have to have been sick yourself to know how to help alcoholics or drug-dependent employees. But you've got to have an empathy born of knowledge of their unique hangups. I think some recovered alcoholics and ex-addicts can be very effective in assisting the employee who is drinking or strung out. They are good at talking to the family, getting into and understanding the goals of AA. But there is more to a company's program for the alcoholic or the drug abuser than this. Sometimes you've got to be tough, and often ex-addicts don't have the stomach for it. So when it comes to handling this aspect of a company program, most recovered alcoholics and ex-addicts fall down because they don't have the heart for it; it takes guts for an ex-alcoholic to say to a man, "Well, I'm sorry, today's your last day with the company; we've both tried for months, but you just aren't making it." They are too close to it — always another chance, the one that is the turning point. I don't say that this holds true with everyone in the field, but it does for many.

It is too bad because a recovered alcoholic or ex-addict can talk their language, which you have to be able to do. There is no way you can get to the root of the problem otherwise. And let's face it, booze and drugs are only symptoms, not causes, of problems. But the problem, whatever it is, has to be brought out into the open — both the employee's side of it and the company's.

So we learned as much as we could about drugs and then we started thinking about a policy. We talked to our supervisors about their problems and to some employees using drugs who came to us voluntarily. We found out, for example, that the junkie is largely unemployable. We didn't think we would have too many people who were really hooked applying for a job because they know they can't hack it. They live for dope; when they have it they are no good, and when they don't have it they are looking for it.

So at that time we weren't too concerned with the junkie, and we began to formulate our policy based on our experience with the alcoholic, who *is* employable: you can work with him or deal with him, for he is a familiar problem. The alcoholic starts as a social drinker, he advances to a moderate drinker, then he goes on to a heavy drinker. Finally he crosses the line into alcoholism. But this doesn't happen overnight.

This was our first mistake — thinking that dependency on drugs can't happen overnight. We began to tie our position on drugs to performance, just as we do with alcoholism. We felt that all drug users except perhaps junkies were employable; they could function like some drinkers and alcoholics and they could be helped if caught in time. It seemed to us that most of our youngsters, for example, were experimenting with drugs. They were weekend, recreational users. In other words, they were at the midpoint, not junkies. We felt that if we could pick up some of these problems and perhaps get them into a rehabilitation program, we could help some people. This would be progress rather than just terminating them on the basis of poor attendance or poor behavior. Our whole approach to the thing is still based on performance and rehabilitation; this is the most effective way, at least in our judgment.

When we hire an individual to do a job, we have an unwritten contract saying we expect him to work so many hours a day and meet our standards. But if he doesn't, we don't just fire him immediately; we try first to find out what's wrong. This goes for anyone. If your supervisor can be trained to discuss problems with his people — poor performance, lateness, absenteeism — you can get an open discussion, or communication, going. This is true in all walks of life. We ask our supervisors to be honest with employees. Tell them how they feel about a problem; ask the employee a few simple questions, such as are we bugging you, do you have any problems at home, don't you feel well, anything on your mind? If the employee admits to a problem, and many of them will if someone really shows an interest in them, we're off and running. We want to help, but in the final analysis we must expect certain performance, and if we don't get it, we have to terminate. And nine times out of ten it shakes something out. It improves whatever the problem might be, at least temporarily.

Pushers Must Go

We disagree with first offense discharge for drug use. Pushers go immediately. This policy is working for us. It may not work for everybody;

it depends on the particular industry you are in. For example, I've been told, well, we are in the airline business and we can't afford to give warnings for drug use. It gets down to that. We feel we can afford to give warnings and should. Now I know the banks take a pretty hard line and I can appreciate why. What a spot for a shrewd junkie or pill popper with a costly habit. They can get their hands on some money. So the banks have a little different problem, although my impression is that some of them are beginning to soften on this a bit, strictly because of manpower needs. It's a tradeoff; manpower needs versus risk. There is a bank in New York, for example, that every year draws over 50 percent of its new employees from minority groups.

I think, too, that managements throughout the country are becoming more sophisticated about drugs. Their first reaction was one of fear — get rid of drug users; don't hire them. But during the last few years there has been so much publicity and information that people now realize that this is a problem that can be handled.

I think you have to realize that most of the employees who are on drugs are pretty placid, even the heroin addicts. The person who is probably the most dangerous is the guy or gal who is on barbiturates. This drug is probably more potent in respect to deterioration of physical and mental abilities than heroin. It is relatively easy to come off heroin. But it is a hell of a thing to come off the barbs. You have to be under medical supervision for three or four weeks to come down safely. But we have found from actual experience in going out to help an employee who is high that they are very passive and there is no trick getting them off the company premises and home. It surprised us at first; we thought we'd have to deal with raving lunatics.

So we wrote a policy based on performance and rehabilitation, and then we sat down and devised an approach to educate our supervisors about drugs. Like us, they knew nothing; drug abuse was alien to their experience. Supervisors should know what to look for. Parents should too. For example, many parents — especially of our younger girls — will come to us and say they suspect that their teenagers are on drugs and they don't know how to cope with the situation; but as you talk with them, you find out that there have been obvious signs they have missed along the way, or ignored. It is an easy thing to ignore something you are afraid of. For instance, I talked with one employee whose daughter was away in college. The daughter didn't smoke cigarettes. But when she came home, her mother would find bottle caps and burnt matches in her room, and she never put this together. But the last time the daughter was home, she overdosed with heroin and they took her to a hospital, not knowing what was wrong. When the doctor told them, they were horrified. And the father asked me what he had missed. I told him that every parent today should educate himself about drugs. Don't just say, "Not my daughter."

If he had talked with her intelligently early in the game when they suspected something, or even before — as routine as a mother's talk about sex — maybe they might have done something. The girl is down in Greenwich Village now. They just couldn't reach her.

So from this point, we felt that if the parents didn't understand their kids and the drug scene, our supervisors certainly didn't. We talked with some of our supervisors, and we were amazed at both their lack of knowledge and their unwillingness to face up to the problem. We devised a program; we invited our medical director and we met with several groups of about 30 supervisors. It was quite a chore, but eventually we went through the entire company. We sat down and talked informally. First the medical director told the medical aspects, what he saw, what he believed, and what the medical profession thought about the whole problem. And then we discussed things from a personnel standpoint. Little by little, our supervisors then began to refer suspected drug users to us, or at least they called and said that, "Well, I don't know what to do, but I suspect someone is in trouble." This was progress.

The first questions we asked a supervisor who called were, "How old is the employee, how long has he been with us, and what has your experience been with him?" We found that many or most of the drug problems were with kids who had only been with us for a month or so. They'd have peculiar behavior patterns — being giddy or horsing around or hanging out in the ladies room or in the lunchroom where they'd have unusual numbers of visitors, both from other departments and outside the company. They'd pass all sorts of things back and forth, and we had a pretty good idea about what was getting all the attention.

Companies Afraid

We checked with some other companies to see if they were experiencing similar problems with their young people, and in what numbers. But we got nowhere. There is this fear, a reluctance to talk about the drug problem. They don't want their company or bank to be known as a haven for junkies. That is why most companies don't want to quote statistics or acknowledge that they have a drug problem. But if they are realistic about it, they should realize that there is always a certain percentage of young people on drugs. I estimate maybe 25 to 30 percent. I think we are all realistic enough to know that probably 50 to 75 percent of all young people use marihuana. I'm beginning to wonder if there is much we can do about that. However, we do not condone or permit the use of pot on company premises; we make that very clear. But it is still here. You'd be surprised; every once in a while, somebody will come right out with it —

pull out a reefer and start smoking, right in front of everyone. Almost as though they want to get caught. It is very difficult to detect the other drugs, the pills especially. The only defense we have to handle people is administrative procedures based on performance — what we expect of them as employees.

Detection of heroin is tough, too, once users are on the job. The other day a girl came to us after she had talked with her supervisor, and she acknowledged she had a problem; she rolled up her sleeve and showed us the track marks. Now you wonder how she had gotten into the company. But I'm sure when she came here she was not using heroin. She may have been smoking pot or popping pills, and it is very easy to get by the doctors on that. But after she came here, she began to shoot and she had pretty nasty-looking arms. They'll always wear long sleeves. And that is one of the things we tell supervisors; it doesn't make sense for a girl to wear long sleeves all during the summer. You can't go over to them and say, "Roll up your sleeves." But it is a clue, and you keep an eye on them. If their work is satisfactory, we are kind of stuck with it. So you say, "The hell with it, wear long sleeves," as long as her work is satisfactory. This is what we have to keep coming back to — performance.

But this particular girl started shooting heroin once she was in the company. That is why I think strict medical screening of applicants is good, but sometimes overplayed. I'd be a liar if I told you that we don't have in-house pushers. Our experience is that most of it is peer-to-peer sales. We are convinced that some of our employees are making a living at it. Not the professional pusher as most of us visualize him — the shady character who hangs around the corner inducing kids to start on drugs. It is the youngsters themselves who are dealing, to pay for their habits. What better place to push than in a large company? There are a lot of young people and it is a good place to get lost in, to circulate. Our experience has been that a lot of our drug trafficking starts in our mail rooms because these kids can run all over the place. But there is dope pushed and used in more sophisticated areas, too. In our computer facilities, for instance. Computer people are a peculiar breed, very liberal-minded, generally speaking. But they are an isolated group and they don't have much truck with the rest of the people in the company. They stay by themselves and usually don't spread the stuff. But it is not uncommon for a boy who has been here for about a year to be transferred to another locale or department. Before you know it, you find out that a department that was "clean" isn't anymore. The kid is pushing. So they fan out and you've got to keep on top of it, because if you don't, the damn thing becomes widespread and entrenched.

Too Many Visitors

It is difficult to nail the pusher. Our internal security people work on it. They watch the lounges and the lunchrooms, supposedly undercover. But the dealers have an extra sense about this sort of thing; they can smell security people a block away. But the security workers keep trying. They look for the obvious. For example, it doesn't make sense when girls and boys from different departments come to lunch and greet each other affectionately or shake hands all the time. You have to be stupid not to suspect something is being passed around. We also keep an eye on people who have an unusual number of visitors every day — perhaps, the same guy.

Perhaps a supervisor observes somebody from another department coming into his department on a regular basis. He thinks he is pushing and he goes up to him and accuses him of dealing. Unless you can prove it, you're in trouble. Don't accuse anybody. We tell our supervisors to tell *us* about their suspicions. If we should find heroin or some unknown drug, we turn it over to the police for evaluation. It may be aspirin; we don't know. But for heaven's sake, never accuse anybody because your company could be open for all kinds of suits on various counts.

Actually, you have to catch a pusher red-handed, transferring stuff. This is a rare, rare thing, at least with industry's present security capability. This is a new concept for management, because I don't think in the past business has been too security-minded. The defense industries, yes, but not the others. But this is going to have to change, because in today's society drug abuse is only one problem; you have militant behavior, bomb threats, sky-rocketing theft, all sorts of things. So supervisors, as well as the security people, have to learn to be more observant. This is part of their job. A lot of them will disagree because many are young, too, and they look at things quite differently. But we have to hammer away at it and we do. We have our training programs, and as new supervisors are taken on, they are briefed on this and told about company policy and what we expect.

If it comes to a case where we have a pretty definite suspicion about a pusher and we have observed him for some time — not just overnight, but for some time — then we sit down and decide if this is a case for the police. But you have to have something solid. The police won't come in and handle your personnel problems for you. They just haven't the time to follow up every suspicion. They've got more than they can handle outside. So it is important that companies focus on security. You have to have the guts to do what has to be done. Don't forget, we have 20 thousand people in this company. That's equivalent to a good-size town like Ridgewood, New Jersey. The police have their own problems; we have to take care of ours. We may not always be right and we are going to make mistakes, but, nevertheless, it has to be done. Security has to be our own bag.

For example, our company's theft rate over the past three years has doubled, skyrocketed. We think a great portion of it can be pinned on drugs. It is mostly radios, clocks, table machines, calculators, typewriters, small tools, this sort of thing. How they get some of this stuff out, I just don't know. But they do.

Frankly, while we are on this security and law enforcement angle, I don't think we will ever minimize the drug problem simply by enforcing the law. It requires education, counseling, and reaching young people. It's got to be a preventive thing; stop them before they start. We are trying this.

Cynical Group

Our supervisors gave fifty-five talks last year. I don't know how effective they were. We also publish articles in our house organ, distribute literature, and all that. Little by little, maybe the youngsters' cynicism is worn down with the right kind of message. No question about it, we are dealing with a highly cynical group. You can't use scare tactics; it just doesn't work on this generation. And the thing I find so different about them — this generation — is that regardless of how bad something may be, like drug abuse, they still feel, even the nonusers, that it is a matter of individual choice. They feel every man has a right to do his own thing, and they mean that sincerely.

Well, you might ask, if that's true, what's the rationale for trying to help or rehabilitate somebody? It is a two-edged sword. You can get somebody in here who is spreading this sickness and you've also got somebody who is in need of help, and wants it. We make an offer of help when somebody is on drugs, but is not a pusher. That's a law enforcement problem, and we don't offer rehabilitation to them. But the offer is made to users, and if they cooperate in every respect in their rehabilitation and their perform- ance, we'll go along with it.

Let me give you our initial thinking on this point about rehabilitation. We recognized we had a drug problem and we believed we had to face up to it; otherwise it would just get worse. We believed we had to meet the problem in the same way we faced up to alcoholism, because all we would be doing if we found people on drugs and fired them would be to pass the buck to some other segment of society, most of whom have their hands full. That's not progress. Not that we are out to rehabilitate all the young people or change society, but somebody somewhere had to get started on this thing. The same question came up as to what our policy should be if a former addict applied for a job. Should we hire him? We agreed that business and industry has to start somewhere; you just can't keep turning people down who are honest enough to say, "Well, I was on drugs for five years, but I've been clean for a year and I'll show you I can pass a medical." If you continue to turn these people down, all you are doing is turning them back on the street; and they have no choice but to go back to what they were doing to earn a living. So we will consider a limited number of ex-addicts for employment. We can't open up completely and create a haven for ex-junkies; we have to be selective, and we are. But we'll take a close look at ex-addicts of heroin, some with police records. We may not be too happy if one of the agencies refers somebody to us who has been convicted of attempted murder or assault, but we may take on a person who in the past was caught stealing, in possession, and similar offenses. If we are convinced that they really are motivated and they are really trying — that they have changed their mode of living, they have left their old neighborhood, they have dropped their old friends, they are planning to get married, or they are living with their family again — we'll put them on.

And they have to be getting the support of counseling from the agency that's sponsoring them, and this should be a continuing thing. They have to report for methadone treatment, or whatever, and we keep tabs on their progress for a whole year.

We have one ex-addict who is terrific. He is going to be one of our top men one of these days — a very bright young man. He was in a federal penitentiary for 15 months for forging checks to support his habit. He was recommended to us by the Department of Justice. They said he was highly motivated — he was going to continue his education, he was a model prisoner, and he worked very hard. He wanted to get back into the mainstream and he was willing to do anything. We talked with him and came to the same conclusions. His aptitude test score was one of the highest we have ever seen. Three months after he came with us, his supervisor said, "Gee, can you get me any more?" He has been with us two years now, and he has progressed very well.

Some of the other ex-addicts we've hired are just fair. You have to stay on them and there are many hangups; a return to drugs may be one thing, but there are also family, psychological, and financial hangups. But you keep trying, because gainful employment has got to be the final step in rehabilitation — otherwise, what good is it? And if industry doesn't do it, we are not going to get very far with this problem. A man has to be able to work. The same thing happened with the alcoholic; until industry got into it and organized programs, the alcoholic was considered a moral leper, a no-good bum. But when industry took an interest, then people became better educated about the problem and we came to find out that alcoholism is treatable and beatable.

Not Like Alcoholics

I must say that industry has some leverage with alcoholics that we don't seem to have with the drug generation. We can hold a man's job over an alcoholic's head. But that is not as important in the drug scene, because you are dealing with a younger person who has less service and the job is less important to him. With the alcoholic, you're talking about people maybe 35 to 55 years old. They have been with the company for several years, the job is important to them. They've got obligations, a family. You can't use this leverage with the kids. It has to be factual information about drugs, no preaching. "Do your thing if you have to, but, Buster, do you know where you are going?"

It is a tough job convincing the kids that drugs are bad for them. They are against the law enforcement people and any legislation against drug use; they feel that drugs should be legalized and everybody should be able to make up his own mind about using them or not, like cigarettes or booze. If you go in the other direction, they just turn off.

We have shown them shock films on drugs, and they just laugh. I feel that you've got to organize a program in the schools — a program the kids actually participate in. Let them kick it around themselves. They relate to one another, but as soon as somebody over 35 starts to preach the dangers of drug abuse, they turn off.

One of our young guys is president of the young lawyers association, and they do exactly that. They get out into the community and into the schools. They usually have a doctor and an attorney and they just rap with the students. The kids get involved themselves, and this is far more effective than a lecture.

Good education is the answer, participatory education. We considered using a film that shows the horrors of drug abuse. It is not participatory education, but the film is dramatic as hell. We wondered whether the film was appropriate to show to our new hires. We have an indoctrination program for new employees, most of whom are youngsters. Well, some of my people thought it was too pointed, too dramatic, too grim. It's factual, no question about it. God, I think it would scare the hell out of you; it did me.

Some people objected to the fact that we were showing the extreme end of drug abuse — what happens when you get on drugs all the way. The film shows addicts, and some of my people said that most drug users in industry are not addicts; they are recreational users, they are experimenters. We don't deal with addicts; they aren't employable for the most part. But, I thought the film underscored this fact, that addicts aren't employable. It starts by discussing marihuana; users talk about how they started on marihuana. And how they went to the ups and the downs and to speed and to acid and then finally to heroin. The film holds back nothing; you have to have a strong stomach, so maybe it is a little bit too ghastly, I don't know. Would it be good education or just another scare tactic that doesn't work?

Rap Sessions Are Best

The best drug education programs are rap sessions with the kids — small groups with good counseling. This, of course, is difficult if you are a small company that has a small personnel staff and no counseling capability. It's tough then to help employees on drugs because you don't have anyone who knows anything about the scene, anyone with a feel. These companies should have good contact with social agencies and rehabilitation centers, like Greenwich House, Phoenix House, Daytop Village, some of the storefront operations. If you don't have access to these types of things, you can get help from government agencies and private hospitals. You can check with your board of health or police department. Most hospitals today have clinics with drug education programs. Quite a few of the smaller companies are hiring a minister or a priest who does community work and counseling, and he'll work as an employee of the company either on a part-time or full-time basis. These are people who are exposed to all these problems. A small company can refer employees to them for counseling, and this involves not just drug abuse, gambling or alcoholism, but any kind of counseling.

We have one man in our office now who was in a Catholic church for years, and he's doing private counseling on his own, very successfully. He has a knack for reaching young people.

Any good manager should also have the directory that lists all the services in the nation available for drug abusers. It is very easy to get. All you have to do is write your regional office of the U. S. Bureau of Narcotics. But I think smaller companies have to lean on their supervisors for counseling, if somebody's abusing and wants to talk about it. If they want help, fine; then the supervisor and the personnel department can make a referral. You don't have to have a medical director. You can make your referral, same as we do with the alcoholic, directly to AA or one of the other organizations that will be helpful.

The American Social Health Association puts out a booklet that every manager should have. It breaks down the different types of drug abusers and indicates what type of therapeutic facility to send them to. It is a good booklet for the layman, if he takes a little time to study it. As I said, he should also visit the hospitals and talk with junkies and doctors. You've got to get the feel of it. If you don't have the feel, you might as well forget about it. This takes time and effort, but it pays off in the long run.

I often hear a company say, "Well, we're not large enough to have a drug program"; and I say, "Oh, that's a lot of baloney." You can have a two-man operation and have a drug program. If you have an employee using drugs, you can certainly get him some outside counseling or rehabilitation at night. We have one fellow who's going to one nightly session a week, which is not enough. But it is a beginning. Then you get a few more to attend.

There's also the angle of multiple-company action. You can form some sort of a drug council. Three or four companies can get together and at the very least open one of those store-front clinics we were talking about. Four or five companies get involved and they split the cost of a clinic, a store-front, out-patient rehabilitation center, to which employees can be referred. It's only good for outpatients; if an employee is really hooked, he has to go to a hospital. He has to be away for 18 months or longer with the understanding that if he is clean when he comes back and can pass the medical, we'll consider him, but we can't make any promises. If it's an employee at the midpoint who can be treated on an outpatient basis, someone who can withdraw easily and by counseling or methadone or whatever can get back on the job, fine, then we'll keep him and demand performance. If he doesn't come up with performance, he is through. That's all there is to it.

So I'm all for trying to help people, even in the smallest company. And it can be done. Some of my counterparts in other companies think I am soft on drugs. I'm not, I'm realistic. In their companies, for example, their policies say they will not hire anybody with a drug history. This is unreal. A very large percentage of young people who are applying for your jobs have some experience with drugs somewhere along the line. They're not going to tell you this. This doesn't mean we don't try to keep people with drug problems out. We do. We never make any commitment as far as a job is concerned without the total package — you've got to get through your initial interview, pass your SRA test, and pass a medical, and there's still no commitment made. When we get to medical if everything else seems to be in order, then a commitment can be made, but not before.

It's like buying a pig in a poke anytime you hire somebody new. He could be an alcoholic. He could be an ex-con. He could have an arrest record for drug use or sale. But he doesn't come right out and tell you this. Drug abusers are going to get into your company, policy or no policy. Some companies give every applicant a urine test for drug use. We don't. It seems to me that urinalysis must be given to *everyone*. You can't just select a certain number, a certain group; urinalysis means testing every-one. Otherwise, it could be discriminatory, particularly if you give it only to the Blacks from the urban areas; then you're in trouble.

Medical Department Screens

Our medical department sees all our people and they have to be medically approved, but it's a routine test that every employee is given when he comes in. However, if during this examination the doctor becomes suspicious or if he notes track marks or puncture marks, he then decides whether he feels that further tests should be made. He asks for a voluntary urine specimen. If the specimen shows heroin use, the applicant is turned down medically. It's as simple as that. If the doctor feels that it's a case of recreational using, he would refer the person to us for evaluation and discussion. And if we agree with the doctor's evaluation, we might hire him, but we have the problem out in the open; we know where it is. It's sort of a liberal policy, but we don't want to give every youngster that comes in here a drug test. It means we are suspicious of every employee. And their parents would probably raise hell if they knew their kid was being tested for drug use. Anyway, I wonder how effective urinalysis really is. Anybody who's been on heroin knows — and believe me these kids are sophisticated — that if they remain drug free for a couple of days, it's not going to show up in urinalysis. We've had situations where they bring in somebody else's urine. So, there are ways of getting around it.

Now, as I mentioned, we do take on a few so-called rehabilitated or recovered drug users or abusers or addicts. We'll put them on for at least a year, on a probationary basis. When we say probationary, we mean that they are not covered under our insurance, medical expense coverage, hospitalization, or retirement program for that year because if they get sick we're liable for disability. To make it easier to place them within the company, our personnel division assumes the salary charge for the first year. Then we can go out to a department or division and say, look, you're getting an employee free for a whole year. We're going to assume the charge. This way, we have a better chance of placing the guy.

This is only a pilot program with a very small number of people. We also have a year's probationary period — and personnel pays the salary — for the rehabilitated employee. It depends upon his performance, and when his year is over, we ask for a recommendation from his supervisor. If they say he's satisfactory, then he's on their payroll. He's their problem, the same as any other employee. He's covered for everything at that time — retirement, hospitalization, and so on.

Now, you say, if short-term rehabilitation is needed for an employee, requiring time off the job for special treatment and counseling, is the employee continued on the payroll? If he's an outpatient, yes, we go along for a reasonable period of time. The first four or five days he's out he is paid salary under the company program the same as any other employee. And, if it takes a week or two, we go along with a reasonable period like that. That's a leave-of-absence without pay. However, if the employee is in a hospital or under medical supervision, he can file his claim under the program which he is entitled to file; and as long as he is under medical supervision, he would get his disability benefits. Now, I certainly don't think you would expect any company with a program such as this to keep it open-ended indefinitely; you have to be practical.

It's true of the alcoholic, too. We don't go along indefinitely. We might pay him benefits two or three times. But if in a given year he's out five or six times, always for getting boozed up, you're going to call a halt. Some of my friends have said that to have benefits for somebody who is sick because of drugs is a very unusual thing. Most companies don't. But to be practical about it, how many doctors will report to you that this is a heroin addict or a drug abuser? The employee is usually in a hospital for hepatitis, kidney infections, etc. But you know damn well, based on medical experience, that employable young people from the ages of 16 to 25 don't usually have hepatitis, so this is how we become aware of drug use. When you see 40 or 50 or 60 cases of young people in a hospital for hepatitis, well, there's something wrong. A lot of bum needles.

Everything Confidential

But the key is to work with young people before they have to be hospitalized. And we do, sometimes without the knowledge of the supervisor, or even without our medical department knowing. A kid comes to us and says, "I'm in a jam, can you help me?" Fine, that's what we're here for. We're glad to get her here on her own. Everything is confidential. Ultimately, we clue the supervisor in and ask for his cooperation in followup.

We check with each other; and the big thing is, is the supervisor satisfied with performance? Has attendance improved, has behavior improved, is our medical department, which also assists in the follow-up, satisfied? We will talk with the rehabilitation agency, if one is being used. What's their experience? How do they feel? With these facts, we keep on top of it.

One thing we do in our alcoholism program, which is very effective and which we are trying in our drug program, is to give employees one or two warnings, and then have what we call a confrontation. Usually the medical director runs it; we're present, and so is the employee's supervisor. We all meet with the employee and tell him it's a final warning; he can't play off one against the other because we're all here and we're all agreed. We tell him what we expect in terms of performance and rehabilitation cooperation, and if we don't get it, it's going to lead to discontinuance of active employment.

Generally speaking, we expect immediate sustained improvement, as well as full cooperation in his rehabilitation. Then we follow up. If anything goes wrong in any area, we decide what action should be taken. We might put him on disability, or he might be forced to retire. He might just terminate, not because he's an alcoholic or drug abuser, but because now he has complications, organic conditions that develop. We try to leave it open.

Perhaps we have a man who is diagnosed as an addict and we get him into a rehab organization on an outpatient basis. He's cooperating, and he's clean, and everything's going along fine. His job performance is OK. Now two years go by, and then he has a slip. It would be stupid to fire him. So he's had one slip in two years. We don't make our judgments on whether he is absolutely clean or not but on his performance — again we get back to this. How long since he had the last slip? How quickly did he get back on the job? Is supervision satisfied? If so, fine, he stays. But if we get five or six quick slips, then it's obvious to us the guy is really back, he's hooked again. We're not getting the cooperation. Then we would move in with our confrontation — final warning.

But if you want to help people, you've got to be flexible. Each problem is an individual one. We think helping our employees is important. If we can help a guy with outside problems, then probably he will be a much better employee in the long run. And it makes the supervisor's job smoother. I think over the years this policy has proved out.

And I think in the years ahead, business and industry must become more people-oriented. Otherwise, the 1970s are going to be a horrible experience for management. This is only my opinion. There are going to be many problems emerging. Drugs is one, and it is here to stay. We're going to have to learn to live with it, and to handle it.

The Extent
of Drug Abuse
in Business and
Industry

If you yourself have never really been confronted with the drug problem but have only heard or read about it, or have only been exposed on the periphery, you're likely to wonder just what are the real dimensions of the drug abuse problem in the workforce.

The true nature and full extent of drug abuse in business and industry can never be known. To assume, however, that no problem exists in any specific business or industry ignores the evidence of rapid increases in drug abuse among our young people and the extensive nature of all forms of drug use by adults. It no longer seems appropriate to assume that the 50 percent of all high school graduates who admit to drug abuse and the 30 percent of all adults who regularly use one or more of the tranquilizers, sedatives, and stimulants are not having some impact on business and industry. We believe the abuse of legal and illegal drugs by employees in all occupational groups is occurring throughout business and industry.

Most attempts to establish the nature and dimensions of the problem of drug abuse in business and industry have been limited by focusing upon a specific industry, specific workers, or specific drugs. However, recent empirical studies conducted by the Division of Research of the New York State Narcotic Addiction Control Commission have provided a data base for projecting the prevalence, incidence, frequency, and situational content of all types of drug use within the general population.[1] These survey studies permit projections of the use of various drugs within seven general occupational groups:

1. Professionals, technical workers, managers and owners
2. Clerical and other white collar workers
3. Skilled and semiskilled workers
4. Unskilled workers
5. Service and protective workers
6. Sales workers
7. Farmers

For the first time, drug survey specialists have made an empirical assessment of drug use which includes the incidence of drug use while *on the job*. It is now possible to begin to meaningfully address the very major issues of workers' health, industrial security, industrial safety and job performance. While the data which we will present was generated for New York State workers, we believe they have applicability throughout the United States. While the incidence of actual use may vary somewhat, the rate of use on the job among users will probably be fairly constant.

I. The Use of Illegal Drugs by Employed Workers

The survey data permits a discussion of the use of four illegally manufactured and/or distributed drugs; marihuana, heroin, LSD and methedrine (speed).

1. *Marihuana*

The various Cannabis sativa preparations (marihuana, hashish, dagga, charas, bhang, etc.) are the most widely used illegal drugs in the world. Similarly, in the United States the use of marihuana exceeds the use of any other illegal drug and quite probably the abuse of the legally manufactured drugs.

1. Chambers, C. D., *An Assessment of Drug Use in the General Population.* New York: New York State Narcotic Addiction Control Commission, 1971, and Chambers, C. D., *Differential Drug Use Within the New York State Labor Force.* New York: New York State Narcotic Addiction Control Commission, 1971.

For the purposes of this survey, any use of a Cannabis preparation was recorded as the use of marihuana. This was done when it became apparent that some respondents used the terms interchangeably, or were at times uncertain as to which preparation had been used. This is, of course, consistent with our awareness that the marihuana grown, sold and used is not a single uniform substance. It contains varying mixtures of the seeds, flowers, leaves and stems of the plant. The drug subsequently produces a wide variation of hallucinogenic effects.

While it is obvious the hallucinogenic effects of the marihuana are related to the amount and potency of the drug ingested, individual reactions are also influenced by the setting in which use occurs, the emotional and intellectual maturity of the user and the previous experience of the user. These combine to prevent meaningful prediction of harmful psychological or physiological effects of use. At the present time and with our current state of knowledge, it is apparent there are some psychological and physiological "costs" which accompany marihuana use. The extent of these "costs" remains to be documented.

These data would tend to confirm various popular hypotheses that the primary usage pattern in the United States appears to be long-term, infrequent use of low-potency marihuana.

EXTENT OF USE BY EMPLOYED WORKERS

The number of employed workers in New York State estimated to have smoked marihuana on at least one occasion is 889,000, or 12.1% of all employed workers. Of these 889,000 workers, 624,000, or 70.2%, are contemporary users (having used during the past six months), and 293,000, or 33.0%, are current regular users (using at least six times per month). Of these 293,000 employed workers who report themselves as regular users of marihuana, *78,000, or 26.6%, also report they have smoked marihuana while on the job.*

Those workers who reportedly smoked marihuana while on the job were most frequently under the age of 25 (66.3%), whites (77.6%), males (73.5%) and high school graduates (69.4%).

Although the rate of having ever used marihuana was found to be the highest among unskilled workers (1,470 per 10,000 workers), the rate of current regular use is highest among sales workers (860 per 10,000 workers). Use on the job is also the highest among the sales workers:

Table 1. Prevalence and Incidence of the Use of Marihuana

Occupational Group	Never Used (% of total)	Former User (No use in 6 months) (% of total)	Infrequent User (1 but not 6 times per month) (% of total)	Regular User (At least 6 times per month) (% of total)	No Data (% of total)	Total (% of total)	Regular Users (Using while at work) (% of regular) users)
Professionals, technical workers, managers and owners	1,469,000 (86.8)	62,000 (3.7)	64,000 (3.8)	48,000 (2.8)	49,000 (2.9)	1,692,000 (100.0)	10,000 (20.8)
Clerical and other white collar workers	1,217,000 (85.6)	50,000 (3.5)	69,000 (4.9)	57,000 (4.0)	29,000 (2.0)	1,422,000 (100.0)	20,000 (35.1)
Skilled and semiskilled workers	2,040,000 (84.3)	112,000 (4.6)	127,000 (5.2)	86,000 (3.6)	56,000 (2.3)	2,421,000 (100.0)	19,000 (22.1)
Unskilled workers	271,000 (83.1)	12,000 (3.7)	19,000 (5.8)	17,000 (5.2)	7,000 (2.1)	326,000 (100.0)	6,000 (35.3)
Service and protective workers	790,000 (89.3)	23,000 (2.6)	28,000 (3.2)	35,000 (4.0)	9,000 (1.0)	885,000 (100.0)	1,000 (2.9)
Sales workers	494,000 (85.3)	6,000 (1.0)	23,000 (4.0)	50,000 (8.6)	6,000 (1.0)	579,000 (100.0)	22,000 (44.0)
Farmers	63,000 (98.4)	— —	1,000 (1.6)	— —	— —	64,000 (100.0)	— —
Total employed	6,344,000 (85.9)	265,000 (3.6)	331,000 (4.5)	293,000 (4.0)	156,000 (2.1)	7,389,000 (100.0)	78,000 (26.6)

Table 2. Rate of Marihuana Use Per 10,000 Employed Workers

Occupational Group	Prevalence Rate (Ever Used)	Incidence Rate (Regular Use)
Professionals, technical workers, managers and owners	1,030	280
Clerical and other white collar workers	1,240	400
Skilled, semiskilled workers	1,340	360
Unskilled workers	1,470	520
Service and protective workers	980	400
Sales workers	1,360	860
Farmers	160	—
Total employed	1,210	400

44.0% of the sales workers who regularly smoke marihuana do so while on the job. By sales workers, we mean any persons employed in sales (including retail sales) excluding sales managers and sales executives.

2. *Heroin*

Heroin is a highly addictive white crystalline powder prepared by acetylation from morphine. The drug was first produced in 1898 and marketed as a nonaddicting substitute for morphine and codeine. Subsequent experience has shown the drug to be twice as potent as morphine at any given quantity. Tolerance develops very rapidly. In fact, there is considerable agreement that heroin has a higher addiction liability than morphine. As tolerance increases, the heroin user typically uses the drug in increasing amounts, and most of his waking hours are spent in drug-centered behavior. With the exception of drug-related phenomena, the addicted user becomes insensitive to his environment and indifferent to his personal situation.

Our current knowledge suggests that the use of heroin is rising

Table 3. Prevalence and Incidence of the Use of Heroin

Occupational Group	Never Used (% of total)	Former User (No use in 6 months) (% of total)	Infrequent User (1 but not 6 times per month) (% of total)	Regular User (At least 6 times per month) (% of total)	No Data (% of total)	Total (% of total)	Regular Users (Using while at work) (% of regular users)
Professionals, technical workers, managers and owners	1,636,000 (96.7)	9,000 (0.5)	— —	4,000 (0.2)	43,000 (2.5)	1,692,000 (100.0)	— —
Clerical and other white collar workers	1,378,000 (96.9)	2,000 (0.1)	— —	9,000 (0.6)	33,000 (2.3)	1,422,000 (100.0)	— —
Skilled and semiskilled workers	2,335,000 (96.4)	23,000 (1.0)	3,000 (0.1)	8,000 (0.3)	52,000 (2.1)	2,421,000 (100.0)	— —
Unskilled workers	315,000 (96.6)	3,000 (0.9)	2,000 (0.6)	1,000 (0.3)	5,000 (1.5)	326,000 (100.0)	— —
Service and protective workers	865,000 (97.7)	13,000 (1.5)	— —	— —	7,000 (0.8)	885,000 (100.0)	— —
Sales workers	560,000 (96.7)	— —	— —	12,000 (2.1)	7,000 (1.2)	579,000 (100.0)	12,000 (100.0)
Farmers	64,000 (100.0)	— —	— —	— —	— —	64,000 (100.0)	— —
Total employed	7,153,000 (96.8)	50,000 (0.7)	5,000 (0.1)	34,000 (0.5)	147,000 (2.0)	7,389,000 (100.0)	12,000 (35.3)

throughout the country, and is increasingly becoming associated with younger individuals of all ethnic groups and socioeconomic classes.

EXTENT OF USE BY EMPLOYED WORKERS

The number of employed workers in New York state estimated to have used heroin on at least one occasion is 89,000, or 1.3% of all employed workers. Of these 89,000 workers who have a history of heroin use, 39,000, or 43.8%, are contemporary users (having used heroin during the past six months), and 34,000, or 38.2%, are current regular users of heroin (using at least six times per month). Of these 34,000 employed regular users of heroin, *12,000, or 35.3%, reported they had used the drug while on the job*.

All of the regular heroin users who reported using the drug while on the job were sales workers. These approximately 12,000 sales workers were most frequently above age 25 (58.3%). All were white, 83.3% were females and 83.3% were high school graduates.

The rate for having ever used heroin and the rate of current regular use of heroin were both highest among the sales workers. No heroin use

Table 4. Rate of Heroin Use Per 10,000 Employed Workers

Occupational Group	*Prevalence Rate (Ever Used)*	*Incidence Rate (Regular Use)*
Professionals, technical workers, managers and owners	70	20
Clerical and other white collar workers	70	60
Skilled, semiskilled workers	140	30
Unskilled workers	180	30
Service and protective workers	150	—
Sales workers	210	210
Farmers	—	—
Total employed	130	50

was detected among farmers, and no regular heroin use was detected among the service and protective users, e.g., policemen, firemen, etc. Some regular use was detected among professionals, technical workers, managers and owners, among clerical and other white collar workers, among skilled and semiskilled workers and among unskilled workers, but none reported using heroin while on the job. This would suggest that these workers were either recent initiates to heroin use or were able to avoid becoming dysfunctionally involved with the drug. Such might not be the case with the sales workers where all regular users were also users while on the job, possibly indicating the *necessity* for using the drug at regular intervals.

3. *LSD*

LSD — D-lysergic acid diethylamine — is a semisynthetic derivative from one of the ergot alkaloids whose hallucinogenic properties were accidentally discovered in 1943. Ergot is a fungus which grows as a rust on rye and other cereals. The drug is relatively easy to manufacture in clandestine laboratories and has become one of the most widely used illegal drugs. With the exception of federally approved research projects, all use of LSD is unlawful.

To date neither the mode nor site of action of LSD is completely known. Drug-induced activity, i.e., distortions of perception, emotionality and rationality, generally lasts eight to twelve hours. The most intense and bizarre changes apparently occur during the first half of the experience, while the latter part is characterized by introspection and hypersuggestibility.

LSD is not physically addicting as are barbiturates and opiates. The dependence is psychological, not physical. Tolerance develops rapidly after a few days of repeated use, but is usually lost in two or three days. Some users have reportedly built up their LSD doses to 1000 and 2000 mcg. over a period of days. The first or threshold dose is about 25 mcg., and an average dose is 200 to 400 mcg. Paradoxically, some users report a state of increased sensitivity to LSD once they have lost their tolerance. Unexpected return of the drugged state after months or even a year without ingestion of LSD has been reported.

The literature reports three different kinds of experiences under

LSD: (1) the good trip — a predominantly pleasant experience; (2) the bad trip — a dysphoric experience characterized by anxiety, panic, feelings of persecution, fears of loss of ego boundaries, loss of control and time perception, and impaired performance; and (3) an ambivalent state where the subject may simultaneously experience contrasting feelings such as happiness and despair, relaxedness and tenseness.

EXTENT OF USE BY EMPLOYED WORKERS

The number of employed workers in New York state estimated to have used LSD on at least one occasion is 191,000, or 2.6% of all employed workers. Of these 191,000 workers who have used LSD, 118,000, or 61.8%, are contemporary users (having used the drug during the past six months), and 25,000, or 21.2%, are current regular users (having taken the drug at least six times during the past month). Of these 25,000 employed workers who report themselves as regular users of LSD, *5,000, or 20.0%, also report using LSD while on the job*. The workers in this study who reportedly used LSD while on the job were all above age 25, were most frequently white (60.0%), most frequently females (80.0%), and all were high school graduates.

No LSD use was reported by the farmers surveyed in this study. Some use, both former and contemporary, was reported by members of all the other occupational groups. Current regular use was reported in all these occupational groups except among clerical and other white collar workers. Some use on the job was reported in only two occupational groups — by professionals, technical workers, managers and owners and by sales workers.

The highest rate of having ever used LSD was among the unskilled workers (430 per 10,000). The rate of current regular use is, however, much higher among sales workers than any other occupational group (230 per 10,000).

4. *Methedrine* (*Speed*)

Methedrine, a brand name for methamphetamine, is a central nervous system stimulant more potent, but chemically related to the amphetamines — amphetamine sulfate (Benzedrine) and d-amphetamine sul-

Table 5. Prevalence and Incidence of the Use of LSD

Occupational Group	Never Used (% of total)	Former User (No use in 6 months) (% of total)	Infrequent User (1 but not 6 times per month) (% of total)	Regular User (At least 6 times per month) (% of total)	No Data (% of total)	Total (% of total)	Regular Users (Using while at work) (% of regular users)
Professionals, technical workers, managers and owners	1,624,000 (96.0)	10,000 (0.6)	12,000 (0.7)	2,000 (0.1)	44,000 (2.6)	1,692,000 (100.0)	1,000 (50.0)
Clerical and other white collar workers	1,357,000 (95.4)	24,000 (1.7)	13,000 (0.9)	—	28,000 (2.0)	1,422,000 (100.0)	—
Skilled and semiskilled workers	2,298,000 (94.9)	27,000 (1.1)	36,000 (1.5)	4,000 (0.2)	56,000 (2.3)	2,421,000 (100.0)	—
Unskilled workers	307,000 (94.2)	4,000 (1.2)	9,000 (2.8)	1,000 (0.3)	5,000 (1.5)	326,000 (100.0)	—
Service and protective workers	853,000 (96.4)	4,000 (0.5)	18,000 (2.0)	3,000 (0.3)	7,000 (0.8)	885,000 (100.0)	—
Sales workers	548,000 (94.6)	4,000 (0.7)	5,000 (0.9)	15,000 (2.6)	7,000 (1.2)	579,000 (100.0)	4,000 (26.7)
Farmers	64,000 (100.0)	— —	— —	— —	— —	64,000 (100.0)	— —
Total employed	7,051,000 (95.4)	73,000 (1.0)	93,000 (1.3)	25,000 (0.3)	147,000 (2.0)	7,389,000 (100.0)	5,000 (20.0)

Table 6. Rate of LSD Use Per 10,000 Employed Workers

Occupational Group	Prevalence Rate (Ever Used)	Incidence Rate (Regular Use)
Professionals, technical workers, managers and owners	140	10
Clerical and other white collar workers	260	–
Skilled, semiskilled workers	280	20
Unskilled workers	430	30
Service and protective workers	280	30
Sales workers	420	260
Farmers	–	–
Total employed	260	30

fate (Dexedrine). The drug was first used widely by the German army during World War II to counter fatigue among combatants. The drug is currently marketed for its appetite-suppressing effects, its potential for reducing mild symptoms of mental depression, its potential as a mood elevator, as an analeptic in sedative overdose, and to raise abnormally low blood pressure, i.e., in anesthetized patients.

Unfortunately, the primary use of this drug is nonmedical, unsupervised, illicit abuse by habitual high-dose amphetamine users. It is the drug of choice among those persons who use amphetamines by intravenous injection only for their euphoric effects. Psychological dependence and tolerance have been well documented. High doses over extended periods of time engender acute or chronic psychoses and loss of memory and powers of concentration. Violent behavior is also commonly seen. There are reports to indicate that methedrine abusers may experience damage to their brains and arteries.

EXTENT OF USE BY EMPLOYED WORKERS

The number of employed workers in New York state estimated to have used *speed* on at least one occasion is 147,000, or 2.0% of all em-

Table 7. Prevalence and Incidence of the Use of Methedrine

Occupational Group	Never Used (% of total)	Former User (No use in 6 months) (% of total)	Infrequent User (1 but not 6 times per month) (% of total)	Regular User (At least 6 times per month) (% of total)	No Data (% of total)	Total (% of total)	Regular Users (Using while at work) (% of regular users)
Professionals, technical workers, managers and owners	1,627,000 (96.2)	15,000 (0.9)	5,000 (0.3)	2,000 (0.1)	43,000 (2.5)	1,692,000 (100.0)	1,000 (50.0)
Clerical and other white collar workers	1,364,000 (95.9)	25,000 (1.8)	6,000 (0.4)	3,000 (0.2)	24,000 (1.7)	1,422,000 (100.0)	—
Skilled and semiskilled workers	2,312,000 (95.5)	33,000 (1.4)	16,000 (0.7)	—	60,000 (2.5)	2,421,000 (100.0)	—
Unskilled workers	311,000 (95.4)	7,000 (2.1)	2,000 (0.6)	1,000 (0.3)	5,000 (1.5)	326,000 (100.0)	1,000 (100.0)
Service and protective workers	860,000 (97.2)	16,000 (1.8)	2,000 (0.2)	—	7,000 (0.8)	885,000 (100.0)	—
Sales workers	558,000 (96.4)	6,000 (1.0)	4,000 (0.7)	4,000 (0.7)	7,000 (1.2)	579,000 (100.0)	4,000 (100.0)
Farmers	64,000 (100.0)	—	—	—	—	64,000 (100.0)	—
Total employed	7,096,000 (96.0)	102,000 (1.4)	35,000 (0.5)	10,000 (0.1)	146,000 (2.0)	7,389,000 (100.0)	6,000 (60.0)

ployed workers. Of these 147,000 workers, 45,000, or 30.6%, are contemporary users (having used during the past six months) and 10,000, or 6.8%, are current regular users (using at least six times per month). Of these 10,000 employed workers who report themselves as regular users of methedrine, *6,000, or 60.0%, also report they have used this drug while on the job.*

Those workers who reportedly used speed while on the job were most frequently above the age of 25 (83.3%), whites (100.0%), females (66.7%) and high school graduates (100.0%).

Although the rate of having ever used speed was found to be the highest among unskilled workers (300 per 10,000 workers), the rate of current regular users is highest among the sales workers (70 per 10,000 workers). Use while on the job is equally high among the current regular users in both occupational groups. All the unskilled workers and all the sales workers who reported themselves as regular users of this drug also reported they had used it while on the job.

No current regular use of this drug was detected among the skilled and semiskilled workers, the service and protective workers, and farmers.

Table 8. Rate of Methedrine Use Per 10,000 Employed Workers

Occupational Group	Prevalence Rate (Ever Used)	Incidence Rate (Regular Use)
Professionals, technical workers, managers and owners	130	10
Clerical and other white collar workers	240	20
Skilled, semiskilled workers	210	—
Unskilled workers	300	30
Service and protective workers	200	—
Sales workers	240	70
Farmers	—	—
Total employed	200	10

In summary, these data on the use of four illegal drugs by employed workers indicated:

1. Some 12.1% (approximately 889,000) of all employed workers have smoked marihuana. Some 4.0% (approximately 293,000) of all employed workers are current regular users of marihuana, and one-fourth of these regular users report smoking marihuana while on the job. The highest rate of regular marihuana use and the highest incidence of use while at work occur among sales workers.

2. Some 1.3% (approximately 89,000) of all employed workers have used heroin on at least one occasion. Some 0.5% (approximately 34,000) of all employed workers are current regular users of heroin, and over one-third of these regular users report the use of heroin while on the job. The highest rate of regular heroin use is among sales workers, and sales workers were the only workers detected who used heroin while at work.

3. Some 2.6% (approximately 191,000) of all employed workers have used LSD on at least one occasion. Some 0.3% (approximately 25,000) are current regular users of LSD, one-fifth of whom report the use of LSD while on the job. The highest rate of regular LSD use is among sales workers, and sales workers contribute the greatest number of on-the-job users.

4. Some 2.0% (approximately 147,000) of all employed workers have used methedrine (speed) on at least one occasion. Some 0.1% (approximately 10,000) of all employed workers are current regular users of methedrine (speed), and almost two-thirds of these regular users report the use of methedrine (speed) while on the job. The highest rate of regular methedrine (speed) use is among sales workers, and sales workers contribute the greatest number of on-the-job users.

The involvements outlined above must be considered minimal estimates of the number of employed workers actually using these four illegal drugs. There is an understandable reluctance on the part of some people to discuss illegal behavior. Nonetheless, the data do reveal a substantial number of workers in all nonfarm occupational groups who are contemporary and regular users of marihuana, heroin, LSD and methedrine. The data also reveal this use is not restricted to social and recreational use after working hours or on weekends. Use of these drugs is also occurring on the job.

II. The Use of Legal Drugs by Employed Workers

The survey data also contained an assessment of the use of a variety of the legally manufactured and distributed drugs: barbiturates, other sedative-hypnotics, relaxants or minor tranquilizers, major tranquilizers, antidepressants, pep pills, diet pills and narcotics other than heroin.

1. *Barbiturates*

The barbiturates are central nervous system depressants which when taken in small doses have a sedating effect and at higher doses have a hypnotic effect. That is, through their action they quiet the user or put him to sleep. As such the barbiturates are applied in the management of a number of medical conditions where these results are desired. However, with the advent of the newer antianxiety and antipsychotic agents, they are now less widely used in the treatment of minor psychiatric disturbances.

Psychic dependence on the barbiturates can occur at any dose level, but physical dependence normally does not when prescribed doses are taken. At higher or abuse dosage levels, drunkenness, not unlike that seen with alcohol, and toxic psychosis, occur. With continued high-dose utilization, tolerance and physical dependence emerge.

The withdrawal syndrome associated with barbiturate addiction is considered more life-threatening than that associated with addiction to the opiates and can include convulsions, delirium and psychosis. The withdrawal process requires close medical supervision and chemotherapeutic assistance. Toxic overdose with the barbiturates can result in death. Indeed, barbiturates are a leading cause of accidental poison death as well as one of the main vehicles for committing suicide.

A danger associated with barbiturate use is that barbiturates and alcohol potentiate one another's actions. Accidental overdose can occur under these circumstances.

EXTENT OF USE BY EMPLOYED WORKERS

The number of employed workers in New York state estimated to have taken a barbiturate on at least one occasion is some 1,392,000, or 18.9% of all employed workers. Of these 1,392,000 workers, 498,000,

Table 9. Prevalence and Incidence of the Use of Barbiturates

Occupational Group	Never Used (% of total)	Former User) (No use in 6 months) (% of total)	Infrequent User (1 but not 6 times per month) (% of total)	Regular User (At least 6 times per month) (% of total)	No Data (% of total)	Total (% of total)	Regular Users (Using while at work) (% of regular users)
Professionals, technical workers, managers and owners	1,254,000 (74.1)	288,000 (17.0)	68,000 (4.0)	44,000 (2.6)	38,000 (2.2)	1,692,000 (100.0)	5,000 (11.4)
Clerical and other white collar workers	1,096,000 (77.1)	187,000 (13.2)	86,000 (6.0)	23,000 (1.6)	30,000 (2.1)	1,422,000 (100.0)	1,000 (4.3)
Skilled and semiskilled workers	2,035,000 (84.1)	211,000 (8.7)	90,000 (3.7)	27,000 (1.1)	58,000 (2.4)	2,421,000 (100.0)	2,000 (7.4)
Unskilled workers	272,000 (83.4)	18,000 (5.5)	19,000 (5.8)	7,000 (2.1)	10,000 (3.1)	326,000 (100.0)	—
Service and protective workers	748,000 (84.5)	80,000 (9.0)	22,000 (2.5)	33,000 (3.7)	2,000 (0.2)	885,000 (100.0)	—
Sales workers	391,000 (67.5)	107,000 (18.5)	7,000 (1.2)	71,000 (12.3)	3,000 (0.5)	579,000 (100.0)	8,000 (11.3)
Farmers	60,000 (93.8)	3,000 (4.7)	1,000 (1.6)	— —	— —	64,000 (100.0)	— —
Total employed	5,856,000 (79.3)	894,000 (12.1)	293,000 (4.0)	205,000 (2.8)	141,000 (1.9)	7,389,000 (100.0)	16,000 (7.8)

or 35.9%, have taken a barbiturate during the past six months and 205,000, or 14.9%, are current regular users (using at least six times per month). Of these 205,000 employed workers who report themselves as regular users of barbiturates, *16,000, or 7.8%, also report taking barbiturates while on the job*. Use on the job appears to be highest among the clerical and other white collar workers. This use is not, however, necessarily abuse. The survey data do not distinguish between legitimate use of this sedating medication and the dysfunctional abuse of it. What effect this has on job performance, etc., is not known at this time.

Although the rate of having used a barbiturate was found to be highest among professionals, technical workers, managers and owners (2,360 per 10,000 workers), the rate of current regular use is the highest among sales workers (1,230 per 10,000 workers).

2. *Nonbarbiturate Sedative-Hypnotics*

What can be said about the barbiturates is generally also appropriate for the nonbarbiturate sedative-hypnotics (e.g., Doriden). This would

Table 10. Rate of Use Per 10,000 Barbiturates

Occupational Group	*Prevalence Rate (Ever Used)*	*Incidence Rate (Regular Use)*
Professionals, technical workers, managers and owners	2,360	260
Clerical and other white collar workers	2,080	160
Skilled, semiskilled workers	1,350	110
Unskilled workers	1,340	210
Service and protective workers	1,520	370
Sales workers	3,200	1,230
Farmers	630	—
Total employed	1,890	280

Table 11. Prevalence and Incidence of the Use of Nonbarbiturate Sedative-Hypnotics

Occupational Group	Never Used (% of total)	Former User (No use in 6 months) (% of total)	Infrequent User (1 but not 6 times per month) (% of total)	Regular User (At least 6 times per month) (% of total)	No Data (% of total)	Total (% of total)	Regular Users (Using while at work) (% of regular users)
Professionals, technical workers, managers and owners	1,455,000 (86.0)	116,000 (6.9)	52,000 (3.1)	21,000 (1.2)	48,000 (2.8)	1,692,000 (100.0)	— —
Clerical and other white collar workers	1,253,000 (88.1)	69,000 (4.9)	43,000 (3.0)	12,000 (0.8)	45,000 (3.2)	1,422,000 (100.0)	2,000 (16.7)
Skilled and semiskilled workers	2,168,000 (89.5)	91,000 (3.8)	70,000 (2.9)	21,000 (0.9)	71,000 (2.9)	2,421,000 (100.0)	— —
Unskilled workers	297,000 (91.1)	4,000 (1.2)	6,000 (1.8)	6,000 (1.8)	13,000 (4.0)	326,000 (100.0)	— —
Service and protective workers	801,000 (90.5)	48,000 (5.4)	25,000 (2.8)	10,000 (1.1)	1,000 (0.1)	885,000 (100.0)	— —
Sales workers	523,000 (90.3)	36,000 (6.2)	2,000 (0.3)	1,000 (0.2)	17,000 (2.9)	579,000 (100.0)	1,000 (100.0)
Farmers	62,000 (96.9)	1,000 (1.6)	— —	1,000 (1.6)	— —	64,000 (100.0)	— —
Total employed	6,559,000 (88.8)	365,000 (4.9)	198,000 (2.7)	72,000 (1.0)	195,000 (2.6)	7,389,000 (100.0)	3,000 (4.2)

be the case whether the examples were for legitimate medical use or the effects of misuse.

While most of these drugs are indeed physically addicting when misused, available evidence suggests this addiction will occur only at dose levels considerably in excess of those therapeutically prescribed. Once addiction has occurred, the "abstinence syndrome" (withdrawal) can include convulsions, delirium, psychoses and even death unless the detoxification is medically managed.

EXTENT OF USE BY EMPLOYED WORKERS

The number of employed workers in New York state estimated to have used one of the nonbarbiturate sedative-hypnotics at least once is 635,000, or 8.6%, of all employed workers. Of these 635,000 workers, 270,000, or 42.5%, have used these drugs during the past six months and 72,000, or 26.7%, are current regular users (using at least six times per month). Of these 72,000 workers who regularly use these sedating medications, *only 3,000, or 4.2%, reported using them while at work*. We would again emphasize that these data do not distinguish between legitimate medical use and abuse.

Table 12. Rate of Nonbarbiturate Sedative-Hypnotic Use Per 10,000 Workers

Occupational Group	Prevalence Rate (Ever Used)	Incidence Rate (Regular Use)
Professionals, technical workers, managers and owners	1,120	120
Clerical and other white collar workers	870	80
Skilled, semiskilled workers	760	90
Unskilled workers	480	180
Service and protective workers	930	110
Sales workers	670	20
Farmers	320	160
Total employed	860	100

Table 13. Prevalence and Incidence of the Use of Relaxants and Minor Tranquilizers

Occupational Group	Never Used (% of total)	Former User (No use in 6 months) (% of total)	Infrequent User (1 but not 6 times per month) (% of total)	Regular User (At least 6 times per month) (% of total)	No Data (% of total)	Total (% of total)	Regular Users) (Using while at work) (% of regular users)
Professionals, technical workers, managers and owners	1,257,000 (74.3)	226,000 (13.4)	114,000 (6.7)	50,000 (3.0)	45,000 (2.7)	1,692,000 (100.0)	18,000 (36.0)
Clerical and other white collar workers	1,065,000 (74.9)	129,000 (9.1)	119,000 (8.4)	81,000 (5.7)	28,000 (2.0)	1,422,000 (100.0)	3,000 (3.7)
Skilled and semiskilled workers	1,995,000 (82.4)	190,000 (7.8)	149,000 (6.2)	36,000 (1.5)	51,000 (2.1)	2,421,000 (100.0)	5,000 (13.9)
Unskilled workers	273,000 (83.7)	16,000 (4.9)	20,000 (6.1)	10,000 (3.1)	7 000 (2.1)	326,000 (100.0)	3,000 (30.0)
Service and protective workers	721,000 (81.5)	91,000 (10.3)	26,000 (2.9)	38,000 (4.3)	9,000 (1.0)	885,000 (100.0)	14,000 (36.8)
Sales workers	417,000 (72.0)	61,000 (10.5)	59,000 (10.2)	25,000 (4.3)	17,000 (2.9)	579,000 (100.0)	9,000 (36.0)
Farmers	62,000 (96.9)	1,000 (1.6)	1,000 (1.6)	— —	— —	64,000 (100.0)	— —
Total employed	5,790,000 (78.4)	714,000 (9.7)	488,000 (6.6)	240,000 (3.2)	157,000 (2.1)	7,389,000 (100.0)	52,000 (21.7)

As with the use of barbiturates, the professionals, technical workers, managers and owners have the most experience with these drugs — 1,120 per 10,000 have used them. Quite unexpectedly, the unskilled workers were found to have the highest rate of current regular use — 180 per 10,000.

3. *Relaxants and Minor Tranquilizers*

Considerable professional disagreement exists as to classification distinctions between the relaxants and minor tranquilizers and the sedative-hypnotics. For the purpose of this report, the following drugs were categorized as relaxants and minor tranquilizers:

Generic Name	*Brand Name*
Chlorodiazepoxide	Libritabs
Chlorodiazepoxide hydrochloride	Librium, Librax
Diazepam	Valium
Hydroxyzine hydrochloride	Atarax
Meprobamate	Miltown, Equanil, Meprotabs, Meprospan

The relaxants and minor tranquilizers can be viewed as agents which reduce the less severe manifestations of anxiety and tension. They do not possess analgesic or anesthetic properties but do potentiate the effects of opiates, sedative-hypnotics and alcohol. Physical dependence occurs with the abuse of these drugs only at dose levels considerably in excess of those therapeutically prescribed. The withdrawal illness resembles that seen with the barbiturates and the other sedative-hypnotics.

EXTENT OF USE BY EMPLOYED WORKERS

The number of employed workers in New York state estimated to have used one of the relaxants and minor tranquilizers at least once is 1,442,000, or 19.5% of all workers. Of these 1,442,000 workers, 728,000, or 50.5%, report having used them within the past six months and 240,000, or 33.0%, are current regular users (using at least six times per month). Of the 240,000 regular users of these relaxants and minor tranquilizers, *52,000, or 21.7%, use them while they are on their jobs*. Since the study did not assess functioning, we do not know what either positive or negative effect this use has upon work performance.

The highest rate of use of these drugs is among sales workers — 2,500 per 10,000 — but current regular use is highest among clerical and other white collar workers — 570 per 10,000.

4. *Major Tranquilizers*

The major tranquilizers, e.g., Thorazine, modify the symptoms of psychosis and are important drugs used in the treatment of acute and chronic psychosis. In the psychotic patient, they reduce panic, fear, hostility, agitation, and the patient's adverse reactions to hallucinations and delusions. They also serve to regularize thinking and ameliorate disorganized behavioral patterns.

The major tranquilizers have not demonstrated a significant tendency to cause psychic dependence and become drugs of abuse. The abuse potential and addiction liability for these drugs are undoubtedly reduced because of the unpleasant side effects readily discernible by nonpsychotic individuals.

Table 14. Rate of Relaxants and Minor Tranquilizer Use Per 10,000 Workers

Occupational Group	*Prevalence Rate (Ever Used)*	*Incidence Rate (Regular Use)*
Professionals, technical workers, managers and owners	2,310	300
Clerical and other white collar workers	2,320	570
Skilled, semiskilled workers	1,550	150
Unskilled workers	1,410	310
Service and protective workers	1,750	430
Sales workers	2,500	430
Farmers	320	—
Total employed	1,950	320

Table 15. Prevalence and Incidence of the Use of Major Tranquilizers

Occupational Group	Never Used (% of Total	Former User (No use in 6 months) (% of total)	Infrequent User (1 but not 6 times per month) (% of total)	Regular User (At least 6 times per month) (% of total)	No Data (% of total)	Total (% of total)	Regular Users (Using while at work) (% of regular users)
Professionals, technical workers, managers and owners	1,574,000 (93.0)	53,000 (3.1)	17,000 (1.0)	3,000 (0.2)	45,000 (2.7)	1,692,000 (100.0)	— —
Clerical and other white collar workers	1,324,000 (93.1)	35,000 (2.5)	10,000 (0.7)	20,000 (1.4)	33,000 (2.3)	1,422,000 (100.0)	3,000 (15.0)
Skilled and semiskilled workers	2,294,000 (94.8)	33,000 (1.4)	14,000 (0.6)	15,000 (0.6)	65,000 (2.7)	2,421,000 (100.0)	— —
Unskilled workers	307,000 (94.2)	8,000 (2.5)	3,000 (0.9)	1,000 (0.3)	7,000 (2.1)	326,000 (100.0)	— —
Service and protective workers	851,000 (96.2)	11,000 (1.2)	4,000 (0.5)	4,000 (0.5)	15,000 (1.7)	885,000 (100.0)	4,000 (100.0)
Sales workers	539,000 (93.1)	— —	— —	12,000 (2.1)	28,000 (4.8)	579,000 (100.0)	— —
Farmers	62,000 (96.9)	2,000 (3.1)	— —	— —	— —	64,000 (100.0)	— —
Total employed	6,951,000 (94.1)	142,000 (1.9)	48,000 (0.6)	55,000 (0.7)	193,000 (2.6)	7,389,000 (100.0)	7,000 (12.7)

Table 16. Rate of Use Per 10,000 Major Tranquilizers

Occupational Group	Prevalence Rate (Ever Used)	Incidence Rate (Regular Use)
Professionals, technical workers, managers and owners	430	20
Clerical and other white collar workers	460	140
Skilled, semiskilled workers	260	60
Unskilled workers	370	30
Service and protective workers	220	50
Sales workers	210	210
Farmers	310	–
Total employed	320	70

The major tranquilizers potentiate the actions of the central nervous system depressants. They may also impair the mental and physical skills required to perform coordinated tasks such as driving, machine operation and so on.

EXTENT OF USE BY EMPLOYED WORKERS

The number of employed workers in New York state estimated to have used one of the major tranquilizers at least once is 245,000, or 3.2% of all the workers. Of these 245,000 workers, 103,000, or 42.0%, have used these drugs within the past six months and 55,000, or 53.4%, are currently doing so on a regular basis (at least six times per month). Of the 55,000 employed regular users of major tranquilizers, *7,000, or 12.7%, report they use them while on the job.* Since there is little or no abuse of these medications, we can assume most of this on-the-job use is medically supervised. We cannot assess what effects, negative or positive, this use has on job performance.

Clerical and other white collar workers have the highest rate of major tranquilizer use — 460 per 10,000 — but sales workers have the highest rate of current regular use of them — 210 per 10,000.

Table 17. Prevalence and Incidence of the Use of Antidepressants

Occupational Group	Never Used (% of total)	Former User (No use in 6 months) (% of total)	Infrequent User (1 but not 6 times per month) (% of total)	Regular User (At least 6 times per month) (% of total)	No Data (% of total)	Total (% of total)	Regular Users (Using while at work) (% of regular users)
Professionals, technical workers, managers and owners	1,613,000 (95.3)	16,000 (0.9)	20,000 (1.2)	— —	43,000 (2.5)	1,692,000 (100.0)	— —
Clerical and other white collar workers	1,363,000 (95.9)	18,000 (1.3)	7,000 (0.5)	4,000 (0.3)	30,000 (2.1)	1,422,000 (100.0)	— —
Skilled and semiskilled workers	2,305,000 (95.2)	28,000 (1.2)	20,000 (0.8)	8,000 (0.3)	60,000 (2.5)	2,421,000 (100.0)	— —
Unskilled workers	313,000 (96.0)	3,000 (0.9)	1,000 (0.3)	1,000 (0.3)	8,000 (2.5)	326,000 (100.0)	— —
Service and protective workers	872,000 (98.5)	4,000 (0.5)	2,000 (0.2)	— —	7,000 (0.8)	885,000 (100.0)	— —
Sales workers	554,000 (95.7)	10,000 (1.7)	— —	— —	15,000 (2.6)	579,000 (100.0)	— —
Farmers	64,000 (100.0)	— —	— —	— —	— —	64,000 (100.0)	— —
Total employed	7,084,000 (95.9)	79,000 (1.1)	50,000 (0.7)	13,000 (0.2)	163,000 (2.2)	7,389,000 (100.0)	— —

5. *Antidepressants*

The introduction of antidepressants, generally known as mood elevators, has greatly facilitated the management of a wide variety of depressive states. These drugs have chemical structures quite different from the amphetamines and have largely replaced them in the treatment of depression. In clinical practice antidepressants are continued for three to six months after optimal improvement in the patient's condition has been attained. They are then gradually withdrawn. Tolerance and physical dependence to these substances have yet to be documented.

A wide variety of undesirable effects have been reported with the use of antidepressant drugs. The type of reaction tends to depend upon the compound used. Adverse reactions most commonly reported include blurred vision, dizziness, hypertension, dry mouth and increased sweating. Some of these effects would, of course, retard the individual's physical performance capability.

The antidepressants potentiate the effects of alcohol, amphetamines, sedatives, and a number of other substances. Care must be exercised

Table 18. Rate of Antidepressant Use Per 10,000 Workers

Occupational Group	Prevalence Rate (Ever Used)	Incidence Rate (Regular Use)
Professionals, technical workers, managers and owners	210	—
Clerical and other white collar workers	210	30
Skilled, semiskilled workers	230	30
Unskilled workers	150	30
Service and protective workers	70	—
Sales workers	170	—
Farmers	—	—
Total employed	200	20

Table 19. Prevalence and Incidence of the Use of Prescription Pep Pills

Occupational Group	Never Used (% of total)	Former User (No use in 6 months) (% of total)	Infrequent User (1 but not 6 times per month) (% of total)	Regular User (At least 6 times per month) (% of total)	No Data (% of total)	Total (% of total)	Regular Users (Using while at work) (% of regular users)
Professionals, technical workers, managers and owners	1,509,000 (89.2)	90,000 (5.3)	37,000 (2.2)	14,000 (0.8)	42,000 (2.5)	1,692,000 (100.0)	4,000 (28.6)
Clerical and other white collar workers	1,291,000 (90.8)	64,000 (4.5)	24,000 (1.7)	12,000 (0.8)	31,000 (2.2)	1,422,000 (100.0)	— —
Skilled and semiskilled workers	2,228,000 (92.0)	74,000 (3.1)	55,000 (2.3)	9,000 (0.4)	55,000 (2.3)	2,421,000 (100.0)	2,000 (22.2)
Unskilled workers	296,000 (90.8)	13,000 (4.0)	6,000 (1.8)	1,000 (0.3)	10,000 (3.1)	326,000 (100.0)	— —
Service and protective workers	798,000 (90.2)	46,000 (5.2)	28,000 (3.2)	7,000 (0.8)	6,000 (0.7)	885,000 (100.0)	4,000 (57.1)
Sales workers	536,000 (92.6)	11,000 (1.9)	15,000 (2.6)	8,000 (1.4)	9,000 (1.6)	579,000 (100.0)	8,000 (100.0)
Farmers	62,000 (96.9)	1,000 (1.6)	1,000 (1.6)	— —	— —	64,000 (100.0)	— —
Total employed	6,720,000 (90.9)	299,000 (4.0)	166,000 (2.2)	51,000 (0.7)	153,000 (2.1)	7,389,000 (100.0)	18,000 (35.3)

Table 20. Rate of Pep Pill Use Per 10,000 Workers

Occupational Group	Prevalence Rate (Ever Used)	Incidence Rate (Regular Use)
Professionals, technical workers, managers and owners	830	80
Clerical and other white collar workers	700	80
Skilled, semiskilled workers	580	40
Unskilled workers	610	30
Service and protective workers	920	80
Sales workers	590	140
Farmers	320	–
Total employed	690	70

when such compounds and the antidepressants are used concurrently. Some mixtures are contraindicated.

EXTENT OF USE BY EMPLOYED WORKERS

The number of employed workers in New York state estimated to have taken an antidepressant on at least one occasion is 142,000, or 2.0% of all workers. Of these 142,000 workers, 63,000, or 44.4%, have used these drugs in the past six months and 13,000, or 20.6%, are current regular users (using at least six times per month). *No employed user of antidepressants reported using them while at work.*

The skilled and semiskilled workers reported the highest rate of antidepressant use — 230 per 10,000. Current regular use was equally high among clerical and other white collar workers, skilled and semi-skilled workers and unskilled workers — 30 per 10,000.

6. *Prescription Pep Pills*

For the purposes of this survey, pep pills were defined as those prescription amphetamines, excluding methamphetamine and the diet pills, which were taken for their stimulant effects on the central nervous system. Only two drugs were encountered with any regularity, amphetamine sulfate (Benzedrine) and dextroamphetamine (Dexedrine).

As with all the amphetamines, the pep pills have as their characteristic the excitation or stimulation of the central nervous system. In addition to stimulation, usually perceived as increased alertness, these drugs produce feelings of wellbeing and confidence. While the prevention of sleepiness and fatigue seems to be the reason the drugs are commercialized, their use to reduce anxiety by making the individual feel confident and secure, to "feel better," should not be minimized.

With the continued intake of the pep pills, tolerance develops and psychic dependence occurs. Although physical dependence has not been demonstrated, withdrawal of these agents from abusers may unmask symptoms of chronic fatigue followed by drowsiness and prolonged sleep. At high doses toxic psychosis may develop.

EXTENT OF USE BY EMPLOYED WORKERS

An estimated 516,000 employed workers in New York state have used prescription pep pills on at least one occasion. This estimate is 6.9% of the total employed workers in the state. Of these 516,000 workers, 217,000, or 41.1%, have used one of these drugs in the past six months and 51,000, or 23.5%, are current regular users (using at least six times per month). Among the 51,000 regular users of pep pills, *18,000, or 35.3%, report they use these drugs while on the job.* Again, since the survey did not assess job performance, we are not able to discuss the effects of this drug use on the job.

Service and protective workers reported the highest rate of pep pill use — 920 per 10,000. Sales workers, however, more frequently report using pep pills on a regular basis — 140 per 10,000.

7. *Prescription Diet Pills*

Diet pills most often consist of an amphetamine-like substance alone or in combination with a central nervous system depressant. When combined this way, the stimulant acts to reduce appetite and the depressant serves to counteract any overstimulation which might otherwise occur. The effect of amphetamine-containing diet pills appears to be related

Table 21. Prevalence and Incidence of the Use of Prescription Diet Pills

Occupational Group	Never Used (% of total)	Former User (No use in 6 months) (% of total)	Infrequent User (1 but not 6 times per month) (% of total)	Regular User (At least 6 times per month) (% of total)	No Data (% of total)	Total (% of total)	Regular Users (Using while at work (% of regular users)
Professional, technical workers, managers and owners	1,469,000 (86.8)	134,000 (7.9)	24,000 (1.4)	34,000 (2.0)	31,000 (1.8)	1,692,000 (100.0)	4,000 (11.8)
Clerical and other white collar workers	1,196,000 (84.1)	125,000 (8.8)	44,000 (3.1)	35,000 (2.5)	22,000 (1.5)	1,422,000 (100.0)	1,000 (3.5)
Skilled and semiskilled workers	2,180,000 (90.0)	108,000 (4.5)	63,000 (2.6)	21,000 (0.9)	49,000 (2.0)	2,421,000 (100.0)	1,000 (14.3)
Unskilled workers	296,000 (90.8)	14,000 (4.3)	9,000 (2.8)	2,000 (0.6)	5,000 (1.5)	326,000 (100.0)	—
Service and protective workers	814,000 (92.0)	46,000 (5.2)	15,000 (1.7)	4,000 (0.5)	6,000 (0.7)	885,000 (100.0)	—
Sales workers	481,000 (83.1)	48,000 (8.3)	8,000 (1.4)	21,000 (3.6)	21,000 (3.6)	579,000 (100.0)	6,000 (28.6)
Farmers	63,000 (98.4)	1,000 (1.6)	—	—	—	64,000 (100.0)	—
Total employed	6,499,000 (88.0)	476,000 (6.4)	163,000 (2.2)	117,000 (1.6)	134,000 (1.8)	7,389,000 (100.0)	13,000 (10.7)

Table 22. Rate of Diet Pill Use Per 10,000 Workers

Occupational Group	Prevalence Rate (Ever Used)	Incidence Rate (Regular Use)
Professionals, technical workers, managers and owners	1,130	200
Clerical and other white collar workers	1,440	250
Skilled, semiskilled workers	800	90
Unskilled workers	770	60
Service and protective workers	740	50
Sales workers	1,330	360
Farmers	160	—
Total employed	1,020	160

to their ability to create a sense of wellbeing. As such they may be useful when applied for short periods of time. However, their long-term effectiveness in weight control may be properly questioned.

A variety of other compounds have been used in the treatment of overweight patients. These include thyroid, diuretics, antispasmodics and digitalis. Although all of these have been used in the past for the treatment of overweight, they are not effective and are no longer used in such treatment.

EXTENT OF USE BY EMPLOYED WORKERS

The number of employed workers in New York state who have used a prescription diet pill on at least one occasion is 756,000 workers, or 10.2% of all employed workers. Of these 756,000 workers, 280,000, or 37.0%, have used diet pills in the last six months and 117,000, or 41.8%, are current regular users (at least six times per month). Of these 117,000 regular users of diet pills, *13,000, or 10.7%, report using these drugs while at work*. No assessment of the effect on job performance has been attempted.

Clerical and other white collar workers have the highest rate of pre-

Table 23. Prevalence and Incidence of the Use of Controlled Narcotics (Nonheroin)

Occupational Group	Never Used (% of total)	Former User (No use in 6 months) (% of total)	Infrequent User (1 but not 6 times per month) (% of total)	Regular User (At least 6 times per month) (% of total)	No Data (% of total)	Total (% of total)	Regular Users (Using while at work) (% of regular users)
Professionals, technical workers, managers and owners	1,431,000 (84.6)	174,000 (10.3)	21,000 (1.2)	4,000 (0.2)	62,000 (3.7)	1,692,000 (100.0)	3,000 (75.0)
Clerical and other white collar workers	1,319,000 (92.8)	59,000 (4.1)	8,000 (0.6)	1,000 (0.1)	35,000 (2.5)	1,422,000 (100.0)	—
Skilled and semiskilled workers	2,234,000 (92.3)	106,000 (4.4)	12,000 (0.5)	5,000 (0.2)	64,000 (2.6)	2,421,000 (100.0)	—
Unskilled workers	306,000 (93.9)	9,000 (2.8)	2,000 (0.6)	1,000 (0.3)	8,000 (2.5)	326,000 (100.0)	—
Service and protective workers	818,000 (92.4)	43,000 (4.9)	15,000 (1.7)	3,000 (0.3)	6,000 (0.7)	885,000 (100.0)	—
Sales workers	523,000 (90.3)	36,000 (6.2)	1,000 (0.2)	5,000 (0.9)	14,000 (2.4)	579,000 (100.0)	—
Farmers	63,000 (98.4)	1,000 (1.6)	—	—	—	64,000 (100.0)	—
Total employed	6,694,000 (90.6)	428,000 (5.8)	59,000 (0.8)	19,000 (0.3)	189,000 (2.6)	7,389,000 (100.0)	3,000 (15.8)

Table 24. Rate of Controlled Narcotic (Nonheroin) Use Per 10,000 Workers

Occupational Groups	Prevalence Rate (Ever Used)	Incidence Rate (Regular Use)
Professionals, technical workers, managers and owners	1,170	20
Clerical and other white collar workers	480	10
Skilled, semiskilled workers	510	20
Unskilled workers	370	30
Service and protective workers	690	30
Sales workers	730	90
Farmers	160	–
Total employed	690	30

scription diet pill use — 1,440 per 10,000 — but sales workers most frequently are regular users — 360 per 10,000.

8. *Controlled Narcotics* (*Nonheroin*)

The controlled narcotics are very potent analgesics that are generally classified as *natural* or *synthetic*. The natural narcotics include opium, two alkaloid components of opium-morphine and codeine, and semisynthetic derivatives of them such as heroin, oxymorphone (Numorphan), hydromorphone (Dilaudid). The synthetic narcotics are related compounds that are morphinelike in their effects, i.e., methadone (Dolophine), meperidine (Demerol), and anileridine (Leritine).

All of these drugs produce euphoria, analgesia, respiratory depression, tolerance, psychic dependence, and physical dependence. In addition, they exhibit cross tolerance, the ability of one drug to substitute for another in a tolerant individual. Tolerance develops rapidly and occurs within therapeutic dose ranges. The severity of withdrawal is positively related to the amount of drug taken.

Increased awareness among physicians prescribing these medications has greatly reduced the number of medical addicts — persons accidentally addicted to these drugs during a therapeutic regimen. Predictability in this area is limited, however. The degree to which levels of euphoria are perceived and the extent to which this sensation or feeling becomes defined as pleasurable and desirable appears to vary widely among persons exposed to these drugs. Within limits, the perception of withdrawal distress and the reaction to this distress during detoxification from these drugs also appears to vary widely even among persons who have been on very high dose regimens.

EXTENT OF USE BY EMPLOYED WORKERS

The survey revealed some 506,000 employed workers in New York state had used a controlled narcotic. This is some 6.9% of all the employed workers. Of these 506,000 workers, some 78,000, or 15.4%, had used a controlled narcotic within the last six months and 19,000, or 24.4%, were current regular users (at least six times per month). Of these 19,000 regular users, *3,000, or 15.8%, were using the drugs while at work.*

Professionals, technical workers, managers and owners report the highest rate of controlled narcotic use — 1,170 per 10,000. Sales workers, however, have the highest rate of current regular use — 90 per 10,000.

III. The Demographic Characteristics
of the Regular Drug Users
Within Each Occupational Group

To assist those who utilize employees in only certain occupational groups, we have chosen to also describe all our drug-use data with the specific occupational group as the focus. Recognizing a managerial need to predict high-risk groups, we have also provided various characteristics associated with those workers in each occupational group who are regular users of each of the drugs.

Table 25. Characteristics of Regular Drug Users Among 1,692,000 Professionals,
Technical Workers, Managers and Owners in % of Regular Users

Drug	Number of Regular Users	Age Distribution		Ethnicity		Sex		High School Graduates		Any Use of the Drug on the Job
		-25	25+	White	Nonwhite	Males	Females	Yes	No	
Barbiturates	44,000	6.8	93.2	97.7	2.3	90.9	9.1	95.5	4.5	11.4
Other sedative-hypnotics	21,000	4.8	95.2	95.2	4.8	85.7	14.3	95.2	4.8	–
Minor tranquilizers	50,000	6.0	94.0	100.0	–	58.0	42.0	96.0	4.0	36.0
Major tranquilizers	3,000	–	100.0	100.0	–	100.0	–	100.0	–	–
Antidepressants	–	–	–	–	–	–	–	–	–	–
Pep pills	14,000	21.4	78.6	92.9	7.1	28.6	71.4	85.7	14.3	28.6
Diet pills	34,000	11.8	88.2	100.0	–	44.1	55.9	91.2	8.8	11.8
Narcotics (Nonheroin)	4,000	25.0	75.0	100.0	–	–	100.0	75.0	25.0	75.0
Marihuana	48,000	27.1	72.9	87.5	12.5	58.3	41.7	93.8	6.2	20.8
LSD	2,000	50.0	50.0	100.0	–	50.0	50.0	100.0	–	50.0
Methedrine	2,000	50.0	50.0	100.0	–	50.0	50.0	50.0	50.0	50.0
Heroin	4,000	100.0	–	25.0	75.0	100.0	–	50.0	50.0	–

A. Most frequently used of the *legal* drugs of 50,000 regular users of
relaxants or minor tranquilizers
36% report taking the drug while at work
94% are age 25 or above
100% are whites
58% are males
96% are high school graduates

B. Most frequently used of the *illegal* drugs of 48,000 regular users
of marihuana
20.8% report using the drug while at work
72.9% are age 25 or above
87.5% are whites
58.3% are males
93.8% are high school graduates

Table 26. Characteristics of Regular Drug Users Among 1,422,000
Clerical and Other White Collar Workers

Drug	Number of Regular Users	Age Distribution		Ethnicity		Sex		High School Graduates		Any Use of the Drug on the Job
		-25	25+	White	Nonwhite	Males	Females	Yes	No	
Barbiturates	23,000	4.3	95.7	69.6	30.4	43.5	56.5	91.3	8.7	4.3
Other sedative-hypnotics	12,000	25.0	75.0	91.7	8.3	–	100.0	100.0	–	16.7
Minor tranquilizers	81,000	14.8	85.2	87.7	12.3	14.8	85.2	84.0	16.0	3.7
Major tranquilizers	20,000	–	100.0	100.0	–	30.0	70.0	60.0	40.0	15.0
Antidepressants	4,000	–	100.0	100.0	–	–	100.0	50.0	50.0	–
Pep pills	12,000	25.0	75.0	100.0	–	50.0	50.0	100.0	–	–
Diet pills	35,000	40.0	60.0	82.9	17.1	2.9	97.1	88.6	11.4	3.5
Narcotics (Nonheroin)	1,000	100.0	–	100.0	–	100.0	–	100.0	–	–
Marihuana	57,000	63.2	36.8	50.9	49.1	71.9	28.1	87.7	12.3	35.1
LSD	–	–	–	–	–	–	–	–	–	–
Methedrine	3,000	–	100.0	–	100.0	100.0	–	100.0	–	–
Heroin	9,000	100.0	–	–	100.0	88.9	11.1	55.6	44.4	–

A. Most frequently used of the *legal* drugs of 81,000 regular users of
relaxants and minor tranquilizers
    3.7% report taking the drugs while at work
    85.2% are age 25 or above
    87.7% are whites
    85.2% are females
    84.0% are high school graduates

B. Most frequently used of the *illegal* drugs of 57,000 regular users
of marihuana
    35.1% report using the drug while at work
    63.2% are younger than 25
    50.9% are whites
    71.9% are males
    87.7% are high school graduates

Table 27. Characteristics of Regular Drug Users Among 2,421,000
Skilled and Semiskilled Workers

Drug	Number of Regular Users	Age Distribution		Ethnicity		Sex		High School Graduates		Any Use of the Drug on the Job
		-25	25+	White	Nonwhite	Males	Females	Yes	No	
Barbiturates	27,000	37.0	63.0	85.2	14.8	59.3	40.7	92.6	7.4	7.4
Other sedative-hypnotics	21,000	28.6	71.4	66.7	33.3	76.2	23.8	66.7	33.3	–
Minor tranquilizers	36,000	13.9	86.1	100.0	–	72.2	27.8	69.4	30.6	13.9
Major tranquilizers	15,000	60.0	40.0	100.0	–	100.0	–	100.0	–	–
Antidepressants	8,000	50.0	50.0	100.0	–	50.0	50.0	100.0	–	–
Pep pills	9,000	88.9	11.1	88.9	11.1	44.4	55.6	100.0	–	22.2
Diet pills	21,000	61.9	38.1	61.9	38.1	28.6	71.4	90.5	9.5	14.3
Narcotics (Nonheroin)	5,000	40.0	60.0	100.0	–	40.0	60.0	40.0	60.0	–
Marihuana	86,000	84.9	15.1	76.7	23.3	83.7	16.3	80.2	19.8	22.1
LSD	4,000	50.0	50.0	50.0	50.0	50.0	50.0	100.0	–	–
Methedrine	–	–	–	–	–	–	–	–	–	–
Heroin	8,000	–	100.0	–	100.0	100.0	–	100.0	–	–

A. Most frequently used of the *legal* drugs of 36,000 regular users of
relaxants or minor tranquilizers
13.9% report taking the drugs while at work
86.1% are age 25 or above
100.0% are whites
72.2% are males
69.4% are high school graduates

B. Most frequently used of the *illegal* drugs of 86,000 regular users
of marihuana
22.1% report using the drug while at work
84.9% are younger than 25
76.7% are whites
83.7% are males
80.2% are high school graduates

Table 28. Characteristics of Regular Drug Users Among
326,000 Unskilled Workers

Drug	Number of Regular Users	Age Distribution		Ethnicity		Sex		High School Graduates		Any Use of the Drug on the Job
		-25	25+	White	Nonwhite	Males	Females	Yes	No	
Barbiturates	7,000	–	100.0	28.6	71.4	85.7	14.3	28.6	71.4	–
Other sedative-hypnotics	6,000	16.7	83.3	33.3	66.7	33.3	66.7	–	100.0	–
Minor tranquilizers	10,000	30.0	70.0	50.0	50.0	40.0	60.0	40.0	60.0	30.0
Major tranquilizers	1,000	100.0	–	100.0	–	100.0	–	–	100.0	–
Antidepressants	1,000	–	100.0	100.0	–	100.0	–	100.0	–	–
Pep pills	1,000	100.0	–	100.0	–	–	100.0	–	100.0	–
Diet pills	2,000	50.0	50.0	50.0	50.0	50.0	50.0	–	100.0	–
Narcotics (Nonheroin)	1,000	–	100.0	100.0	–	–	100.0	100.0	–	–
Marihuana	17,000	88.2	11.8	76.5	23.5	76.5	23.5	52.9	47.1	35.3
LSD	1,000	100.0	–	–	100.0	100.0	–	–	100.0	–
Methedrine	1,000	100.0	–	100.0	–	100.0	–	100.0	–	100.0
Heroin	1,000	100.0	–	–	100.0	–	100.0	–	100.0	–

A. Most frequently used of the *legal* drugs of 10,000 regular users of relaxants or minor tranquilizers
   30.0% report taking the drugs while at work
   70.0% are age 25 or above
   50.0% are whites
   60.0% are females
   60.0% are *not* high school graduates

B. Most frequently used of the *illegal* drugs of 17,000 regular users of marihuana
   35.3% report using the drug while at work
   88.2% are younger than 25
   76.5% are whites
   76.5% are males
   52.9% are high school graduates

Table 29. Characteristics of Regular Drug Users Among 885,000
Service and Protective Workers

Drug	Number of Regular Users	Age Distribution		Ethnicity		Sex		High School Graduates		Any Use of the Drug on the Job
		-25	25+	White	Nonwhite	Males	Females	Yes	No	
Barbiturates	33,000	–	100.0	100.0	–	42.4	57.6	84.8	15.2	–
Other sedative-hypnotics	10,000	–	100.0	100.0	–	20.0	80.0	80.0	20.0	–
Minor tranquilizers	38,000	–	100.0	100.0	–	36.8	63.2	60.5	39.5	36.8
Major tranquilizers	4,000	–	100.0	100.0	–	–	100.0	100.0	–	100.0
Antidepressants	–	–	–	–	–	–	–	–	–	–
Pep pills	7,000	57.1	42.9	100.0	–	57.1	42.9	100.0	–	57.1
Diet pills	4,000	50.0	50.0	100.0	–	50.0	50.0	100.0	–	–
Narcotics (Nonheroin)	3,000	–	100.0	100.0	–	–	100.0	100.0	–	–
Marihuana	35,000	51.4	48.6	71.4	28.6	80.0	20.0	57.1	42.9	2.9
LSD	3,000	–	100.0	100.0	–	–	100.0	100.0	–	–
Methedrine	–	–	–	–	–	–	–	–	–	–
Heroin	–	–	–	–	–	–	–	–	–	–

A. Most frequently used of the *legal* drugs of 38,000 regular users of relaxants or minor tranquilizers

    36.8% report taking the drugs while at work

    100.0% are age 25 or above

    100.0% are whites

    63.2% are females

    60.5% are high school graduates

B. Most frequently used of the *illegal* drugs of 35,000 regular users of marihuana

    2.9% report using the drug while at work

    51.4% are younger than 25

    71.4% are whites

    80.0% are males

    57.1% are high school graduates

Table 30. Characteristics of Regular Drug Users
Among 579,000 Sales Workers

Drug	Number of Regular Users	Age Distribution		Ethnicity		Sex		High School Graduates		Any Use of the Drug on the Job
		-25	25+	White	Nonwhite	Males	Females	Yes	No	
Barbiturates	71,000	9.9	90.1	88.7	11.3	57.7	42.3	69.0	31.0	11.3
Other sedative-hypnotics	1,000	–	100.0	100.0	–	100.0	–	100.0	–	100.0
Minor tranquilizers	25,000	8.0	92.0	100.0	–	24.0	76.0	48.0	52.0	36.0
Major tranquilizers	12,000	–	100.0	100.0	–	–	100.0	100.0	–	–
Antidepressants	–	–	–	–	–	–	–	–	–	–
Pep pills	8,000	12.5	87.5	50.0	50.0	–	100.0	100.0	–	100.0
Diet pills	21,000	23.8	76.2	100.0	–	28.6	71.4	61.9	38.1	28.6
Narcotics (Nonheroin)	5,000	–	100.0	100.0	–	100.0	–	–	100.0	–
Marihuana	50,000	56.0	44.0	92.0	8.0	38.0	62.0	82.0	18.0	44.0
LSD	15,000	–	100.0	73.3	26.7	–	100.0	100.0	–	26.7
Methedrine	4,000	–	100.0	100.0	–	–	100.0	100.0	–	100.0
Heroin	12,000	41.7	58.3	100.0	–	16.7	83.3	83.3	16.7	100.0

A. Most frequently used of the *legal* drugs of 71,000 regular users of barbiturates
    11.3% report taking the drugs while at work
    90.1% are age 25 or above
    88.7% are whites
    57.7% are males
    69.0% are high school graduates

B. Most frequently used of the *illegal* drugs of 50,000 regular users of marihuana
    44.0% report using the drug while at work
    56.0% are younger than 25
    92.0% are whites
    62.0% are females
    82.0% are high school graduates

Table 31. Characteristics of Regular Drug Users Among 64,000 Farmers

Drug	Number of Regular Users	Age Distribution		Ethnicity		Sex		High School Graduates		Any Use of the Drug on the Job
		-25	25+	White	Nonwhite	Males	Females	Yes	No	
Barbiturates	–	–	–	–	–	–	–	–	–	–
Other sedative-hypnotics	1,000	–	100.0	100.0	–	100.0	–	–	100.0	–
Minor tranquilizers	–	–	–	–	–	–	–	–	–	–
Major tranquilizers	–	–	–	–	–	–	–	–	–	–
Antidepressants	–	–	–	–	–	–	–	–	–	–
Pep pills	–	–	–	–	–	–	–	–	–	–
Diet pills	–	–	–	–	–	–	–	–	–	–
Narcotics (Nonheroin)	–	–	–	–	–	–	–	–	–	–
Marihuana	–	–	–	–	–	–	–	–	–	–
LSD	–	–	–	–	–	–	–	–	–	–
Methedrine	–	–	–	–	–	–	–	–	–	–
Heroin	–	–	–	–	–	–	–	–	–	–

For all intents and purposes, one can report virtually no regular use of any drug among farmers.

IV. The Summary Distributions of
All the Regular Users of Drugs
Within Each Occupational Group

A. Summary analyses within each *occupational* group indicating the drugs most frequently being used on a regular basis are as follows:

Professionals, technical workers, managers and owners
Relaxants or minor tranquilizers
(50,000 regular users — 36.0% report use while at work)

Clerical and other white collar workers
Relaxants or minor tranquilizers
(81,000 regular users — 3.7% report use while at work)

Skilled and semiskilled workers
Marihuana
(86,000 regular users — 22.1% report use while at work)

Unskilled workers
Marihuana
(17,000 regular users — 35.3% report use while at work)

Sales workers
Barbiturates
(71,000 regular users — 11.3% report use while at work)

Farmers
Other sedative-hypnotics
(1,000 regular users)

B. Summary analyses within each drug group indicating which of the groups contribute the greatest number of current regular users to the total are as follows:

Marihuana
Skilled and semiskilled workers
(86,000 regular users — 22.1% who use while at work)

Heroin
Sales workers
(12,000 regular users — 100% who use while at work)

LSD
Sales workers
(15,000 regular users — 26.7% who use while at work)

Methedrine (speed)
Sales workers
(4,000 regular users — 100% who use while at work)

Barbiturates
Sales workers
(71,000 regular users — 11.3% who use while at work)

Nonbarbiturate sedative-hypnotics
Professionals, technical workers, managers and owners;
Skilled and semiskilled workers
(21,000 regular users in both groups with no use reported for either group while at work)

Relaxants or minor tranquilizers
Clerical and other white collar workers
(81,000 regular users — 3.7% who use while at work)

Major tranquilizers
Clerical and other white collar workers
(20,000 regular users — 15.0% who use while at work)

Antidepressants
Skilled and semiskilled workers
(8,000 regular users — no use while at work)

Pep pills
Professionals, technical workers, managers and owners
(14,000 regular users — 28.6% who use while at work)

Diet pills
Clerical and other white collar workers
(35,000 regular users — 3.5% who use while at work)

Narcotics (nonheroin)
Skilled and semiskilled workers
Sales workers
(5,000 regular users in each group but no use while at work in either group)

Table 32. Summary Table — Numerical and Percentage Distribution of Regular Drug Users (At Least Six Times Per Month)

	Marihuana	LSD	Methedrine	Heroin	Barbi-turates	Other Sedatives	Minor Tran-quilizers	Major Tran-quilizers	Anti-depres-sants	Pep Pills	Diet Pills	Narcotics (Non-heroin)
Professionals, technical workers, managers and owners	48,000 (9.9)	2,000 (4.0)	2,000 (5.9)	4,000 (9.8)	44,000 (11.7)	21,000 (12.1)	50,000 (9.5)	3,000 (3.5)	–	14,000 (12.7)	34,000 (15.1)	4,000 (19.0)
Clerical and other white collar workers	57,000 (11.8)	–	3,000 (8.8)	9,000 (22.0)	23,000 (6.1)	12,000 (6.9)	81,000 (15.4)	20,000 (23.5)	4,000 (10.8)	12,000 (10.9)	35,000 (15.6)	1,000 (4.8)
Skilled and semiskilled workers	86,000 (17.7)	4,000 (8.0)	–	8,000 (19.5)	27,000 (7.2)	21,000 (12.1)	36,000 (6.9)	15,000 (17.6)	8,000 (21.6)	9,000 (8.2)	21,000 (9.3)	5,000 (23.8)
Unskilled workers	17,000 (3.5)	1,000 (2.0)	1,000 (2.9)	1,000 (2.4)	7,000 (1.9)	6,000 (3.5)	10,000 (1.9)	1,000 (1.2)	1,000 (2.7)	1,000 (0.9)	2,000 (0.9)	1,000 (4.8)
Service & protective workers	35,000 (7.2)	3,000 (6.0)	–	–	33,000 (8.8)	10,000 (5.8)	38,000 (7.2)	4,000 (4.7)	–	7,000 (6.4)	4,000 (1.8)	3,000 (14.3)
Sales workers	50,000 (10.3)	15,000 (30.0)	4,000 (11.8)	12,000 (29.3)	71,000 (18.8)	1,000 (0.6)	25,000 (4.8)	12,000 (14.1)	–	8,000 (7.3)	21,000 (9.3)	5,000 (23.8)
Farmers	–	–	–	–	–	1,000 (0.6)	–	–	–	–	–	–
Total employed	293,000 (60.4)	25,000 (50.0)	10,000 (29.4)	34,000 (83.0)	205,000 (54.4)	72,000 (41.6)	240,000 (45.7)	55,000 (64.6)	13,000 (35.1)	51,000 (46.4)	117,000 (52.0)	19,000 (90.5)

MORE DATA IS NEEDED, BUT . . .

It is apparent that business and industry must immediately address the issues which these data frame: worker safety, job performance, absenteeism, inventory shrinkage, contagion to nonaffected workers, and drug selling, to mention a few. The data also raise a number of researchable items which demand immediate attention: Where and when does the drug use occur? Why does this use remain undetected or unreported? What use is occurring with legal drugs such as barbiturates, amphetamines and tranquilizers? What are the differences between workers who use drugs on the job and those who do not? Why are users found more frequently in certain occupations? While we acknowledge these reported findings relate specifically to New York state where the use of illegal drugs is known to be unusually high, there is ample evidence that the problem already exists in most parts of the United States and is developing throughout the country. An understanding of all these issues is therefore of critical importance. Yet business and industry cannot afford to wait for all the answers to emerge before adopting policy; the problem demands that companies take specific positions now, and be prepared to adapt policy as new data are revealed. What is the most appropriate policy for your company? It depends on a number of factors.

Organizing a Community Drug Program

If your company is seriously committed to combating your own in-house drug problem, you must look beyond the confines of your plants and offices for serious, long-term solutions. No company is an island when it comes to drug abuse; it functions as part of a community and shares with it the problems of its people, many of whom are your employees, or will be.

The drug problem is really a people problem and the solution requires community resources and participation. For this reason, you must understand not only your company's drug problem, but the problem as it exists within the context of your community. And you must go beyond understanding it; you must help solve it. You should work with other community leaders in clearly setting forth programs that will forestall the spread of drug abuse, keeping in mind that a worthwhile drug program must be preventative as well as rehabilitative.

The alliance between business and the community in formulating and implementing programs to fight drug abuse is a new one. There is very little history or precedent by which to be guided, or to which one can refer for established criteria. But there are some examples worth consideration, one of which we will discuss here. Keep in mind, however, that there are no quick solutions, only hard work, ahead. Organizing and implementing a community drug council — even with the help of other businessmen in your area — can be a frustrating endeavor; but it can also be rewarding, both from your own personal viewpoint and that of your company's.

One of the more successful community action programs of this kind is the Greater Lawrence (Massachusetts) Community Drug Council — an alliance of three large companies in the area and thirty community leaders in five towns who represent education, medicine, law enforcement, social agencies, and the news media. How this drug council was formed and how it is now operating are facts that should provide you with stepping-stone techniques for organizing a similar community program.

According to the by-laws of the Greater Lawrence Community Drug Council, its purpose is "to establish, coordinate and maintain community resources in combating the abuse of harmful and dangerous drugs in the Greater Lawrence area." The council today is made up of three organizations that operated independently in the community before the formation of the present council. One of the organizations is a drug rehabilitation center for young people called Reality, Inc.; the second principal organization (now dissolved) was a joint hospital committee on drugs that worked closely with the United Fund; and the third group was a committee made up of industrial relations representatives from three area companies, and the editor of the local newspaper. The goal of the latter group was to coordinate all of the communities' efforts into a single organization, encompassing what everyone felt were all of the communities' interested facets.

The present board of directors of the council reflects the variety of the communities' "interested facets." It includes a director of one community's mental health commission, a district court judge, the head of social services at the local hospital, the president of the area pharmaceutics association, and four student representatives from area high schools. The purpose here is to have a senior from each school as a voting member of the board, backed by a member of the junior class of their school who is being primed for participation the following year. The council has used its board meetings as an educational vehicle to consolidate the board in its thinking, and has had presentations on psychiatry, psychology, probation, police work, rehabilitation, and so forth. When the students did not agree with what was said, they were most vocal and very helpful in giving the "establishment" members of the council their point of view.

In addition to four high school seniors, the council board also includes a junior-college senior and a college senior, doctors from the staffs of two local hospitals, an attorney, and a probation officer from the district court.

The area's three largest industries are also represented on the board. Though the members from industry have been very active in the organization of the drug council, the council expects to get its biggest pay back from industrial representatives when it graduates rehabilitated drug addicts and a place is made for them to work in industry.

The council includes a doctor of psychology from a local college, and the secretary of the organization is the managing editor of the local newspaper. Members of the board of trustees of two local hospitals are also members of the council.

In Greater Lawrence there is a rapidly growing, Spanish-surnamed population. To have a direct liaison with these 6,000 to 8,000 people, the council board includes a member whose full-time job is interpreting and coordinating the efforts of the Spanish community of Greater Lawrence in the city's Division of Employment Security Office. The council also has one doctor representing the Lawrence Medical Society, and the captain of detectives in charge of a narcotic squad of the Lawrence Police Department. One school superintendent represents the superintendents of all school systems. The vice president of the organization is the Lawrence city planner. The council only recently hired a full-time program administrator.

One of the prime movers of the council is Dr. James A. O'Shea, a local pediatrician. Dr. O'Shea reflects the thinking of the entire council when he discusses drug abuse:

Drug abuse is not just a medical, educational, law enforcement, parental or industrial problem. It is everyone's problem demanding total community involvement. All facilities and personnel within a community which can aid in supporting and helping citizens with drug problems must be called upon and utilized efficiently and economically. This can best be accomplished by a nonprofessional, nonpolitical community council. Such a council *should be independent* of hospitals, the mental health department, religious or social agencies, city or state government; yet it should have adequate representation and work with all such existing facilities.

What the Council Found Out

Before establishing a program of action, the council first set out to determine the nature and scope of its community drug problem. While the actual numbers of community drug abusers are irrelevant here, the thinking behind the council's program is of value.

The council asked itself, "Why are our young people and many adults copping out chemically with drugs and becoming academic, social and employment drop outs?" The council's conclusions — some controversial and perhaps peculiar to its community — were these:

Communication: Lack of communication between people — especially between our youth and adults — certainly is the major factor for allowing drug abuse to become epidemic today. More than ever our youth need interested and well-informed people to rap with regarding feelings, problems and fears. It gives them a chance to verbalize and compare, to understand themselves. When young people have no adults they can rap with, they are compelled to look to their peer group for answers that may not be the right ones.

When failure of communication goes deeper, when adolescents become strangers in their homes, fail in school, or on the job, when they fall behind in social skills, find no source of pleasure or self-esteem, they too frequently turn to drugs and become "drop-outs" in order to deal with their emptiness or inner tensions.

No purpose in life: In this affluent society, very often our young people's material and academic needs are met before they know what they want, and parental motivation overshadows self-motivation. No one takes the time to ask what our young people's ambitions or interests are. We insist that all students conform to a highly structured educational system which has little room for self-expression or personal motivation and where compulsory attendance defeats, in many cases, emotional growth.

With such a pace, proper values are often lost, making it difficult for youth to identify with life's true meaning and difficult to find a real purpose in life for them to seek.

Human need not being met: It must be remembered that when any institution fails to meet the human needs of its people, the people no longer need the institution. This is what is happening in many families, schools, companies, and churches. Kids are turned off because nobody really cares. Material things and dogmas seem to take precedence. A helping hand, someone to listen, is what is needed. Is it any wonder that youth turn to each other for humanizing experiences?

Peer-group pressures: One of the most common reasons given by young people today for copping out with drugs is peer-group pressure. They have a strong need for belonging and being accepted, and presently the in thing is the drug scene, giving youth a cultural behavior they can identify with, a group sharing, a symbol of defiance. Unfortunately, many adolescents are driven by peer-group pressures into disaster situations; they become trapped only to experience more hopelessness and fear.

Permissiveness: Permissiveness in our homes and educational institutions has been confused with intellectual freedom when in effect it is resorted to because of fear and failure on the part of the parents, educators, and others to relate to the real human needs of youth. Such permissiveness is leading to confusion, emotional unrest, lawlessness, and lack of respect. Dr. O'Shea explained:

Permissiveness is truly an adult cop-out; parents have confused permissiveness for love and punishment for discipline. Today, more than ever, we need responsible love, and guts enough to say *no.* Unfortunately, many adults have too many personal hang-ups to properly communicate love or their feelings with youth. When kids don't feel loved they get feelings of rejection with a lot of hurt emotions which lead to hostility or withdrawal. Parents and others should also realize that discipline is essential for emotional maturity. Responsible discipline evidences concern and caring. It is discipline with a purpose, a growth experience to teach right from wrong. And, of course, with lack of discipline comes lack of control, so evident today among our youth.

Lack of confidence and responsibility: Youth who are being treated for drug abuse have a low self-image. They have failed to achieve personal objectives and hence lack a sense of accomplishment so necessary for successful maturation. They lack responsibility because they have been given none. In this affluent society, parents and institutions continue to infantilize youth well beyond the age when it is necessary or appropriate. This enforced dependence makes for adolescent revolt.

"So what we should really be treating today," said Dr. O'Shea, "is not drug abuse, which is merely a symptom, but 'youthful crisis' with the following character disorders: low self-image, immaturity, fear, hostility, and withdrawal."

With this as a backdrop, the council then proceeded to outline their general objectives and a specific action program. The general objectives are:

1. To share and learn from each others' successes and failures.
2. To give support when support is needed.
3. To gather meaningful statistics for research and knowledge.
4. To make known our financial needs and more uniformly, equitably, and realistically seek local, state and federal funds.
5. To unite the community against drug abuse, so necessary if the job to be done is done right.

A specific five-point action program called for the establishment of:

1. A community education program
2. A hot line
3. Medical walk-in clinics
4. Ambulatory rehabilitation
5. Residential rehabilitation

Educational Program

In keeping with the concept of a comprehensive community drug treatment and prevention program, the area of education must receive primary concern and attention. Educational approaches (i.e., advertising), after all, have been used with great success in convincing the American public of the *benefits* of over-the-counter drugs.

The fact that practically all Americans are drug users cannot be disputed, and an intelligent understanding of drug use, as well as drug abuse, demands recognition of this fact. In a chemical era, such as the present, we need all the information that exists about the nature of drugs and of drug effects in order to make wise decisions affecting our own health and welfare and that of others. The body of relevant, scientific information is vast, ever-changing, and, at times, confusing. Although answers to many questions are not yet available, there are many basic facts and concepts with which everyone should be familiar.

The council's first consideration in community drug education was the enumeration of objectives to be attained. However, before this enumeration could be meaningful, a methodology was developed whereby education became a participatory experience. Although the council's objectives will be modified as more is learned about the nature of drugs and the community environment, the following goals are receiving top priority today:

1. Coordinate all drug educational efforts (formal and informal) in the community.
2. Dispel the prevailing misconceptions about drug use — both pro and con.
3. Provide a basic understanding of the effects and hazards of drug abuse.
4. Develop within the community the concept that the "drug problem" is really a "people problem" and that the solution to this problem demands total community participation.

Guiding the council's community education program is Dr. Joseph A. Harrington, Director of Psychological Services of Merrimack College in Lawrence. He says:

Human behavior is highly complex and often quite difficult to understand. We can, for example, predict with certainty that there will be no simple answers to problem behavior. Development of an educational program must keep this fact in mind, for any program offering "cookbook" solutions is doomed to failure. In the absence of extensive local research and evidence, hypotheses and assumptions must be imaginatively and creatively set forth and programmed in the local community. These hypotheses and assumptions must be tested and then modified in the light of new or additional evidence.

To achieve success in an educational program, the council decided that substantial effort should be directed toward prevention of drug abuse. Prevention demands understanding the motivations that lead to this type of undesirable behavior. For both humanitarian and financial reasons, the council's education program set out to show the benefit to the individual and to society in the positive sense of constructive changes brought about in people and not just symptom amelioration.

"An educational program must, therefore, suggest positive alternatives to drug use," says Dr. Harrington. "Successfully developed and communicated, the sharing of information, attitudes, and values will lead to the perception of drug taking itself as a less desirable species of behavior, and emotional ends formerly served by drugs will be satisfied in the interpersonal or intrapersonal process."

The council also considered a most important secondary gain to be derived from this educational objective: whatever its success on drug experimentation, the efforts of the education program will make a contribution to desirable health practices that can be applied throughout a person's lifetime.

Dr. Harrington first contacted the local school systems and colleges and, at present, the education committee is made up of the chief health officer from each school system and two colleges, plus the student representatives from the council (a total of six adults and six students, as well as the chairman). The committee meets every other Friday from 10:30 A.M. to 12 noon. This has provided a forum for the exchange of ideas and for the coordination of many programs throughout the school systems. For example, each school system has a distinct drug policy, but all systems shared ideas and problems before drawing up that policy. This caused better policy formulation and decreased the chance of criticism about the policy and the individuals most responsible for its construction and implementation.

Although the council's educational objectives will be more specifically defined as the needs of the community are further studied, the following considerations are receiving top priority today:

1. Coordinate drug education efforts in the five local school districts.
   a. Develop a spirit of cooperation.
   b. Develop those aspects of a program which would be usable in all programs.

   c. Collect and disseminate drug education programs existing in other school systems.

   d. Keep abreast of legislation related to drug use and abuse.

2. Develop an educational program designed to create community readiness for a positive and active involvement with drug abusers and potential drug abusers.

   a. Put forth positive reasons why the general public must get involved.

   b. Suggest positive approaches that the police, courts, and churches can take in dealing with drug abusers.

   c. Survey what is being done in other communities and adapt what is pertinent to this community's needs.

3. Develop an in-service training program for drug education for the faculties of the five school districts.

   a. Survey existing in-service programs.

   b. Stimulate cooperation among the school systems to share professional resources, that is, consultants.

   c. Arrange for consultants to be brought in.

4. Develop a speakers' bureau. This would involve organizing and coordinating the efforts of knowledgeable people from all organizations and groups within the community.

   a. Stimulate knowledgeable persons to take part in this program.

   b. Check their competence and effectiveness in functioning on this bureau.

   c. Fulfill requests from various groups and organizations to provide a speaker(s).

5. Develop an audio-visual aids library.

   a. Develop appropriate films, literature, tapes, and so forth, with particular emphasis on the local area. For example, a film depicting local parks and streets with anonymous shots of local youngsters experimenting with drugs would have far greater impact than impersonal cities like New York or Chicago.

   b. Make these appropriate films, tapes, literature, and equipment available for loan to school systems and other organizations (service organizations, industry, and so forth).

   c. Create appropriate spot announcements for radio, T.V., and newspapers.

6. Develop the educational program within the residential treatment facility for addicts. This will be a most important function. Rehabilitation cannot be meaningful without preparing the individual to live and compete in an open society. Experience has shown that meaningful education can be provided with addicts and that even the slightest improvement in their educational skills greatly enhances their re-entry into society.
   a. Explore possibility of sending addicts to local schools or of bringing local teachers into the residential treatment center.
   b. Explore possible curriculum programs which will be meaningful for this type of population.
   c. Encourage a volunteer system of staffing the school program.
   d. Plan an informal educational program — that is, speakers, projects, reading matter, and so forth.
   e. Develop a manual arts training program in conjunction with the sheltered workshop.
7. Work with the local colleges to encourage development of courses for teachers, guidance counselors, parents, and students. A local college recently conducted a crime control institute which provided lecture and field-work experience for approximately fifty policemen. This program dealt with juvenile delinquency and was extremely successful. Development of a drug control institute would be a real possibility and every effort should be made to encourage the establishment of such an institute. Academic work would be undertaken at the college and practical work in various units of the local hospital.
8. Make a particular effort to develop appropriate educational procedures and programs to meet the needs of the poorly educated, the Spanish-speaking, and the Blacks.
   a. Consult with the leaders of these groups.
   b. Develop self-educational programs.
   c. Determine present needs and resources.

The education committee has two major events planned for the future. The students on the committee plan to hold a two-day "rap in" with other students from the area schools. The noncommittee students would be chosen by their peers to represent their school at the conference. From this, the council hopes the young people will advise the schools and the community as to what they feel constitutes the best methods of preventing drug abuse. Approximately sixty students will participate in this program.

A second event will feature a five-part conference for teachers and administrators: 1. a panel of professionals in the field of drug education; 2. a panel of students who had participated in the student "rap in"; 3. small group discussions of what was presented by the panels; 4. summarization of the ideas presented at the conference, after which a request for proposals and recommendations from the floor to be used by the committee toward the further development of community programs; 5. finally, those individuals interested in taking a more active role in educating the community will be invited to join the council's education committee.

It would be well at this point to state that the council's education committee does not interfere with independent educational efforts, but rather acts as a resource to them. For example, the committee works with the Lawrence school department and a group of students who call themselves "Decisions Unlimited." This group of high school students have been trained by professionals in the field of drug education and rehabilitation, and their purpose is to talk with youngsters as far down as the third grade about the dangers of drug abuse.

Recently, a town not connected with the council contacted the education committee, requesting an educational program. A health officer and a teacher from the education committee spoke with the system's school teachers. Dr. Harrington spoke to a meeting of interested and concerned townspeople, and nine students from "Decisions Unlimited" spoke to 17 classes of grades three, four, and five. Reactions from the outside community revealed that programs of this nature are quite valuable.

It is apparent that the council's educational efforts have just begun and that much work lies ahead. The council does not pretend to have the best, or even an outstanding, educational program at this point in time. "However," says Dr. Harrington, "we do have an impressive number of adults and kids talking *with* each other and working together. We hope to increase these numbers. We feel we can win this battle. And let's face it — we just can't afford to lose!"

Hot Line

The second aspect of the council's five-point action program was the creation of a "hot line" — the concept for which began in 1968. A telephone service called "hot line" was initiated in Los Angeles by Dr. Dale Garell, Chief of the Adolescent Clinic, Children's Hospital, to serve as an experiment — hoping to help young people in crisis situations.

The idea for a hot line grew out of an awareness of the seemingly increased alienation of youth and the relative lack of effective avenues of communication during stress (including the traditional helping agencies).

The council's hot line committee adopted the same service and approach as initiated at Children's Hospital in Los Angeles. The approach followed in assisting callers is based on a number of assumptions related to youth in general, to those who would make use of the service specifically, and to what constitutes effective interaction toward problem solving. Among these assumptions are the following:

1. In general, those who would call the service do so because they face some kind of conflict or uncertainty about an issue which they have not been able to resolve on their own.
2. Effective resolutions of problems can only evolve out of the context of the individual's own life experience.
3. Individuals with problems are little, if at all, benefited from advice-giving, ready-made solutions, or any other unilateral impositions which, in effect, displaces responsibility.
4. Unconditional regard and respect effectively communicated are absolute prerequisites to constructive interaction.

The hot line workers must provide "creative listening," which implies a catalytic progress that is neither passive nor impositional, wherein the listener's primary function is that of encouraging an attitude of self-examination and exploration. The listener's job is to assist the caller in recognizing the realities of the situation he confronts and exploring strategies open to him in resolving the problem. The listener may throw out ideas for consideration (or even give personal opinions if these are solicited), but the focus is always placed on the caller's own resources and experiences. In this way, the caller not only remains the responsible agent, but the coping strategies developed have meaningful anchorage in his own world as well.

Suffice to say that the process involves a good deal of active listening and the asking of questions which are designed both to clarify the problem and to stimulate the development of coping strategies.

The approach described above obviously does not apply when the caller simply requests information on matters of fact. In these instances, the facts are given if they are known to the hot line worker, or the caller is referred to a resource where such information is available. In no case, however, is medical, legal, or other advice offered.

Structure and Procedure

1. Hours — The service operates from 6 P.M. to 12 midnight every day of the week with the exception of Friday and Saturday nights, when the hours extend to 2 A.M. the following morning. Twenty-four-hour coverage is provided by an answering service taking messages from individuals who may call outside of hot line hours. These messages are picked up by the hot line staff at the beginning of each evening shift.

2. Equipment and materials
   a. Telephone facilities — The hot line utilizes three phones with four incoming lines with consecutive numbers. The telephone exchange service, which provides 24-hour coverage, utilizes standard switchboard equipment.
   b. Data forms — Insofar as possible, pertinent information on each call is recorded on forms especially designed to facilitate data recording. In addition to whatever identifying information the caller may voluntarily give (name, age, sex, area, etc.), the worker indicates the nature of the problem or problems presented and the strategies discussed in dealing with the problem. The form also asks for the listener's judgment of the caller's affect, how the call was terminated, and the effectiveness of the interaction.

c. Resource directories — A directory of community agencies (for example, hospital, police, public health, mental health, etc.) is maintained in the hot line office. In addition, a catalog of resource material, including current teenage language, facts and figures related to frequent problems encountered, etc., is maintained for immediate use.

d. Caller file — All completed data forms are kept on file in sequence. In addition, a separate file is kept for frequent callers.

e. Message board — The hot line office is equipped with a message board. If a person calls and wishes to speak with a specific listener who is not working, the worker in question returns the call when he comes on duty. The board is also used for communication between workers on different shifts as, for example, when a worker wishes to be patched in at home if a particular person calls when he is not on duty.

3. Staff

a. Schedule of staff — Three individuals are on duty during each shift. Each staff person works one shift per week so that the total regular staff contingent is twenty-one. In addition to this number, there is a small pool of reserve standbys who fill in for assigned staff when the latter cannot work the shift by reason of illness, vacation, or other unavoidable circumstances. Thus far the turnover in staff has been very small. Regular staff members are replaced, when necessary, by those who have been serving as reserves. The staff is paid nominal stipend wages.

b. Selection of staff — Any individual is free to apply for a position on the hot line staff. Usually such application is prompted by a keen interest in the program, by a desire to gain experience in working with young people and/or develop professional skills, by the feeling that the individual has something to offer and would enjoy assisting youth in dealing with their problems.

In general, applications come from individuals who have been recommended to the service by various graduate schools in local colleges and universities (e.g., Departments of Psychology, Social Work), by members of the professional advisory board, or by hot line staff members themselves. Selection criteria are weighted heavily by factors other than formal professional training and experience, although such a background is obviously not disregarded. Primary emphasis is placed on judgments of the applicants' capacity to engage in effective communication with young people. This is best achieved when there is a minimum of defensiveness and need to be judgmental and authoritarian, where there is an openness and sensitivity to minimal but significant cues in the verbal exchange, where there is skill in enlisting the *caller's* resources toward the end of evolving possible solutions to the problems presented, and where unconditional warmth and regard are comfortably and spontaneously communicated.

The applicants are judged against the selection criteria primarily by means of an interview procedure. Each applicant under consideration is interviewed twice and evaluated independently by professional members of the advisory board. Consensus ratings are then generated and final selections made. The interviews take approximately forty-five minutes and make use of role-playing techniques, along with open-ended questioning and other more conventional techniques of inquiry.

4. Training — Training is seen as an on-going process. There are, however, two formal, three-hour sessions prior to any work on the service. These sessions are designed to introduce the staff to: (1) general issues related to youth culture; specific topics such as the drug and hippie scenes, venereal disease, unwed pregnancy, juvenile law, community resources; (2) crisis intervention theory and general principles of interviewing; (3) the concept of creative listening and techniques involved. Much of the time during these meetings is devoted to role-playing with simulated phone calls, using equipment in the facility which allows for monitoring.

In addition to the introductory sessions for new staff, regular training meetings are held once a month on an on-going basis for all workers. These are informal and deal primarily with technique: reviewing principles and drawing heavily upon hot line experiences that raise questions or have constituted problems. The monthly meetings are also used to introduce any modification in the program, deal with logistical problems that come up periodically, and, most importantly, to allow for free exchange of ideas and experiences between hot line workers themselves.

A final avenue of training is on the job. Members of the training faculty make periodic visits to the hot line during working shifts and provide individual consultation. This has proven to be the single most effective training mode, no doubt because of the combination of one-to-one exchange and the opportunity for the immediate translation of theory into practice via the live calls.

5. "On-call" professional consultation — Professional specialists in fields relevant to youth (for example, law, medicine, mental health, religion, community resources) are available to hot line workers for immediate consultation. This is accomplished by means of a phone patch-in system handled by the exchange switchboard. The primary function of the consultant is to assist the hot line worker in the course of a difficult call. The listener may seek suggestions on handling a call or information relevant to issues the caller has raised. In this case, the caller would be placed on hold while the worker and consultant discuss the matter. In other situations, a three-way conference may be appropriate, involving the consultant, listener, and the caller. Finally, the caller may request to speak directly with a consultant himself.

6. Advisory board — From its conception, the hot line has had an advisory board of community leaders who actively participate in the program. The advisory board meets monthly to discuss policy issues and to evaluate program needs.

Implications

Among the many possible implications of an emergency telephone service for young people, the following are suggested as particularly significant:

1. Young people may receive help in times of crisis that they would not otherwise obtain.
2. The hot line may offer a new form of therapy particularly suited to the unique needs of adolescents.
3. The hot line may serve as a valuable listening post and outlet in times of crisis in the community at large.
4. The program may uncover evidence suggesting the need for resources not presently available in the community.

5. Hot line data may prove to be more representative of the local youth culture than that gained by the more traditional practices (for example, school and clinic statistics).

Since the inception of Dr. Dale Garell's hot line in Los Angeles, its success has been common knowledge, and similar approaches have now been widespread throughout the nation. Its success has been in its unique way of improving communication with youth.

It is the council's feeling presently that hot lines should be an integral part of each community's program and, ideally, such facilities should be in a hospital setting in reasonable proximity to either a medical walk-in clinic or a detoxifying unit in order to most efficiently utilize the professional staff's knowledge by the trained volunteers who will be answering the calls.

Medical Walk-In Clinic

Point three of the council's five-point program was the creation of a medical walk-in clinic. Dr. O'Shea describes the clinic's function:

Less than one year ago kids with drug-related illnesses could not seek medical help without involving their parents. The result was that kids did not seek medical help and doctors did not become involved. I was privileged to author a bill, introduced by our local legislators and passed in the House and Senate in August of 1970, providing minors 12 years of age and older the right to give their consent for hospital and medical care for drug dependency if the dependency was determined by two or more physicians. Methadone maintenance therapy was to be excluded. Doctors are also allowed to give medical care to minors for venereal disease without parental consent. Such legislation has now made medical walk-in clinics for young adults a reality.

The council's purpose in creating a walk-in clinic in the local hospital was to create an atmosphere of informality and trust, and to safeguard a youth's right to privileged communication in his attempt to seek help. "If initially the patient lacks such trust," says Dr. O'Shea, "he or she may go nameless and be identified by a number. It is, however, important that standardized records be kept for the purpose of developing a statistical reporting mechanism which could gather information helpful to the growth of drug programs and useful in research both for our own experiences, and for such regional and state-wide studies."

The council's medical walk-in clinic is the first physical contact with youth in trouble. Their immediate medical or emotional needs are first taken care of. Such medical needs may include serum hepatitis, venereal disease, local or systemic infection and pregnancy; their emotional needs may be fear, anxiety, or drug-induced psychosis; or the chief complaint may be withdrawal symptoms embracing both physical and emotional complaints.

The primary responsibility of the council's clinic is medical, utilizing, of course, specialties of surgery and gynecology, psychiatry, and psychology. The clinic is further supported by nurses, social service workers, and volunteer youth workers.

Ideally, a medical walk-in clinic should be in the confines of a hospital so that a variety of professional skills would be more readily available, X-ray and laboratory departments more accessible, and transfer to the detoxification unit simplified.

The council's medical walk-in clinic also serves as a referral center to the detoxification unit, ambulatory rehabilitation, residential rehabilitation, and methadone maintenance program.

In describing the council's walk-in clinic, Dr. O'Shea makes the following points:

Detoxifying Unit

Hospital detoxifying units are necessary in every community. Such units make the withdrawal of drugs reasonable and safe for the patient. During such detoxification it affords the doctors time to medically and psychiatrically evaluate the drug-dependent patient and make arrangements for proper rehabilitation.

Such units could be used for both drugs and alcoholic detoxification. Isolation facilities are necessary in treating serum hepatitis or other contagious illnesses related to drug abuse. Zoning or isolation from the rest of the hospital is important to control visitors. Patients wtih drug overdose, of course, would initially be treated in the intensive care unit.

Staffing should include a medical team complemented by ex-addicts, social workers, and so forth; a psychiatric or psychological evaluation should be required for every patient; and records should be standardized for research studies.

Methadone Maintenance Program

Methadone maintenance programs are meeting critical needs in urban communities during the past two or three years. Presently, studies are being conducted in Chicago with L–Methadyl Acetate, a long-acting methadone-like substance, which can be administered as infrequently as three times weekly.

Methadone maintenance programs meet the following crises:

1. The substitution of methadone for heroin eliminates the need for drug-related crimes.
2. It makes work possible for the heroin addict.
3. It eliminates some of the medical complications which accompany shooting heroin, including overdose and death.

In reality a methadone maintenance program is merely substitution therapy — an exchange of one narcotic for another supposedly less harmful. Such a program is treating symptoms, not the disease itself, and true rehabilitation of the drug-dependent person while under the influence of methadone is not only difficult, but the success thereof is hard to evaluate.

It has been necessary and realistic to establish methadone maintenance programs, particularly in large cities, because adequate rehabilitation programs just are not available. Rehabilitation programs are costly and require trained personnel who are not available. A methadone maintenance program is much less costly, requiring fewer trained people to service a large number of addicts. In developing community drug programs, methadone maintenance programs should be the last to be considered — not the first. Says Dr. O'Shea, "I think it is a crime to subject a youngster to 'dope therapy' without first giving him a real 'trial of labor' in an adequate rehabilitation program; and before considering anyone for such substitution therapy a board, comprised of an internist or pediatrician, a psychiatrist, and an ex-addict, should make the ultimate decision. Standard procedure should be established in states with identification for each participant so that the addict can't play one program against the other."

Ambulatory Rehabilitation

In creating its ambulatory rehabilitation program to help drug abusers find their way back the council utilized many professional people — psychiatrists, psychologists, nurses, social workers, counselors, and guidance teachers — and nonprofessionals — ex-addicts, clergy and young, interested, trained adults.

Despite one's background, however, there are five important qualifications one must have to be successful in rehabilitation.

1. Ability to relate
2. Willingness to become involved
3. Knowledge of drugs and clinical effects
4. No serious personal hang ups
5. Training and experience in conducting group sensitivity or encounter sessions.

Group therapy has not only become a popular approach in helping young people, but it is very practical and successful. It gives a youngster a chance to compare, reflect, challenge and release inner feelings and tensions with a group he can be comfortable with and trust.

Hostility, fear, love all become expressed with an intensity proportionate to the group's feelings. Youths help themselves by gaining strength in sharing, comparing, and supporting one another. Their self-destructive pattern can be changed when they learn to accept and respect themselves.

The success of group therapy largely depends on two factors: first, it is proportionate to the time spent. A four-hour session is four times as effective as a one-hour session. Secondly, and most important, is the qualifications and the ability of the group leader. The location for such therapy can vary depending on the patient's need and accessibility.

The Dawn Program was one of the first successful ambulatory therapeutic programs to fight drug abuse among school students in this country. It was established in Los Angeles, California, in July 1967 by two high school guidance teachers, Mr. Jordon Paul and Mr. Caldwell Williams. By trial and error, followed by success, they concluded that the best size for groups was between ten and twelve students. These groups met for three hours, two nights weekly for encounter sessions and four hours on either Saturday or Sunday for socializing. The program was conducted only during the school year.

Group therapy is not always needed to turn young people off drugs. Sometimes merely a change of environment, a job, encouragement, or correcting medical problems will suffice. Interest and follow-ups are essential, however.

Residential Rehabilitation

The fifth point in the council's action program is residential rehabilitation, which according to all evidence is absolutely necessary for the severely drug-dependent patient. Their history is usually one of multiple drug use for several years and then daily use of either barbiturates, amphetamines, or opiates (primarily heroin) for several months or longer. It is the exception that heroin addiction can be successfully treated on an ambulatory basis. The average duration for such therapy is approximately eighteen months.

It has been difficult to evaluate the success for such programs because up to now accurate statistics have not been available. Why, then, is such a program so important?

1. It gives the motivated, drug-dependent patient a real chance to be drug free and return to society as a responsible citizen.
2. The house serves as an important area in community education.
3. Residents in the program have been invaluable in working to combat drug abuse within their peer group.

In order to make reasonable evaluations of these programs, however, the following information is needed: 1. a thorough psychological workup on all admissions to better evaluate and research successes or failures, and 2. computerized statistics with follow-up studies for a minimum of five years.

The council's residential rehabilitation program centers around a rehabilitation house called Reality, Inc. — one of the organizations that existed before the formation of the council. It is useful to delve into the background of a house such as this in order to shed some light on the possible perils and pitfalls of inaugurating and operating a residential rehabilitation program.

Reality, Inc., was formed over two years prior to the creation of the council and gained the distinction of being the first community group in the Commonwealth of Massachusetts to develop a drug program under the sponsorship of a medical society, namely the Essex North District Medical Society. A survey conducted by the medical society in 1968 clearly indicated the seriousness of the drug problem among the youth of the Greater Lawrence community.

The charge to the Reality, Inc., board of directors was to promote improved community health with an emphasis on rehabilitation of youthful drug dependents and the education of young people and adults in such a way as to reduce the potential of future drug dependency and other mental health problems. Reality's first task was to make the community aware of the drug problem and obtain broad support for a very necessary drug rehabilitation program.

In the formative period, rehabilitation sessions were initiated with drug-dependent youth and conducted evenings in the offices of Dr. O'Shea. Based on the experience of other apparently successful drug programs across the country, it was evident that an ex-drug addict could play a very important role in the rehabilitation process of drug-dependent individuals. The Reality board decided that their program, if it were to progress rapidly, needed the services of a former drug addict, and the search was on. Reality heard of an ex-addict who was located in a community some fifty miles away and who was interested in a change of jobs.

Reality, Inc., took their newly acquired ex-addict and proceeded to introduce him to every civic, professional, fraternal, and community organization in the Greater Lawrence area. The new director was set up on a temporary basis to do rehabilitation work several evenings a week at the Lawrence Y.M.C.A. This program worked reasonably well, but it became apparent that some of the hard-core heroin addicts needed around-the-clock supervision and rehabilitation treatment. To handle this new development, a storefront was leased, and it very shortly became the assembly point of drug-dependent youth. From the large numbers of youths using the storefront and seeking help there, it was obvious that the storefront would not meet the increasing needs of the rehabilitation program. The search started again to locate a larger, more permanent residential rehabilitation facility.

"I think it is important to point out that up to this time the only funds received to support the program came from donations by industry, business, professionals, fraternal organizations, a parents' group fighting drug abuse, and concerned Greater Lawrence citizens," says Harry Youngman, an executive with a local company, a prime mover in Reality, Inc., and now a council board member. He continued:

With endorsements of our programs by the area hospitals, law enforcement agencies, news media, and all the other segments of the community who heretofore made financial contributions to Reality, Inc., we were able to obtain a lease on a castle in Methuen, Massachusetts. This more spacious, ideally located facility would serve as an excellent residential rehabilitation center for our program. Our director and some additional staff moved into our new center, named Challenge House, in July of 1970. Reality, Inc., was now faced with the task of raising or obtaining a substantial amount of money to operate the new facility. With an expected fifty to seventy-five residents being housed in Challenge House, the salaries for additional staff, cost of necessary renovations, and general operating costs were of serious concern to the Reality, Inc., board.

An application was made to the Massachusetts Department of Mental Health for a grant to meet some of the operating expenses of the drug program. Considerable assistance was received from the staff of the Department of Mental Health and the Merrimack Valley Health Planning Council in developing the information required for the grant application.

"A request for funds was also made to the Greater Lawrence United Fund," Youngman said. "Since these monies, if granted — both from the Department of Mental Health and the United Fund — would not be forthcoming for some time, the money to support the program continued to arrive in the form of donations from the same sources who contributed to our earlier effort." All appeared to be moving along well with the overall drug program.

With the rapid growth of the residential center, the director was instructed to maintain an accurate accounting of all monies and goods received and funds expended. A bookkeeper–administrator was hired by Reality, Inc., to assist in discharging this responsibility. The director was told that major expenditures of any type for the program were not to be made without prior approval of the board of directors. Then problems seemed to develop. Mr. Youngman tells why:

Shortly thereafter the question of "hustling" merchants and firms in the Greater Lawrence community became a problem with many of the local citizens who had been supporting our program for some time. It was the opinion of the director that hustling was a major part of the rehabilitation process for the residents. After much discussion and considerable debate, the Reality board directed that hustling would not be allowed in the Greater Lawrence area. It was also stressed that records would have to be kept of all materials and supplies that were obtained through hustling. This the director agreed to do.

The Reality board then learned that a play was being put on by residents of Challenge House at school halls and churches throughout the community and that the profits of this play were being retained in a separate bank account. When the director was told to use the receipts from the play to pay some of the ever-increasing bills at Challenge House, he would not comply, but indicated that the money belonged to the cast and director of the play.

The next problem came to light following an inspection of the castle by the Massachusetts Department of Public Safety. They insisted that residents not be allowed to sleep on the top floor of the castle. In the interest of the residents' safety, the Reality board had to issue a direct order to the director to move the residents from the top floor. Following the relocation of the residents to sleeping quarters on the lower floors, the director had an elaborate shower installed on the top floor of the castle without the knowledge of the Reality board. After learning that the shower room cost better than $5,000, the director was told again that major expenditures for the program were not to be made without prior approval of the board of directors.

Funds were always short, but the program was continuing with many area vendors extending credit to Reality, Inc. The United Fund contributed $9,000 to the program, which helped to pay some of the bills.

A zoning variance was requested from the town of Methuen to operate our residential center, which had been licensed as a mental hospital by the Department of Mental Health. A temporary variance would be granted by the town if specific renovations to the castle were made.

A grant application was prepared and forwarded to the Governor's Committee on Law Enforcement and the Administration of Criminal Justice to cover the expansion of services of Reality, Inc., and renovations to the castle. Again, we received excellent cooperation from the state, the Lawrence city planner, and the Merrimack Valley Health Planning Council in drawing up the grant application.

The Reality, Inc., board of directors was surprised to learn that the director of Challenge House had employed additional staff and was making arrangements for the leasing of an apartment building to house staff and graduates of the drug program without the knowledge of the Reality board.

The relationship between the Reality board and the director was becoming more strained as time passed. There still was not an acceptable accounting of donations and materials received. Hustling and panhandling by residents was becoming more widespread and was the main activity of some residents. An admission procedure to the program was nonexistent; anyone who applied was admitted by the director. The medical director notified the Reality board that he would not be responsible for the health of the residents since already residents were being admitted with serious contagious venereal diseases.

The director at this time notified the Reality board that he wanted to incorporate his own rehabilitation program and set up branch rehabilitation centers across the country and possibly in foreign countries. It was obvious to the Reality board that the director was more interested in expansion of his empire than in the drug problems of Greater Lawrence, and therefore there would have to be a parting of the ways. Hopefully, this transition could be done quietly in the best interest of the residents and the drug program. This did not occur and much unpleasantness developed over the resultant termination of the director.

During the emotion-packed weeks that followed the termination of the director, the Reality board chose to maintain a discreet silence rather than publicize facts that might jeopardize a long-range, comprehensive drug program for all of Greater Lawrence.

Our residential facility, Challenge House, had remained open during the transition and is still in operation, helping to rehabilitate the young drug-dependent people of Greater Lawrence under the direction of our new staff. We have received the $50,000 grant from the Department of Mental Health and the $75,000 grant from the Governor's Committee on Law Enforcement and the Administration of Criminal Justice.

Youngman sums up the lessons Reality learned by reviewing some of the areas where a community program should direct special attention:

1. An ex-addict has a definite place in the rehabilitation program, but check the ex-addict thoroughly. Remember, if the ex-addict has been

on the street for several years, he approaches things differently than you do.

2. Do not hesitate to obtain professional assistance in drawing up your grant applications. It could make the difference of whether or not you are successful.

3. If you are trying to obtain a residential facility, be extremely selective and aware of zoning requirements, state laws, and insurance coverages. Renovations and insurance are expensive items, so try to find a building that can readily and economically meet your needs.

4. Proposed budgets and accountability of funds and materials donated should receive careful scrutiny by qualified people. This is a very important feature of your agreements with state funding agencies.

5. Purchase orders should be utilized to buy necessary items, and all proposed major expenditures should receive the prior approval of the governing board.

6. An administrator (not the former addict) should be used to conduct the daily business of the organization. He should be responsible for the financial operation of the program.

7. Admission procedures should be clearly defined. Interviews by the director, a psychological evaluation, and a complete physical should be required for every prospective resident.

8. The goal of the residential rehabilitation program should be to return the resident to the status of a responsible member of the community.

9. A parents' group is very helpful to the program, but to be effective it should have specific goals and should keep the governing board informed of its projects.

After hearing of its pitfalls, you probably wonder about the achievements of Reality, Inc.

1. Reality was able to develop a keen awareness of the drug problem in the Greater Lawrence community.

2. Reality was able to rally community involvement in its program.

3. Despite several setbacks and problems, Reality, Inc., was able to get a viable and effective program developed and under way in Greater Lawrence.

Despite its problems, Reality, Inc., acted as the catalyst for the Greater Lawrence Community Drug Council.

The Role of the Ex-addict in Community Drug Programs

It must be remembered that today the ex-addict is not necessarily a criminal, a derelict, or a psychopath; on the contrary, he may be your son or daughter, a typical American youth now ready to help others and be a responsible citizen. Many become the apostles of our time, in this new field of mental health, reaching young people on the street and in the schools where the action is.

The properly rehabilitated, formerly drug-dependent young adult meets all the qualifications for leadership in this field. He has personal knowledge, is sensitive to the hard road back to society, and has developed a strong desire or need to help others. Like the alcoholic, he knows that help cannot wait for an appointment but must be available 24 hours around the clock.

Therapeutic programs in residential rehabilitation centers such as "half-way houses" can be directed by qualified ex-addicts. Their dedication and involvement make them invaluable. Professional personnel — psychiatrists and psychologists — should complement their work and be available on a continuous consulting basis. Full-time professional counselors could also serve to complement the work done in the house, if they are properly in tune with the house concept and can work with the director or co-directors. A business administrator for such a center, of course, is necessary.

The administrator and therapeutic directors of residential treatment centers should be responsible to the community drug council, through their executive director. All such facilities must be under professional and community control since they are dealing with emotionally disturbed young people and distraught parents who are extremely vulnerable and in many instances have been exploited for personal greed or ambition by irresponsible leadership.

Staff Interaction Between Agencies

Ex-addicts or advanced residents at a residential center can and should be used in the medical walk-in clinics and the detoxifying hospital units in a consulting or counseling role.

The psychiatrist and psychologist have professional skills all drug programs need. Their primary role is in consulting and in a supervisory capacity since their therapeutic role is limited to the severely emotionally disturbed young adult.

Nurses have and can play a prominent role in the field of drug abuse. They should be actively involved with all phases of a five-point program.

The social service department can work most effectively out of the medical walk-in clinics and serve to coordinate the various modalities of rehabilitation. They can also intercede with probation officers, courts and various social agencies when necessary.

In concluding the rehabilitation aspect of the council's program, it should be pointed out that the council only has a *voluntary* program — helping people who seek help. "But what do we do with the thousands of young people today who have a bad drug habit but who won't go for treatment?" asked Dr. O'Shea. "In the near future it may be that we will have to direct our attention to compulsory rehabilitation therapy in this state."

Where Does the Money Come From?

Where indeed does the money come from? This is the question that is asked by any new community effort. Even though there are a great deal of volunteer services available, there are always some things which must be purchased, either services or goods. Thus, at some point, volunteer services are not enough for a successful program. This is especially true in attempting to operate an on-going, community-based drug treatment program, with hopes of expansion into a drug-prevention education program. Initial efforts at soliciting funds from a broad cross section of the community will soon show that the large amount of money which is needed cannot be raised by this approach. There are too many other programs attempting to raise funds. As far as the council is concerned, the Reality residential treatment program alone needs some $200,000 per year to operate. A great deal of the future funding will probably come directly from the federal government.

As to methods of obtaining local and state funding, Harry S. Weinroth, a council board member and Lawrence city planner, points out two sources which have funded Reality, Inc., to date. First, the Massachusetts Department of Mental Health awarded $50,000 to Reality, Inc. The Governor's Committee on Law Enforcement and Administration of Criminal Justice, through its project, Community-Based Drug Treatment Program, is the second valuable source. The Criminal Justice effort has allocated $75,000 to Reality, Inc. The latter program required local matching funds of $50,000. Both state agencies fund programs based on applications, which are submitted to them at appropriate times, when projects are open for competitive submission. It is entirely conceivable that in the future, projects which have been funded by these agencies will continue to receive funding on a noncompetitive basis. The council hopes so. However, at this time, the council can only assume that new applications will be annually required to continue funding from these sources. It is also conceivable that no matter how successful any community effort might be, governmental funds may be late in coming or may dry up completely. To counteract these possibilities and to provide matching funds, as well as additional income, it is necessary that other major sources be created.

"I think the most important thing which must be understood by any community which attempts to operate a drug treatment program, is that these programs are most expensive," said Weinroth. "They must provide medical services, food and shelter, as well as many other things for those persons under treatment. The programs can hope to receive some sort of assistance from state or federal sources, but in the long run it will probably be up to the local government to provide continuing funding, either through local tax dollars or from revenue-sharing allocations."

The Greater Lawrence Community Drug Council attempted, on the spur of the moment, to request funds from each of the communities involved in the drug council.

Warrants were submitted to each of the town meetings, requesting a flat $10,000 from each town. Town attorneys and selectmen were faced with a difficult decision. While they concurred with the efforts of the council, they were also aware that state law did not permit them to make a grant to a nonprofit organization for drug treatment. As soon as this information was relayed to the council, warrant requests were withdrawn without prejudice.

With the new knowledge, members of the council journeyed to Boston to discuss with the legislature house counsel the feasibility of introducing legislation which would permit cities and towns to give money to drug councils so that services could be offered to area residents.

The house counsel, while indicating agreement with the basic concept of the proposed legislation, was emphatic that even if such legislation received the approval of the legislature, it would not receive the approval of his office. It was the house counsel's opinion that there was existing state legislation which permitted a city or town to appropriate funds for the payment of health services, which can include the following:

1. In-patient services
2. Out-patient services
3. Emergency services on a twenty-four-hour basis
4. Partial hospitalization services for day and night care
5. Mental health consultation and educational services to community agencies and professional personnel practicing in the area
6. Diagnostic services
7. Rehabilitative services
8. Preventive, precare, and after-care services within the area
9. Research programs, including evaluation of effectiveness and efficiency of the various programs operating within the area.

In order for a drug council to receive the funds which are appropriated for the above-listed services, they must offer all or any of the services and keep itemized records concerning the services rendered. Costs must be allocated by the community to those who are treated. All records will be subject to state audit. This type of contribution offers perhaps the greatest source of supporting income for a drug treatment program, since it can be based on a per capita contribution from each community represented by the drug council.

The question which arises is, at what level will that per capita be established? And what effect will this contribution have on the community's overall tax rate? No matter what the final answer may be, there should be agreements between drug councils and local communities for services so that local programs can continue.

Other sources of obtaining funding other than gifts, solicitations, raffles, and so forth, are those offered through various surplus programs of the federal government, such as the surplus food program, which can provide food to a residential treatment center. Armed Forces surplus equipment, such as vehicles, bedding and any other materials used by the Armed Forces which has been declared to be surplus, can also be made available to a drug-treatment program. There are several ways of obtaining this latter material — either by utilizing a local community's Civil Defense Agency, or by contacting the Defense Department, the state agency for surplus property, or local Congressmen. There are many ways to raise funds. The best and fastest source, however, for obtaining funds on a continuing basis will be through local assistance.

**Sources of Information for
Funding Community Training
and Rehabilitation Programs**

Funding for Rehabilitation

The following is a review of the federal government's grants program (at this writing) on rehabilitation of addicts and drug dependent persons. HEW should be contacted regarding part D, Community Mental Health Act, second section as amended.

The section authorizes grant support for a portion of the cost of professional and technical personnel salaries to staff comprehensive community centers for the training of narcotic addiction and drug abuse prevention programs. A program must provide the following: 1. inpatient, 2. out-patient, 3. professional observation, 4. administrative care, and 5. community consultation and education.

Grants will also be authorized to public and nonprofit private agencies or organizations to fund a portion of the costs of programs for the training and rehabilitation of narcotic-addicted or drug-dependent persons. The projects must include one or more of the following services: 1. detoxification service, 2. institutional (which includes medical, psychological, educational or counseling) services, and/or 3. community-based after-care service.

Priority is given to special project grant applications from states or areas within states having the highest projection of population who are narcotic- or drug-dependent persons.

An interesting part of the total national mental health program is that it is possible to some degree to combine a mental health center with a staff and provide a direct advantage to existing programs and pay only for staffing physicians. The federal government tends to fund special projects that reflect the best needs of a community. For information, write HEW, Washington, D. C. 20201.

Funding of Drug Abuse Education

This funding is primarily handled through the Administration of Grants and Contracts Programs for Drug Addiction Education, Bureau of Educational Personnel Development, Office of Education, which is authorized under P.L. 91–527 of the Drug Abuse Education Act of 1970. The law provides for grants and contracts with higher education, state and local educational agencies, and the public and private educational or research institutions and organizations which support research and pilot projects which are designed to develop, demonstrate, and evaluate new and improved curricula in the problems of the drug addict. The law also provides for drug abuse education and training for members of many communities, agencies, and organizations.

Further information about this funding program may be obtained by writing to:

> Office of Education
> Bureau of Educational Personnel Development
> Drug Education Branch
> Washington, D. C.   20202

The Center for the Studies of Narcotics and Drug Addicts and Drug-Dependent Persons also administers grants and programs for drug education. This is under section 253 of the Comprehensive Drug Abuse Prevention and Control Act — P.L. 91–513. This authorizes grants to states and public or nonprofit private agencies and organizations for the development and evaluation of programs of drug addiction education training for general public-school-age children. For further information write:

> Central Office
> Dept. of Health, Education and Welfare
> 5600 Fischer Lane
> Parklon Building
> Rockville, Md. 20852

Law Enforcement Assistance Administration

The Department of Justice supports certain types of drug addict educational programs relating to the law enforcement aspect of drug abuse. Grants are made available through these funds for community-based treatment for mental health, technical assistance, and drug treatment supplies, as well as case loads for half-way house programs for prevention and evaluation of drug treatment. For information, contact the Bureau of Narcotics and Dangerous Drugs, Department of Justice, in your state capital.

Other Funding

The Economic Opportunity office has grants available for community-based programs for planning, community education, and rehabilitation. Write:

> Economic Opportunity
> 1200 19th Street, N.W.
> Washington, D. C. 20506

Funds are also available from the Model Cities Program, Department of Housing and Urban Affairs, for professional staff, educational treatment, rehabilitation, or evaluation of drug-addicted persons relating to or incorporated in a Model Cities Program. For further information on Model Cities Program, write:

> Model Cities Administration
> 45 Seventh Street, S.W.
> Washington, D. C.   20410

The Office of Research and Demonstration Training of Social and Rehabilitation Service administers grants under sections four and seven of the Vocational Rehabilitation Administration of 1954, and also under Title XI, section 1110–Social Security Act as amended.

Grants under Vocational Rehabilitation Administration are awarded to public and private nonprofit agencies in support of research and demonstration projects which present some unique contribution to present knowledge of theory or practice. The grants program, under which are research and demonstration grants under the Social Security Act as they might apply to drug addiction, is focused toward grants made to state, public and other nonprofit organizations. For further information regarding the program:

> Administrator
> Office of Research Demonstration and Training
> 330 Independence Avenue, S.W.
> Washington, D. C.   20201

One of the objectives that was reflected in the government's recent statement concerning drug addiction was that all federal funding resources should be coordinated so that the government is not funding overlapping programs — two different agencies funding a program within one agency. Work is progressing on this.

Selected Printed References and Audio Visual Materials

There has been an explosion of materials addressing the problems associated with drug use and drug users. As with any complex problem, these materials reflect many biases and many levels of research and writing sophistication. We have selected a representative group of references which, while technically competent works, still reflect the ambiguities and biases so illustrative of the field.

I. Books and Monographs

Abramson, H. A., ed. *The Use of LSD in Psychotherapy and Alcoholism.* Indianapolis: Bobbs-Merrill, 1967.

Ausubel, D. P. *Drug Addiction: Physiological, Psychological and Sociological Aspects.* New York: Random House, 1958.

Ball, J. C., and Chambers, C. D. *The Epidemiology of Opiate Addiction in the United States.* Springfield: Thomas, 1970.

Barber, B. *Drugs and Society.* New York: Russell Sage, 1967.

Blum, R. H. *Utopiates: The Use and Users of L.S.D.* New York: Atherton Press, 1964.

Chambers, C. D. *Differential Drug Use Within the New York State Labor Force.* Albany: New York State Narcotic Addiction Control Commission, 1971.

Chambers, C. D. *An Assessment of Drug Use in the General Population: Special Report No. 1, Drug Use in New York State.* Albany: New York State Narcotic Addiction Control Commission, 1971.

Cohen, S. *The Beyond Within, The LSD Story.* New York: Atheneum, 1964.

Cohen, S. *The Drug Dilemma*. New York: McGraw-Hill, 1968.

Department of Health, Education and Welfare. *Marihuana and Health*. Washington: U.S. Government Printing Office, 1971.

DeRopp, R. S. *Drugs and the Mind*. New York: St. Martin's Press, 1957.

Glueck, S., and Glueck, E. *Delinquents in the Making: Paths to Prevention*. New York: Harper, 1952.

Gross, J. E., ed. *Respect for Drugs*. Washington: U.S. Government Printing Office, 1968.

Grupp, S. E., ed. *Marihuana*. Columbus, Ohio: Merrill, 1971.

Harman, R. E., and Fox, A. M., eds. *Drug Awareness*. New York: Avon Books, 1970.

Kron, J., and Brown, E. M. *Mainline to Nowhere: The Making of a Heroin Addict*. New York: Pantheon Books, 1965.

Leinwood, G., ed. *Drugs*. New York: Washington Square Press, 1970.

Lindesmith, A. R. *The Addict and the Law*. Bloomington: Indiana University Press, 1969.

Lingeman, R. R. *Drugs From A to Z: A Dictionary*. New York: McGraw-Hill, 1969.

Louria, D. B. *The Drug Scene*. New York: McGraw-Hill, 1968.

Maurer, D. W., and Vogel, H. *Narcotics and Narcotic Addiction*. Springfield: Thomas, 1962.

Nowlis, H. H. *Drugs on the College Campus*. New York: Doubleday, 1969.

Smith, D. E. *The New Social Drug*. Englewood Cliffs, N. J.: Prentice-Hall, 1970.

Stearn, J. *The Seekers*. New York: Bantam Books, 1969.

Stewart, W. W., ed. *Drug Abuse in Industry*. Miami: Halos, 1970.

Solomon, D., ed. *The Marihuana Papers*. Indianapolis: Bobbs-Merrill, 1966.

Taylor, N. *Narcotics: Nature's Dangerous Gifts*. New York: Delta, 1963.

Wittenborn, J. R., ed. *Drugs and Youth*. Springfield: Thomas, 1970.

II. Professional Journal Articles

"A Medical Department's Experience in Having Hardcore Unemployed." *American Journal of Public Health*, August 1969.

"A.S.P.A.—B.N.A. Survey: The Employee With Problems." *The Bureau of National Affairs* (Washington, D. C.), December 10, 1970.

Blair, T. S., "Relations of Drug Addiction to Industry." *Journal of Industrial Hygiene*, October 1919.

Chambers, C. D., and Brill, L. "Some Considerations for the Treatment of Non-Narcotic Drug Abusers." *Industrial Medicine and Surgery*, 1970.

Connell, P. H. "Some Observations Concerning Amphetamine Misuse: Its Diagnosis, Management, and Treatment with Special Reference to Research Needs." In Wittenborn, J. R., et al. (Eds.) *Drugs and Youth.* Springfield: Thomas, 1970.

Dembo, R., and Chambers, C. D. "Disabilities to Employment Among Ex-Addicts." *Journal of Employment Counseling,* September 1971.

"Drug Abuse and Industry." *N.A.M. Reports,* I, May 1970.

"Drug Abuse and Industry." *N.A.M. Reports,* II, June 1970.

"Drug Abuse and Industry." *N.A.M. Reports,* III, July 1970.

"Drug Abuse and Industry." *N.A.M. Reports,* IV, August 1970.

Essig, Carl F. "Newer Sedative Drugs that Can Cause States of Intoxication and Dependence of Barbiturate Type." *J.A.M.A.,* 196:714–717 (1966).

Farnsworth, D. L. "The Drug Problem Among Young People." *West Virginia Medical Journal,* December 1967.

Griffith, John. "A Study of Illicit Amphetamine Drug Traffic in Oklahoma City." *American Journal of Psychiatry,* 123(5):560–569 (1966).

Hine, C. H. "The Role of the Industrial Nurse in the Detection and Prevention of Drug Abuse." *Occupational Health Nursing,* April 1969.

Isbell, Harris, and Fraser, Havelock F. "Addiction to Analgesics and Barbiturates." *Journal of Pharmacology and Experimental Therapeutics,* Part II, 99(4):355–397 (1950).

Lasagna, L. "Many Faces of Drug Abuse." *Modern Medicine,* April 1970.

Lemere, F. "The Danger of Amphetamine Dependency." *American Journal of Psychiatry,* 123 (1966).

O'Connor, R. B. "An Alert—Narcotic Usage Among Employees in Industry." *Journal of Occupational Medicine,* October 1968.

Rush, H., and Brown, J. "The Drug Problem in Business." *The Conference Board Record,* March 1971.

Smith, David. "The Trip." *Emergency Medicine,* pp. 27–42 (December, 1969).

Sohn, D. "Drug Screening in Industrial Nursing." *Occupational Health Nursing,* August 1970.

Sweeney, F. E. "Illegal Drug Abuse and Industry." *American Association Industrial Nurses Journal,* August 1967.

III. Pamphlets

Answers to the Most Frequently Asked Questions About Drug Abuse. National Institute of Mental Health, National Clearinghouse for Drug Abuse Information. Rockville, Maryland, 1970.

Barbiturates as Addicting Drugs. Public Health Service publication no. 545, U. S. Dept. of Health, Education and Welfare. Washington, 1961.

Bureau of Drug Abuse Control Fact Sheets. Food and Drug Administration. Washington, 1966.

Darkness on Your Doorstep. Los Angeles County Department of Community Services. Los Angeles.

Desk Reference on Drug Abuse. New York State Department of Health. Albany, 1970.

Drug Abuse as a Business Problem. New York Chamber of Commerce. New York City, 1970.

Drug Abuse: the Chemical Cop-out. National Association of Blue Shield Plans, 1969.

The Drug Abuse Epidemic: A Synopsis of Facts, Figures, and Tables. Prudential Life Insurance Company. Undated.

The Drug Abuse Problem. Food and Drug Administration publication no. 37, Superintendent of Documents. Washington, 1967.

Drug Abuse Resource and Information Guide. Health Insurance Plan of Greater New York, Mental Health Services Division. New York City, 1971.

Drug Facts. American Telephone and Telegraph, Medical Division. New York, 1970.

Drugs of Abuse. Reprint from FDA papers, U. S. Government Printing Office. Washington, 1967.

LSD: The False Illusion, Parts I and II. Reprint from FDA papers, U. S. Government Printing Office. Washington, 1967.

Narcotic Drug Addiction. Public Health Service publication no. 1021, U. S. Dept. of Health, Education and Welfare. Washington, 1963.

Narcotics and Drug Abuse (Task V Force Report). U. S. Government Printing Office. Washington, 1967.

Narcotics and Youth. Brook Foundation. West Orange, New Jersey, 1953.

Prevention and Control of Narcotic Addiction. Bureau of Narcotics, U. S. Treasury Dept. Washington, 1962.

Rehabilitation in Drug Addiction. Public Health publication no. 1013, U. S. Government Printing Office. Washington, 1963.

Resource Book for Drug Abuse Education. National Institute of Mental Health, National Clearinghouse for Mental Health Information. Rockville, Maryland, 1969.

Youthful Drug Use. U. S. Department of Health, Education and Welfare, Social and Rehabilitation Service. Washington, 1970.

IV. Trade Publications

Chemical Week: July 1970, "Attacking Drug Abuse"; November 1970, "Rx for Drug Abuse Problem"; November 1970, "Industry High on Drugs Problem"; December 1970, "Pinpointing the Pill Popper."

Employee Relations Bulletin: June 1970, "Help Hooked Employees Kick the Drug Habit."

Fleet Owner: December 1970, "Can You Employ the Ex-Addict?"

Industry Week: May 1970, "Drug Abuse Problems Invade Industry"; July 1970, "Drug Abuse Is Becoming a Big Problem for Business."

Iron Age: August 1970, "Drugs Fail to Dent Metalworking."
Management Information: August 1970, "Drugs in Industry — A Growing Menace."
Management Resources: July 1970, "Drugs on the Job."
Modern Manufacturing: July 1970, "How Serious Is Drug Abuse in Industry?"
Modern Office Procedures: June 1970, "It's High Time to Have a Drug Policy."
Nation: November 1970, "Drug Threat in Business."
National Safety News: January 1970, "The Problem Employee."
Supervisory Management: July 1970, "Employees Who Use Drugs, A Growing Problem."
Wayfarers Magazine: February 1969, "Tranquilizer Users."

V. Films

Are Drugs the Answer? 1970, color, 20 minutes. Distributed by N.I.M.H. Drug Abuse Film Collection, National A V Center, National Archives and Records Service (GSA), Washington, D. C. 20409.
Beyond LSD: A Film for Concerned Adults and Teenagers. 1968, color, 25 minutes. J. Thomas Ungerleider, professional consultant. Distributed by Bailey-Film Associates, 11559 Santa Monica Blvd., Los Angeles, California 90025.
Bridge from Noplace. 1968, color, 22 minutes. Alfred M. Freedman, professional consultant. Distributed by National A V Center, National Archives and Records Service (GSA), Washington, D. C. 20409.
The Current Scene. 1968, black/white, 26 minutes. Distributed by NET Film Service, Indiana University, Audio Visual Center, Bloomington, Indiana 47401.
A Day in the Death of Donnie B. 1969, black/white, 14 minutes. Distributed by National A V Center, National Archives and Records Service (GSA), Washington, D. C. 20409.
Drugs: Facts Everyone Needs to Know. 1970, color, 29 minutes. Sanford J. Feinglass, professional consultant. Distributed by Fiorelli Films, Research Drive, Stamford, Conn. 06906.
Drugs and the Nervous System, 1966, color, 16 minutes. Distributed by Churchill Films, 662 North Robertson Blvd., Los Angeles, California 90069.
Flowers of Darkness. 1968, color, 22 minutes. Alfred M. Freedman, professional consultant. Distributed by National A V Center, National Archives and Records Service (GSA), Washington, D. C. 20409.
From Pot to Psychedelics. 1968, black/white, 32 minutes. Distributed by NET Film Service, Indiana University, Audio Visual Center, Bloomington, Indiana 47401.

Grooving. 1970, color, 31 minutes. Distributed by Benchmark Films, 516 Fifth Avenue, New York, N. Y. 10036.

Marihuana (CBS Reports). 1968, black/white, 52 minutes. Distributed by Carousel Films, 1501 Broadway, New York, N. Y. 10036.

A Movable Scene. 1968, color, 22 minutes. Alfred M. Freedman, professional consultant. Distributed by National A V Center, National Archives and Records Service (GSA), Washington, D. C. 20409.

Speedscene — The Problem of Amphetamine Abuse. 1969, color, 17 minutes. Distributed by Bailey-Film Associates, 11559 Santa Monica Blvd., Los Angeles, California 90025.

World of the Weed. 1968, black/white, 21 minutes. Distributed by NET Film Service, Indiana University, Audio Visual Center, Bloomington, Indiana 47401.

Drug Glossary

All "in-groups" develop a distinctive vocabulary with which members can identify and communicate with other members. This language evolves in the same manner as more formal languages. The argot or slang vocabulary of the involved drug abusers changes as new people enter the group, as new behaviors are adopted, as new chemicals are abused, and so forth. The following glossary contains those terms which are currently popular among contemporary drug abusers. The glossary is not exhaustive and is primarily presented to familiarize managers with a vocabulary which they may encounter.

Acapulco Gold. High grade of marihuana; refers to the area of Mexico where it is grown; see marihuana.

Acid. LSD, one of the most popular hallucinogens or "psychedelic" drugs; see LSD.

Acid Head. A person who regularly uses acid (LSD); see LSD.

Acid Test. Party at which LSD has been added to the punch.

Addict. A person addicted or "hooked" to regular use of drugs, especially heroin, morphine and opium. Also: Hophead, Hypo, Junkie.

Addiction. Chronic drug use which involves: 1) a desire or need to take the drug, 2) a tendency to take more and more of the drug, 3) a mental – and sometimes physical – dependence on the drug and its effects.

African Black. A grade of marihuana grown in Africa; see marihuana.

Agent. Law enforcement officer. Also: buster, fed, fuzz, the heat, the man, plant, sam, uncle, whiskers.

Agonies. Withdrawal symptoms, usually in early stages; see withdrawal.

Amphetamine. Barbiturate combinations; see French Blue, Greenies.

Amphetamines. Stimulants which increase the activity of the nervous system; used medically to relieve depression or to reduce weight; misuse results in tremors, talkativeness, hallucinations and excitability. Terms and slang names: Dexies, Dominoes, Footballs, Hearts, Roses, Jelly Babies, Jolly Beans, Lid Poppers, Methedrine, Bennies, Oranges, Peaches, Speed, Ups, Wake ups, Whites, Copilots, Dolls, Pillhead, Truck drivers, Blackbirds; see methedrine.

Amytal. Registered trade name for Amobarbitol, a barbiturate; see barbiturate.

Anti-freeze. Heroin; see heroin.

Arsenal. An addict's or pusher's supply of drugs; see works.

Artillery. Equipment (such as a hypodermic syringe) used to inject a drug; see works.

Babysit. To guide a person through his drug experience: see guide, guru.

B, Bee. A penny match box volume, now a measure of marihuana approximately that size.

Back Track. To allow blood to come into the syringe during injection; see flushing.

Bag. 1) Container of drugs; 2) a problem; 3) a specialty; see Dime Bag, Nickel Bag.

Bagman. A drug seller; see pusher.

Bale. A pound of marihuana.

Bang. To inject drugs.

Barbiturates. The most commonly abused depressants (sedatives); medically used to produce sleep or to reduce blood pressure; drowsiness, staggering and slurred speech result when misused. Terms and slang names: Double Trouble, Goofballs, Nimby, Peanuts, Pinks, Rainbows, Red Devils, Sleepers, Tooies, Yellow Jackets, Blue Devils, Candy; see Amphetamine-Barbiturate combinations.

Barbs. Barbiturates; see barbiturates.

Bennies. Capsules or tablets of Benzedrine, a brand of amphetamine; see amphetamines.

Bhang. A grade of marihuana found in India; see marihuana.

Big D. LSD; see LSD.

Big Man. Someone high up – or at the top – in a drug selling ring; see pusher.

Bindle. A packet of narcotics.

Bit. A person's specialty, pastime or favorite drug; a prison sentence.

Blackbirds. Amphetamines; see amphetamines.

Blank. Low-grade narcotics.

Blasted. Under the influence of – or high on – drugs; see drug experiences.

Blocked. Under the influence of a drug, alone or in combination with alcohol; see drug experiences.

Blow a Stick. To smoke a marihuana cigarette; see marihuana.

Blow Your Mind. To experience severe mental effects from a hallucinogenic drug such as LSD; see drug experiences.

Blue Acid. LSD; see LSD.

Blue Cheer. LSD; see LSD.

Blue Devils. Amytal; see Amytal. Also, Blue Angels, Bluebirds, Blue Heaven.

Blue Devils. Blue capsules of Amytal, a brand of barbiturate; see barbiturates.

Blue Velvet. A mixture of paregoric (a preparation which contains opium) and an antihistamine (a drug used to combat allergies).

Bogart a Joint. 1) To salivate on a marihuana cigarette. 2) To retain and not share a marihuana cigarette.

Bombita. Amphetamine-heroin injection.

Bomber. Large, fat marihuana cigarette; see fatty.

Boo. Bu. Marihuana.

Boo Hoo. A leader of the Neo-American Church, an organization which considers hallucinogens to be sacraments; see hallucinogens.

Boot. The temporary elation or thrill experienced by an addict in his early days of using drugs. This experience – like all other claimed "good feelings" – disappears after repeated use; see drug experiences.

Boost. To shoplift.

Bottle. A quantity of tablets or capsules, usually 1,000.

Boxed. Jailed.

Boy. Heroin; see heroin.

Bread. Money, usually in reference to money needed to buy illicit drugs.

Break the Needle. To attempt to break or drop the narcotic habit; see withdrawal.

Brewery. A place where drugs are made, bought or used.

Brick. A kilogram (2.2 pounds) of marihuana; see marihuana.

Bridge. An alligator clip or other device used to hold a marihuana butt; see roach, crutch, roach clip.

Broker. A dealer in drugs; see pusher.

Brought Down. Depressed feeling following elation from drug use; see drug experiences.

Browns. Amphetamines; see amphetamines.

Bugged. 1) To be irritated by someone or something. 2) To be covered by sores and abscesses, caused by repeated injections with unsterile equipment; see drug experiences.

Bummer. A bad experience with hallucinogens.

Bundle. A packet or supply of drugs.

Burned. To obtain weak or contaminated drugs or a harmless substitute.

Bush. Marihuana; see marihuana.

Busted. Arrested by the police.

Buster. Narcotics agent, usually the Federal Bureau of Narcotics; see agent.

Buttons. That part of the peyote cactus containing the hallucinogen, mescaline; see mescaline.

Buzz. The feeling of exhilaration produced by a drug.

"C." Cocaine; see cocaine.

Candy. 1. Barbiturates. 2. A nickname for cocaine; see barbiturates, cocaine.

Cannabis (Sativa). The hemp plant from which marihuana is obtained; see marihuana.

Cannon. The addict's hypodermic syringe; see works.

Cap. A capsule or other drug container or dose.

Cartwheels. Amphetamine sulphate; see amphetamines.

Charas. A grade of marihuana found in India; see marihuana.

Charged Up. "High," or under the intoxicating influence of drugs; see drug experiences.

Chief, The. LSD; see LSD.

Chipping. Taking small doses of drugs irregularly; see dabble.

Chippy. A prostitute; among narcotic addicts, a woman who obtains money to buy drugs through prostitution.

Chloral Hydrate. A barbiturate; see barbiturates.

Christmas Tree. Dexedrine, an amphetamine; see amphetamines.

Chuck. To eat excessively while undergoing withdrawal.

Clean. Off drugs and/or not carrying them at the moment.

Clear Up. To stop drug use; see withdrawal.

Coasting. "High," or under the intoxicating influence of drugs; see drug experiences.

Cocaine. A stimulant drug once widely used medically as a local anesthetic; when abused, it results in excitability, talkativeness and reduction of the feeling of fatigue – and may result in anxiety, fear, violence and hallucinations. Also: "C," Coke, Dust, Gold Dust, Snow, Candy, H and C, Speedball.

Cocktail. Short butt of marihuana cigarette inserted in end of regular cigarette.

Coke. Cocaine; see cocaine.

Cold Turkey. Withdrawal from physically addicting drugs without medication; the drug user feels chilled and is covered with "goose bumps," looking like a plucked turkey; see withdrawal.

Come Down. To lose the drug-induced exhiliration; see drug experiences.

Congo Mataby. African term for marihuana; see marihuana.

Connect. To buy drugs (from a "connection").

Connection. A drug seller; see pusher.

Contact High. The feeling of being "high" on drugs merely by being in contact with someone who is.

Cook Up. 1. Prepare heroin for injection; see heroin. 2. Prepare hashish for inclusion with tobacco by heating in silver paper; see marihuana.

Cooker. A spoon, bottle cap or small cup used to dissolve a narcotic, such as heroin, in water. The solution is "cooked" or heated over a match or candle until the drug-containing powder is dissolved; see works.

Cool. A term of approval; drug users feel they are "cool," while nonusers are termed "square."

Cop. To purchase drugs; to steal.

Cop Out. To avoid responsibility; to plead guilty.

Co-pilots. Amphetamines; refers to the boost or uplift given, much as co-pilot helps an airplane get off the ground; see amphetamines.

Corine. Cocaine; see cocaine.

Cotton. The piece of cotton (or other material) used to filter the dissolved narcotic after it has been "cooked." Addicts often re-use this material, saving it for a time when they are unable to secure drugs. When soaked in water, such material yields a weak solution of the drug; see works.

Crash. To collapse from exhaustion, usually while under the influence of drugs; see drug experiences.

Crash Pad. Temporary residence, usually for one or two nights or for the duration of a drug trip.

Crutch. Device used to hold a marihuana butt.

Crystal. Methamphetamine; see methedrine, speed.

Cubehead. A frequent user of LSD.

Cut. To dilute or adulterate a narcotic before selling it; heroin is often "cut" with milk sugar so that the seller has more portions, or "bags," to sell.

Cyclazocine. A narcotic antagonist, used to block the euphoric effects of narcotics; see narcotics.

DMT. Dimethyltryptamine, a hallucinogen; see hallucinogens.

Dabble. To "chip" or take small amounts of drugs irregularly; see chipping.

Dagga. South African term for marihuana; see marihuana.

Dealer. A drug seller; see pusher.

Deck. A small packet of drugs.

Dexies. Dexedrine, a brand of amphetamine; see amphetamines.

Dextroamphetamine Sulphate. An amphetamine; see amphetamines.

Dime Bag. A supply of drugs which costs $10.

Dirty. Possessing drugs.

Doing. To do or take something.

Dollies. Dolophine, a brand of the narcotic methadone; see heroin.

Dolls. Pills; amphetamines, barbiturates or a combination of these two drugs.

Dominoes. Durophret – an amphetamine, 12.5 mg. capsules; see amphetamines.

Dope. Narcotics used by addicts; see heroin.

Double Trouble. Tuinal, a brand of barbiturate; see barbiturates.

Down. A drug hangover, or coming out of a drug-induced state; see drug experiences.

Downers. Barbiturates; see barbiturates.

Dried Out. To have taken a cure – usually self-regulated (cold turkey); see withdrawal.

Drop Out. To withdraw from the real world while under LSD or other drugs; see drug experiences.

Dropped. Arrested. Also: busted, nailed, snatched.

Dropping. Taking a drug by mouth; in capsules, tablets or pills, or solution in water or alcohol.

Drug. A narcotic substance or preparation which affects the user in various ways.

Drug Experiences. Terms for drug influence; see blasted, blocked, boot, blow your mind, brought down, bugged, coasting, come down, crash, charged up, down, drop out, euphoria, floating, flake out, flattened, flying, freak out, flip out, gassed, happening, high, hopped up, horrors, hung up, lift, on a trip, on the nod, out of it, overcharged, stoned, turned on, up, up tight, wasted.

Duby. Marihuana

Dust. Cocaine; see cocaine.

Dusting. To add strychnine or other substance to marihuana to increase the effect of the drug.

Dynamite. A very powerful dose of drugs.

Eating. Taking a drug, especially by mouth.

Equipment. Items used to prepare and inject a dose of drugs, usually heroin; includes: bent spoon or bottle-cap, for dissolving drug-containing powder, matches, hypodermic needle, eye dropper and cotton; see works.

Euphoria. A feeling of well-being or elation sought by drug users and sometimes found the first few times that certain drugs are taken; see drug experiences.

Explorers Club. A group of LSD users.

Factory. Equipment or instruments for injecting drugs; see works.

Famine. A lack of available drugs resulting from a raid by the police on a supply.

Farmer. Someone naive about drugs; see square.

Fatty. A fat or thick marihuana cigarette.

Fed. An agent or policeman, especially from the Federal Bureau of Narcotics; see agent.

Feed Bag. A container of narcotics.

Feed Store. A place where drugs can be purchased.

Fiend. A regular user of drugs.

Fix. An injection of drugs.

Flake Out. Lose consciousness from misuse of drugs; see drug experiences.

Flash. The intense feeling experienced immediately after injection of a drug, particularly speed; see speed.

Flashback. The unpredictable phenomenon of undergoing again the effects of LSD weeks or even months after the last use of the drug; see LSD.

Flattened. An addict in stupor resulting from overdose; see drug experiences.

Flea Powder. Low quality or weak drugs.

Flip Out. LSD-induced madness; see drug experiences.

Floating. "High," or under the intoxicating influence of drugs; see drug experiences.

Flushing. Drawing blood back into the syringe during an injection – to be sure that a vein has been tapped.

Flying. "High," or under the intoxicating influence of drugs; see drug experiences.

Footballs. Oval-shaped amphetamine tablets; see amphetamines.

Freak Out. To lose contact with reality while on drugs; a bad drug experience; see drug experiences.

French Blue. Amphetamine-barbiturate pill.

Fresh and Sweet. Just out of jail or a treatment center.

Frisco Speedball. 50% heroin, 50% cocaine with a dash of LSD.

Fruit Salad. A variety of capsules or tablets contributed by group members and shared by all.

Fuzz. The police; see agent.

G. A paper funnel placed at the end of an eye dropper used to inject heroin; see works.

G-Shot. A very small dose of drugs, used to stave off sickness until a full dose can be taken.

Gage or Gauge. Marihuana; see marihuana.

Ganja. West Indian name for marihuana; see marihuana.

Garbage. Weak, heavily diluted narcotics.

Gassed. "High," or under intoxicating influence of drugs; see drug experiences.

Gear. Any belongings, but especially supplies of drugs or syringes; see works.

Get Through. To obtain drugs.

Girl. Cocaine

Gold Dust. Cocaine, as the exquisite drug for some users; see cocaine.

Goods. Drugs.

Goof. 1) To give oneself up to police. 2) To spoil an injection, either when making it up or injecting it.

Goofballs. Barbiturates. Large doses make the user sluggish and "goofy" in the same way as someone who is drunk; see barbiturates.

Grass. Marihuana; see marihuana.

Greenies. Green, heart-shaped tablets of a barbiturate-amphetamine mixture.

Ground Control. Guide/caretaker in an LSD session.

Guide. A person who gives guidance or support during a psychedelic drug experience; see LSD.

Gum. Opium.

Gun. Hypodermic needle for "shooting" drugs; see works.

Guru. An experienced LSD user who acts as a companion/guide to one who is on a trip.

H. Heroin; see heroin.

H and C. Hot and cold, heroin and cocaine mixture; see heroin, cocaine.

Habit. Addiction to drugs (physical dependence). Also: Jones, Monkey; see weekend habit, ice-cream habit.

Hallucinogen. A drug which causes hallucinations (seeing things which do not exist), distortions of time, space, color and sound, and rambling speech. Marihuana, LSD, STP and DMT are the most commonly abused hallucinogens (popularly called "psychedelics").

Hang-Up. A personal problem.

Happening. A psychedelic event or "show"; see drug experiences.

Hard Stuff. Strong, narcotic drugs such as heroin, morphine and opium; see heroin.

Hash. Hashish or marihuana; see marihuana.

Hashbury. Haight-Ashbury section of San Francisco.

Hashish. A strong form of marihuana; see marihuana.

Hawk, The. LSD; see LSD.

Hay. Marihuana; see marihuana.

Head. Chronic user of a drug or drugs.

Head-shop. A store which specializes in merchandise popular with drug users.

Hearts. Benzedrine or Dexedrine, brands of amphetamines; see amphetamines.

Heat. The police; see agent.

Heavenly Blues. Morning glory seeds; see hallucinogens.

Hemp. Marihuana; see marihuana.

Herb. Marihuana; see marihuana.

Heroin. A strong depressant, the narcotic drug used by nearly all addicts; it is a white powder which is usually dissolved in water and injected into the body. Also: anti-freeze, boy, dollies, dope, H, H and C, hard stuff, horse, junk.

High. Under the intoxicating influence of drugs; see drug experiences.

Hip. To be "in the know." First used to identify opium smokers, who, because they rested on their right sides while smoking, tended to develop hard callouses on their right hips.

Hippies. Persons believing in a way of life based on love and beauty and considering it possible to gain deep insights into life and themselves.

Hit. To buy drugs or to be arrested.

Hooked. Physically addicted to a drug.

Hop Head. A narcotic addict; restricted to opiate users in addict usage.

Hopped Up. Under the intoxicating influence of drugs; see drug experiences.

Horrors. Terrifying dreams and hallucinations caused by LSD and other hallucinogenic drugs; see drug experiences.

Horse. Heroin; see heroin.

Hot. Wanted by the police.

Hot Shot. A fatal and usually strong – or even full strength – dose of a narcotic or a mixture of a poison and a narcotic given to a troublesome addict or one who has betrayed sellers to the police.

Hung-up. Unable to obtain drugs; depressed, let down, disappointed; see drug experiences.

Hypo. Narcotics addict.

IFIF. The International Federation for Internal Freedom. Created by a Harvard research group for work on LSD. Not associated with the university.

Ice Cream Habit. An off-and-on use of drugs.

In. Being involved or accepted; a popular drug.

Indian Hemp. Inaccurate term popularly used to describe all forms of cannabis; see marihuana.

Instant Zen. LSD; see LSD.

Jack Up. To inject a drug; also Sodium Amytal.

Jones. A drug habit.

Jelly Babies. Amphetamine pills; see amphetamines.

Joint. A marihuana cigarette; see marihuana.

Jolly Beans. Amphetamine pills; see amphetamines.

Joy-pop. To inject small doses of drugs irregularly.

Joystick. Marihuana cigarette; see marihuana.

Juice Head. An alcoholic.

Junk. Narcotics or "hard" drugs,

sometimes refers to poor quality drugs; see heroin.

Junkie. An addict, especially one who sells drugs; see pusher.

K.Y. U.S. Pubilc Health Service Hospital, Lexington, Kentucky, a narcotics treatment center.

Karma. Fate; see Nirvana, Samsara.

Kheef. Hashish; see hashish.

Kick. To stop using drugs; see withdrawal.

Kilo. Kilogram, the equivalent of 2.2 pounds; the usual package of marihuana sold in Mexico.

LSD — Lysergic Acid Diethylamide. One of the most potent hallucinogens known. Terms and slang names for LSD: The Hawk, Instant Zen, Sugar, Acid, The Chief, Big D, Blue Acid. See also: Acid head, Flashback, Niacinamide, Guide, Flip-out, Horrors, Blow Your Mind.

Lay-out. Equipment for taking drugs.

Leapers. Amphetamines; see amphetamines.

Lemonade. Poor heroin.

Lid. One ounce of marihuana.

Lid Poppers. Amphetamines; see amphetamines.

Lift. The temporary escape from mental depression given by some drugs; see drug experiences.

Loco Weed. Marihuana; see marihuana.

Love Weed. Marihuana; see marihuana.

Loused. To be covered by sores and abscesses as a result of unsterile equipment.

M. Morphine.

MDA. A hallucinogen; see hallucinogens.

Machine. Syringe; see works.

Magic Mushroom. The species of a Mexican mushroom which contains psilocybin, a hallucinogen; see hallucinogen, psilocybin.

Mainline. To inject drugs directly into a vein.

Maintaining. Keeping at a certain level of drug effect.

Man, The Man. A policeman (sometimes a drug dealer or anyone with authority); see agent.

Manicured. High-grade marihuana, undiluted by seeds or stems; see marihuana.

Mantra. A hymn, prayer or mystic formula, originally Hindu or Buddhist.

Marihuana. The most popular hallucinogen, smoked in a cigarette or pipe; made from the resin of the female hemp plant. Also: Acapulco gold, cannabis, Congo mataby, dagga, gage, ganga, grass, hash, hashish, hay, hemp, Indian hemp, kief, Mary Jane, Panama red, pot, rope, tea, Texas tea, weed; see also: blow a stick, joint, joystick, pack, reefer, roach, rolling up, stick, brick, cook up, manicured, salt and pepper, stoned, weed-head.

Mary Jane, Mary Warner. Marihuana, see marihuana.

Mescaline. The alkaloid of peyote, a hallucinogen; see hallucinogen, peyote.

Meth. Methedrine, an amphetamine; see methedrine.

Methedrine. A powerful amphetamine. Also: meth, speed; see amphetamine.

Mezz. Obsolete term for marihuana.

Mikes. Micrograms.

Monkey. A drug habit.

Moon. A flat, circular piece of hashish; see hashish.

Morphine. A form of opium.

Mota, Muta. Mexican slang for marihuana.

Mud. Crude opium; sometimes marihuana.

Narco, Nark. Narcotics officer.

Narcoland. The fanciful world of addicts.

Narcotic. A drug that dulls the senses, relieves pain and induces sleep; large doses may result in stupor, coma or convulsions. Heroin, morphine, and opium are narcotics.

Needle. Hypodermic syringe used to inject drugs; see works.

Niacinamide. An antidote for LSD: used to interrupt a bad trip; see LSD.

Nickel Bag. A five-dollar purchase of narcotics.

Nimby. Nembutal, a brand of barbiturate; see barbiturate.

Nirvana. The state of freedom from Karma. The extinction of desire, passion, illusion and individual consciousness. The attainment of rest, truth and unchanging being; see Karma, Samsara.

Number. A marihuana cigarette.

O. Opium.

O.D. Overdose of drugs, results in coma and/or death.

Off. No longer under the influence of drugs; see withdrawal.

On a Trip. Under the influence of LSD or another hallucinogen; see drug experiences.

On the Nod. Under the intoxicating influence of drugs, especially the stupor immediately following the injection of a narcotic such as heroin; see drug experiences.

Oranges. Dexedrine, a brand of amphetamine; see amphetamine.

Orange Sunshine. LSD; see LSD.

Out of It. Not in touch, such as when under the influence of drugs; see drug experiences.

Overcharged. Under the influence of an overdose of narcotics; see drug experiences.

Owsley's Acid. Good quality LSD, originally that manufactured by Augustus Owsley Stanley III.

PCP. Phencyclidine hydrochloride; a powerful hallucinogen which is mixed with parsley and smoked.

P.G. Paregoric; see paregoric, narcotics.

Pack. A pack of marihuana cigarettes; see marihuana.

Panama Red. High grade marihuana; almost as prime as Acapulco Gold; see marihuana.

Panic. A lack or diminished supply of narcotics resulting from a police raid on a supply point.

Paper. A legal prescription for narcotics; see script.

Paregoric. A mild derivative of opium, a narcotic; see narcotics.

Peaches. Benzedrine, a brand of amphetamine; see amphetamine.

Peanuts. Barbiturates; see barbiturates.

Pearly Gates. Morning glory seeds; see hallucinogens.

Pentobarbitol Sodium. A barbiturate; see barbiturates.

Pep Pills. Amphetamines; see amphetamines.

Peyote, Peyotl. A hallucinogen from the peyote cactus; see hallucinogen.

Pick Up. A new customer for drugs; a shot of narcotics usually given another addict as a gift or favor.

Piece. A container of drugs; usually an ounce of narcotics.

Pigs. Police.

Pill Head. Person taking pills, usually amphetamines; see amphetamines.

Pin. Thin, well-rolled marihuana cigarette.

Pinks. Seconal, a brand of barbiturate; see barbiturates.

Plant. An undercover narcotics agent or policeman pretending to be a drug user so as to gain leads or suspects; see agent.

Plastic Hippie. A parttime or weekend hippie.

Pop. To inject drugs, especially under the skin.

Pot. Marihuana; see marihuana.

Pot Head. A chronic user of marihuana.

Psilocybin. A hallucinogen obtained from a Mexican mushroom; see hallucinogen.

Psychedelic. Anything pertaining to the world of the hallucinogens. Usually vivid, undulating colors, strobe lights and acid-rock music.

Purple Hearts. Phenobarbitol, a barbiturate; see barbiturates.

Push. To sell drugs illegally.

Pusher. A person who sells illegal drugs. Also: big man, broker, bag man, dealer, connection, junkie.

Quill. A matchbook cover used in sniffing heroin.

Rainbows. Tuinal, a brand of barbiturate; see barbiturates.

Rap. To talk while under the influence of drugs.

Reader. A legitimate prescription for narcotics used in medicine; morphine is sometimes prescribed.

Red Devils. Seconal, a brand of barbiturate; see barbiturates.

Reds and Blues. Tuinal; see doubletrouble.

Reefer. A marihuana cigarette; see marihuana.

Reentry. Return from an LSD "trip."

Retinal Circus. Visual hallucinations experienced by an LSD user.

Righteous. High quality drugs.

Roach. A butt of marihuana cigarette; these are saved to make new cigarettes; see marihuana.

Roach Clip. Device used to hold a marihuana butt; see bridge, crutch.

Rolling Up. Making a marihuana cigarette; see marihuana.

Rope. Marihuana; see marihuana.

Roses. Benzedrine, a brand of amphetamine; see amphetamines.

Rural Free Delivery (RFD). An addict who visits small-town doctors, attempting to obtain legal prescriptions for narcotics such as morphine.

Rush. The immediate effect of injecting methamphetamine (speed); see flash.

STP. Serenity, Tranquility, Peace. A mixture of methedrine and DOM, six times as strong as LSD; see hallucinogens.

Salt and Pepper. Impure or low-grade marihuana; see marihuana.

Sam. A federal narcotic agent; see agent.

Samsara. The indefinitely repeating cycle of birth, misery and death; see Karma, Nirvana.

Satch Cotton. Cotton used to filter a solution of narcotics before injection; addicts may soak this cotton and use the solution when drugs are not available; see works.

Score. To buy drugs, especially after a long search.

Scratching. Searching for drugs.

Script. A prescription for legitimate drugs.

Secobarbital. Seconal, a barbiturate; see barbiturates.

Shoot. To inject drugs.

Shooting Gallery. A place where addicts gather to inject drugs.

Skag. Heroin; see narcotics.

Skin. Cigarette paper.

Skin-popping. To inject drugs, particularly narcotics, directly under the skin.

Sleepers. Barbiturates in general; see barbiturates.

Smack. Heroin; see narcotics.

Snop. Marihuana.

Snort. To take heroin by sniffing.

Snow. Cocaine; see cocaine.

Snowbird. Cocaine user.

Spaced Out. In a daze, particularly from drug use.

Speed. Methedrine, a powerful amphetamine; see amphetamines, methedrine.

Speedball. A mixture of cocaine and heroin or morphine; see cocaine, heroin.

Spike. Needle; see works.

Square. A person who does not use drugs.

Stardust. Cocaine, implies the high price of the drug.

Stash. A hidden supply of drugs.

Steamboat. Toilet roll used as a roach holder; see bridge, crutch, roach clip, roach.

Stick. A marihuana cigarette; see marihuana.

Stoned; Stoned out of Your Mind. Being under the influence of marihuana; see marihuana, drug experiences.

Straight. A nonuser.

Strung Out. Heavily dependent on, or addicted to, drugs.

Stuff. Drug.

Sugar. LSD; see LSD.

THC. Tetrahydrocannabinol, the active chemical in marihuana; see marihuana.

Tabs. Drugs in tablet form.

Tar. Opium; see narcotics.

Tea. Hashish, a strong form of marihuana; see marihuana.

Teenie Boppers. Adolescents between the ages of 12 and 16. Regarded as dangerous by drug users because of their age.

Texas Tea. Marihuana; see marihuana.

Toke. To smoke a marihuana cigarette.

Tolerance. The phenomenon which occurs as an individual becomes physically dependent on an addicting drug, such as heroin. As his tolerance builds, he needs more and more of the drug for the same effect.

Tooies. Tuinal, a brand of barbiturate; see barbiturates.

Toy. A small, flat, coin-shaped container for opium.

Tracks. Scars along veins which result from repeated drug injections.

Travel Agent. An LSD supplier.

Trey. $3 bag of heroin.

Trigger. To smoke marihuana immediately after taking LSD.

Trip. The experience resulting from hallucinogens or psychedelics such as LSD.

Truck Drivers. Amphetamines; refers to the use of these stimulants by gypsy truck drivers who try to stay behind the wheel for long stretches; see amphetamines.

Tuinal. Amobarbitol and Secobarbitol combination; see double-trouble.

Turkey. A harmless substance sold as a narcotic.

Turned Off. No longer under the influence of drugs; see withdrawal.

Turn On. 1) To alter awareness, with or without drugs. 2) To use drugs.

Uncle. A federal narcotics agent; see agent.

Up. Under the intoxicating influence of drugs; see drug experiences.

Up Tight. Under stress; see drug experiences.

Ups. Amphetamines; see amphetamines.

User. Usually refers to user of drugs, one who takes drugs either regularly or irregularly.

Vibration, Vibs. Feelings coming from another person or from a situation. May be good or bad vibs.

Viper's Weed. Marihuana; see marihuana.

Wake-ups. Amphetamines; see amphetamines.

Wasted. Under the intoxicating influence of drugs; see drug experiences.

Wedges. Wedge-shaped tablets.

Weed. Marihuana; see marihuana.

Weed-head. A frequent user of marihuana; see marihuana.

Weekend Habit. A small, irregular habit.

Weekend Hippie. A person who lives a normal life during the week but who lives the part of a hippie – usually including drugs – on the weekend.

Whiskers. Narcotic agents or local police; see agent.

White Lightning. LSD; see LSD.

White Stuff. Morphine; see narcotics.

Whites. White amphetamine tablets; see amphetamines.

Winging. High on drugs.

Withdrawal. Phenomenon which occurs when an individual who is physically dependent on a drug stops taking that drug. Symptoms include nausea, dizziness, chills, runny nose and itching; see agonies, break the habit, clear up, cold turkey, dried out, kick off, turned off.

Works. Equipment for injecting narcotics; see arsenal, artillery, cannon, cooker, cotton, "G," gun, machine, needle, piece, satch cotton, spike, factory, equipment, gear.

Yellow Jackets. Nembutal, a brand of barbiturate; see barbiturates.

Yen Sleep. A drowsy, restless state occurring after LSD use.

Zap. Totally destroy.

Zig Zag. Brand name of cigarette paper used to roll marihuana cigarettes.

Zonked. Intoxicated by drugs or alcohol.

Sources
for Information
about Drug Abuse

Alcohol and Drug Addiction
Research Foundation
344 Bloor Street West
Toronto, Ontario,
Canada

American Association for
Health, Physical Education
and Recreation
1201 Sixteenth Street, N.W.
Washington. D. C. 20036

American Medical Association
Committee on Alcoholism
and Drug Dependence
535 N. Dearborn Street
Chicago, Illinois 60610

American Orthopsychiatric
Association
1795 Broadway
New York, N. Y. 10019

American Pharmaceutical
Association
2215 Constitution Avenue, N.W.
Washington, D. C. 20036

American Public Health
Association, Inc.
1740 Broadway
New York, N. Y. 10019

American School Health
Association
American School Health Building
P. O. Box 416
Kent, Ohio 44240

Bureau of Narcotics
and Dangerous Drugs
U. S. Dept. of Justice
Washington, D. C. 20537

B'nai B'rith (CUS)
1640 Rhode Island Avenue, N.W.
Washington, D. C. 20036

Chamber of Commerce
of the United States
1615 H Street, N.W.
Washington, D. C. 20006

Institute for the
Study of Drug Addiction
680 West End Avenue
New York, N. Y. 10025

National Association
for Mental Health
10 Columbus Circle
New York, N. Y. 10017

National Clearinghouse for
Drug Abuse Information
Parklawn Building, Room 8C-09
5600 Fishers Lane
Rockville, Maryland 20852

National Coordinating Council
on Drug Abuse Education
and Information, Inc.
1211 Connecticut Ave., N.W.,
Suite 212
Washington, D. C. 20036

National Council of the
Churches of Christ in
the United States of America
475 Riverside Drive
New York, N. Y. 10027

National District Attorneys
Association
211 East Chicago Avenue
Chicago, Illinois 60611

Pharmaceutical Manufacturers
Association
1155 — 15th Street, N.W.
Washington, D. C. 20005

U. S. Department of Defense
1117 North 19th Street
Arlington, Virginia 22209

U. S. Office of Education
400 Maryland Avenue, S.W.
Washington, D. C. 20206

WHO Expert Committee on
Dependence-Producing Drugs
Palais des Nations
Geneva, Switzerland

Department of Economic
and Social Affairs
Division of Narcotic Drugs
United Nations
New York, N. Y., and
Palais des Nations
Geneva, Switzerland

International Narcotics
Control Board
Palais des Nations
Geneva, Switzerland

International Association
of Chiefs of Police
1319 — 18th Street, N.W.
Washington, D. C. 20036

Alaska Drug Abuse
Education Coordinating Office
Pouch A
Juneau, Alaska 99801

Florida Inter-Agency Law
Enforcement Planning Council
(Task Force on Narcotics,
Dangerous Drugs and Alcohol
Abuse)
104 South Calhoun Street
Tallahassee, Florida 32304

Georgia State Board of Pharmacy,
Office of the Chief Drug Inspector
19 Hunter Street, S.W.
Room 212-214
Atlanta, Georgia 30334

Kentucky Department
of Mental Health
P. O. Box 678
Frankfort, Kentucky 40601

Maine Department of
Health and Welfare,
State Health Planning Council
The State House
Augusta, Maine 04330

Maine Department of
the Attorney General,
Criminal Division
The State House
Augusta, Maine 04330

Maryland Drug Abuse Authority
State Office Building
301 West Preston Street
Baltimore, Maryland 21201

Massachusetts Department of
Education, Division of
Health Education
182 Tremont Street
Boston, Massachusetts 02133

Massachusetts Office of
the Attorney General
Drug Abuse Section
State House
Room 373A
Boston, Massachusetts 02133

Michigan Narcotics Addiction
Rehabilitation Coordinating
Organization
18444 West Ten Mile Road
Southfield, Michigan 48075

Michigan State Pharmaceutical
Association
1812 Michigan National Tower
Lansing, Michigan 48933

Minnesota Office of the Governor
The State House
St. Paul, Minnesota 55101

Mississippi Division of
Law Enforcement Assistance
Office of the Governor
345 North Mart Plaza
Jackson, Mississippi 39206

Montana Alcohol and
Drug Dependence Commission
1336 Helena Avenue
Helena, Montana 59601

New Hampshire Program on
Alcohol and Drug Abuse
Division of Public Health
Twitchell Building
105 Pleasant Street
Concord, New Hampshire 03301

New Jersey Bureau of
Narcotic Addiction and
Drug Abuse
167 West Hanover Street
Trenton, New Jersey 08625

New York Narcotic
Addiction Control Commission
Executive Park South
Albany, New York 12203

Pennsylvania Department
of Public Health
P. O. Box 90
Harrisburg, Pennsylvania 17120

South Dakota Commissioner
of Drugs and Substance Control
State Capitol
Pierre, South Dakota 57501

Texas Pharmacy Association
1624 U. S. Highway East
Austin Savings Building
Austin, Texas 79601

U. S. Bureau of Narcotics
and Dangerous Drugs
1405 I Street, N.W.
Washington, D. C. 20537

Washington State Office
of Public Instruction
P. O. Box 527
Old Capitol Building
Olympia, Washington 98501

West Virginia Dept.
of Mental Health
Division of Alcoholism
State Capitol
Charleston, West Virginia 25305

Regional Offices of the Bureau of Narcotics and Dangerous Drugs

Region I — Boston
JFK Federal Bldg., Rm. G-64
Boston, Massachusetts 02203
(617) 223-2170
(Connecticut, Maine, Massachusetts, New Hampshire, Rhode Island, Vermont)

Region II — New York
Suite 605
90 Church Street
New York, New York 10007
(212) 264-7187
(New York, northern New Jersey)

Region III — Philadelphia
605 U. S. Custom House
2nd & Chestnut Streets
Philadelphia, Pennsylvania 19106
(215) 597-4310
(Delaware, southern New Jersey, Pennsylvania)

Region IV — Baltimore
31 Hopkins Place, Rm. 955
Baltimore, Maryland 21201
(301) 962-4800
(District of Columbia, Maryland, North Carolina, Virginia, West Virginia)

Region V — Miami
1200 Biscayne Blvd.
Suite 201
Miami, Florida 33132
(305) 350-4241
(Florida, Georgia, South Carolina, Puerto Rico)

Region VI — Detroit
602 Federal Building and U. S. Courthouse
231 W. Lafayette
Detroit, Michigan 48226
(313) 226–6110
(Kentucky, Michigan, Ohio)

Region VII — Chicago
Suite 1700, Engineering Building
205 W. Wacker Drive
Chicago, Illinois 60606
(312) 353-7875
(Illinois, Indiana, Wisconsin)

Region VIII — New Orleans
546 Carondelet Street
Fourth Floor

New Orleans, Louisiana 70130
(504) 527-2317
(Alabama, Arkansas, Louisiana, Mississippi, Tennessee)

Region X — Kansas City
U. S. Courthouse, Suite 115
811 Grand Avenue
Kansas City, Missouri 64106
(816) 374-2631
(Minnesota, North Dakota, South Dakota, Iowa, Kansas, Missouri, Nebraska)

Region XI — Dallas
1114 Commerce Street
Room 723
Dallas, Texas 75202
(214) 749-3631
(Oklahoma, Texas)

Region XII — Denver
New Customs House
1950 Stout Street
Denver, Colorado 80202
(303) 297-4291
(Arizona, Colorado, New Mexico, Utah, Wyoming)

Region XIII — Seattle
U. S. Courthouse
1010 5th Avenue, Rm. 311
Seattle, Washington 98104
(206) 583-5443
(Alaska, Idaho, Montana, Oregon, Washington)

Region XIV — Los Angeles
Petroleum Building, Suite 1010
714 W. Olympic Blvd.
Los Angeles, California 90015
(213) 688-2650
(California, Hawaii, Nevada)

Region XV — Mexico
American Embassy
Nar Apartado Postal 88 Bis.
Mexico D.F., Mexico

Region XVI — Bangkok
American Embassy
APO San Francisco 96346

Region XVII — Paris
American Embassy, Room 511
APO New York 09777

"I find the great thing in this world is not so much where we stand, as in what direction we are moving. We must sail sometimes with the wind and sometimes against it, but we must sail, and not drift, nor lie at anchor."

Oliver Wendell Holmes
The Autocrat of the Breakfast Table (1858)

Index